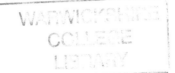

Thinking and Knowing

Grange
BOOKS

This edition published in 2005 by Grange Books
an imprint of Grange Books Plc
The Grange
Kingsnorth Industrial Estate
Hoo, Near Rochester
Kent ME3 9ND
www.Grangebooks.co.uk

ISBN: 1-84013-803-3

Printed in China

Editorial and design:
The Brown Reference Group plc
8 Chapel Place
Rivington Street
London
EC2A 3DQ
UK
www.brownreference.com

FOR THE BROWN REFERENCE GROUP PLC
Editors: Windsor Chorlton, Karen Frazer, Leon Gray,
Simon Hall, Marcus Hardy, Jim Martin, Shirin Patel,
Frank Ritter, Henry Russell, Gillian Sutton, Susan Watt
Indexer: Kay Ollerenshaw
Picture Researcher: Helen Simm
Illustrators: Darren Awuah, Dax Fullbrook, Mark Walker
Designers: Reg Cox, Mike Leaman, Sarah Williams
Design Manager: Lynne Ross
Managing Editor: Bridget Giles
Production Director: Alastair Gourlay
Editorial Director: Lindsey Lowe

PHOTOGRAPHIC CREDITS
Front Cover: Photodisc: National Cancer Institute (tr); Photos.com (br);
Mark Walker (l).
AKG London: 70; **American Psychiatric Association:** Popplestone/
McPherson 138; **Archives of the History of American Psychology:** University
of Akron, Ohio 50, 136; **Art Explosion:** 69tl, 72r; **Chimpanzee & Human
Communication Institute:** 116; **Corbis:** 84, Bettmann 21, 43, 46, 47, 53, 58,
162, Richard Bickel 114, Ron Boardman/FPLA 86t, D. Boone 150, Anna Clopet
153, Owen Franken 155, Lowell Georgia 60, Christel Gerstenberg 139, Tony
Hamblin 88, Robert Holmes 129, Layne Kennedy 158, Gail Mooney 64, Orion
Press 86b, Photex 146, Steve Raymer 69tr, Reflections Photolibrary 59, Roger
Ressmeyer 9, 137, 154, David Samuel Robbins 142, Tim Wright 49; **Corbis
Stockmarket:** Rick Gomez 128; **Ecoscene:** 56; **Empics Sports Agency:** John
Buckle 98; **Hemera Photo Objects:** 87tl, 87tr; **Hutchison Picture Library:**
Isabella Tree 75; **Image Bank:** Jeff Cadge 82, Color Day Production 80t, 85,
Erlanson-Messens 6, Larry Gatz 80b, Larry Dale Gordon 124, Guang Hui
China Tourism Press 10, G. K. & Vikki Hart 54, Romilly Lockyer 62, Real Life
25, Marc Romanelli 34, Sparky 48, Moritz Steiger 18, Cherie Steinberg Cote
26, Steve Dunwell Photography 69c, Ross Whitaker 57; **Impact Photos:** Piers
Cavendish 119, Simon Shepheard 159; **Kobal Collection:** MGM 83b, Mirisch-
7 Arts/United Artists 83t; **Mary Evans Picture Library:** 12, 14, 15, 149;
NHPA: G. I. Bernard 115, Gerard Lacz 74, John Shaw 72l; **Photodisc:**
Geostock 125, Doug Menuez 110, Jeremy Woodhouse 71; **Pictor:** 19, 31, 97,
103, 106, 108; **Rex Features:** Peter Brooker 44; **Science & Society Picture
Library:** Science Museum 11; **Science Photo Library:** Mauro Fermariello
151, Pascal Goetgheluck 38, Hank Morgan 94, Wellcome Dept of Cognitive
Neurology 37, 120; **Still Pictures:** Janet Jarman 156; **Sylvia Cordaiy Photo
Library:** John Howard 40, 55, Chris Parker 79; p. 133 courtesy HarperCollins.

CONTRIBUTORS

Consultant:
Frederike Heuer, PhD
Visiting Professor,
Department of Psychology,
Lewis and Clark College,
Portland, Oregon

Authors:
Gordon D. A. Brown, PhD
Professor of Psychology,
Department of Psychology,
University of Warwick, UK
Problem Solving

Ian Hocking, PhD
School of Psychology,
University of Exeter, UK
The Human Computer

Jonathan K. Foster, DPhil
Academic Psychologist and
Neuropsychologist, Memory & Brain
Laboratory, School of Psychology,
University of Western Australia
Storing Information

Sven L. Mattys, PhD
Lecturer, Department of
Experimental Psychology,
University of Bristol, UK
Language Processing

Sarah E. Milne, PhD
Clinical Psychologist and Lecturer,
Department of Psychology,
University of Bath, UK
Attention and Information Processing

Gary B. Nallan, PhD
Associate Professor of Psychology,
The University of North Carolina at Asheville
Learning by Association

Andy Wills, PhD
Lecturer in Cognitive
Psychology, School of Psychology,
University of Exeter, UK
Representing Information

Contents

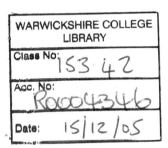

About This Set

volume title

opening quote

introduction

cross-reference

fact box

chapter title

author of opening quote

chapter title

picture caption

general quote

fact box

The diagram above shows the typical elements found within a chapter in this set. The various types of fact box are explained more fully in the box shown opposite.

These pages explain how to use the *Psychology* encyclopedia. There are six volumes in the set, each one illustrated with color photographs and specially commissioned artworks. Each volume has its own contents list at the beginning and a glossary at the back explaining important terms. More information, such as websites and related reference works, are listed in the Resources section, also found at the back of each volume.

To find articles on a particular subject, look for it in the set index at the back of each volume. Once you have started to read a relevant chapter, cross-references within that chapter and in the connections box at the end of the chapter will guide you to other related pages and chapters elsewhere in the set.

Every chapter has several color-coded fact boxes featuring information related to the subject discussed. They fall into distinct groups, which are described in more detail in the box opposite (p. 5).

THE SIX VOLUMES

History of psychology (Volume One) takes a look at psychology's development throughout history. It starts in ancient Greece when concepts of "mind" existed only as a topic of philosophical debate, looks at the subject's development into a separate field of scientific research, then follows its division into various schools of thought. It also explores the effects of scientific developments, discusses recent approaches, and considers the effects of new research in nonwestern cultures.

The brain and the mind (Volume Two) analyzes the relationship between the mind and the brain and looks at how the brain works in detail. The history of neuroscience is followed by a study of the physiology of the brain and how this relates to functions such as thinking. Chapters tackle the concept of the mind as an intangible and invisible entity, the nature of consciousness, and how our perceptual systems work to interpret the sensations we feel. In a chapter entitled Artificial Minds the volume explores whether or not machines will ever be able to think as humans do.

Thinking and knowing (Volume Three) looks at how the brain processes, stores, and retrieves information. It covers cognitive processes that we share with animals, such as associative learning, and those that are exclusive to people, such as language processing.

Developmental psychology (Volume Four) focuses on changes in psychological development from birth, throughout childhood, and into old age. It covers theories of social and intellectual development, particularly those of Jean Piaget and Lev Vygotsky. It also covers social and emotional development and how they can be improved and nurtured.

Social psychology (Volume Five) studies people as unique individuals and as social animals. It analyzes the notions of personality and intelligence as well as considering how people relate to and communicate with each other and society, and the social groups that they form.

Psychologists using a variety of approaches work in different fields (developmental, social, or abnormal, for example), but all study the brain, trying to figure out how it functions and how it influences people's behavior, thoughts, and emotions.

Abnormal psychology (Volume Six) asks what is abnormality? It shows how the number and types of abnormalities recognized as mental disorders have changed over time and examines specific disorders and their causes. It also looks at diagnosis of disorders and treatments, which can be psychological (talking cures) or physical (drugs and surgery). The social issues associated with abnormality and how society deals with people who have mental disorders are also explored.

 KEY DATES
Lists some of the important events in the history of the topic discussed.

 KEY POINTS
Summarizes some of the key points made in the chapter.

 KEY TERMS
Provides concise definitions of terms that appear in the chapter.

 KEY WORKS
Lists key books and papers published by researchers in the field.

 FOCUS ON
Takes a closer look at either a related topic or an aspect of the topic discussed.

 EXPERIMENT
Takes a closer look at experimental work carried out by researchers in the field.

 CASE STUDY
Discusses in-depth studies of particular individuals carried out by researchers.

 BIOGRAPHY
Provides historical information about key figures mentioned in the chapter.

 PSYCHOLOGY & SOCIETY
Takes a look at the interesting effects within society of the psychological theories discussed.

 CONNECTIONS
Lists other chapters in the set containing information related to the topic discussed.

The Human Computer

In principle the computer and the brain are two of a kind

The branch of cognitive psychology called the information-processing approach is based on the idea that the human brain works much like a computer. Obviously there are differences, and the comparisons between the two are not always rigorously scientific; but efforts to explain the brain in terms of a computer have produced some immensely interesting research.

People do not have a limited warranty, plug into the wall for power, and crash when third-party software is installed. But while the human computer is physically quite different from a PC or Mac, it often operates on similar principles.

Imagine that an intelligent alien had been sent to Earth to observe the planet's life forms. What would it make of humans? At first glance the alien might regard us as quite unremarkable creatures. Although people have five senses and sophisticated mechanisms for using them, no human sense is the best of its kind on the planet. Hawks have better eyesight, dogs have a stronger sense of smell, and bats hear much better than people do. Neither is the human physically dominant. Pound for pound, many other animals are stronger, faster, and more efficient at what they do. So the naked human is a pretty average mammal with a poor tolerance for heat and cold, wind and rain, and injury.

While the humans' genetic cousins—a few million great apes such as gorillas and chimpanzees—seem happy to lead quiet, tribal lives, the six billion people on the planet construct cities, elect presidents, build business empires, listen to music, and question their own existence. Rapid advances in technology at the end of the 20th century even propelled three men to the Moon and back. The alien may find these contradictions inexplicable, but it can scarcely fail to be impressed by them.

All these amazing achievements were produced by minds that, on closer examination, resemble machines. Many people think this analogy dehumanizes what it means to be a person. It is true that humans have little in common with automobiles or production-line robots. But people are similar to machines in the sense that they are physical systems composed of interacting elements.

Information processing

Modern philosophers and psychologists have argued convincingly that the machine with which the brain shares the most characteristics is the computer. This may sound odd, but humans and computers are alike in many ways. Both have a hardware component—the brain in humans and the complex electronic circuitry inside computers. Both also have a software component—the mind can be likened to computer programs. The brain is the most complex structure yet discovered. But the mind is also necessary. Both the brain and the mind use this built-in hardware and software to process all sorts of information.

> *"It might have been necessary a decade ago to argue for the commonality of the information processes that are employed by such disparate systems as computers and human nervous systems. The evidence for that commonality is now overwhelming."*
> —*Herbert Simon, 1980*

Let's examine how we process visual information. Your eyes collect light—data about colors, contours, movement, and depth. But light in itself is not all you need to recognize what you are looking at. You also need to process the visual data. Imagine you are at a football game. Sunlight reflects off the surface of objects and flies in all directions. Your eyeballs

collect some of the reflected light shining right at you. The brain's visual pathways—the hardware—kick into action. Information processing begins. First, the eyeballs register the incoming stimulation. The outer protective layer of each eye—the cornea— focuses and sharpens the image. Like a camera, the eyes also have fine-focusing mechanisms called lenses. The light then reaches the back inside cover of each eyeball—the retina. There it stimulates light-sensitive cells. Some cells respond to contrast; others to color. They are all information processors. The cells transform the light into nerve signals that pass electrical impulses down each optic nerve to the visual cortex at the back of the brain. In addition, you have the software— information from other parts of the brain that adds inferences, deductions, and interpretations to what you have seen.

KEY POINTS

- Information processing is any change or transformation to sensory stimuli or the impulses derived from sensory stimuli.
- The information-processing approach likens the human brain to a machine. The brain is seen as the human version of a computer and the mind as software that processes data.
- The information-processing approach allows psychologists to explain the mind, a nonphysical entity, in terms associated with a physical entity like a computer.
- Cognitive psychologists believe that the brain symbolizes information. These symbols are then processed by the mind.
- Cognitive psychologists examine objective measures and work backward to posit the subjective. They use the transcendental method proposed by Kant. Given a set of facts, they propose probable sequences of information-processing events, which can then be tested.
- The information-processing approach is applied to a wide range of disciplines, including perception, attention, memory, mental representation, problem solving, and language.
- Connectionist theories suggest ways in which networks of nerve cells process information. They have major implications in areas such as artificial intelligence and linguistics.
- One of the main arguments against the information-processing approach is reductionism. The critics argue that it is too simplistic to suggest that the physical laws governing nonliving objects can be applied to living things.

The visual cortex "finishes" the processing by piecing together all the information. At this point—just a fraction of a second after the light from the football field hits your eye—you see the ball being caught in the end zone. Touchdown!

If we accept the proposition that human brains are like computers, information can be defined as any incoming sensory data that passes through the network of neurons that constitute our brains. Light entering our eyeballs, sound waves entering our ear canals, and molecules entering our mouth and nostrils are all examples. The term also includes any impulses derived from the incoming sensory data, for example, the electrical signals that travel down each optic nerve. Information processing is any change to, or transformation of, these data. For this analogy to work, we must also assume that the human brain contains mechanisms, or software, for processing the information. This processing is called cognition and, in its widest definition, encompasses all forms of thinking about the world around us.

Imagine you are a computer. Your task is to add two numbers together and display the result. Adding is a form of information processing because it involves the transformation of input data. You register the two numbers, for example, 2 and 4. To add the two numbers, you must first make them compatible with what might be called your addition program. Theoretically, it is possible that the brain could store every answer individually ($1 + 1 = 2$, $8 + 2 = 10$, $83 + 91 = 174$, etc.), but this would take up far too much room in the memory banks. So the human computer has stored a framework by which the sum of any two numbers can be figured out. It is a cognitive process. To add, we know that it is necessary to take the two numbers and figure out their sum— in symbolic form: $A + B = C$. So taking our two numbers 2 and 4, we substitute 2 for A and 4 for B, and arrive at the answer C, which in this case is 6.

The mind as a machine

The brain is much more complicated than simple pieces of computer hardware and software. However, the analogy works sufficiently well to describe the function of the brain using terms associated with computer processing. This provides psychologists with new ways of describing behavior and explaining data. For example, cognitive psychologists would argue that the brain and a computer are

> *"Under pressure from the computer, the question of mind in relation to machine is becoming a central cultural preoccupation. It is becoming for us what sex was to Victorians—threat, obsession, taboo, and fascination."*
> —*Sherry Turkle, 1995*

similar because they process information in a goal-orientated, intentional, and systematic way. This does not fit with the theories of behavioral psychologists (*see* Vol. 1, pp. 74–89), who describe humans as rather passive—their thoughts and actions are mainly a result of environmental factors. Cognitive psychologists have also found ways to conduct experiments that reveal the processes involved in thinking. Behavioral psychologists do not believe that the mind can be observed or measured in any way.

Cognitive psychologists think that like computers, our brains act as symbol processors. Computers use number binary digits (zeros and ones) to represent any kind of information. The numbers are processed by computer programs and switch on tiny pulses of electricity inside the computer. Humans also use symbols to represent information. These symbols are processed by the mind—the human equivalent of a computer program. Finally, they end up as millions of nerve impulses flying around the pathways of the brain. Different computer programs enable you to perform many different tasks. For example, a word-processing program enables you to write a letter; a game program lets you fight evil creatures in an imaginary world. In a similar way the programs hardwired into the human brain can process all sorts of different information. They enable you to make decisions, recognize objects, solve problems, and use language.

The programs and symbols uncovered by cognitive psychologists have physical form, but they can be described without reference to them. In other words, information-processing explanations are abstract. In our vision example a physiologist may talk about information being processed in the eye, along the optic nerve, and in the visual cortex. But a cognitive psychologist can describe these three areas equally well—if less specifically—as A, B, and C. In fact, cognitive psychologists often describe absolutely everything of importance about visual processing without reference to physiology at all. Sure, to build a visual system we would need something to gather the light at one end: An eye or a camera will both do the same job. At the other end we would need a collection of programs to do the work of the visual cortex and piece together the processed information. A physical computing machine is needed to process this information, but cognitive psychologists believe that any general computing device can do it. If this is true, any general computer should be able to copy the function of the brain. All we need to do is feed the general computer the same programs—human computer programs discovered by psychologists using the information-processing approach.

The limitations

Theories of information processing have many critics. One of the charges most commonly leveled against it is that of reductionism. Reductionists attempt to explain the processes of living organisms using physical laws usually applied to

Just like the stars in the sky, everything on Earth consists of the same basic elements. According to the reductionist theory, human beings are simply the result of the interaction of all these elements—processes governed by the fundamental forces of nature.

nonliving objects. Psychologists who adhere to the information-processing approach also look to explain complex relationships between an organism, its mind, and its environment in terms of a nonliving object—computer. This approach may be seen as inaccurate, but the overall benefits are widely regarded as worth the risk.

Any information-processing system is limited in speed and capacity. A program must have a limited capacity to be specific and efficient. For example, you could not

Bottom-up and top-down

By convention, a hierarchy is used to differentiate between things and groups of things. The cognitive system is based on a hierarchy. Information that gets processed, such as auditory and visual sensory stimuli, is located at the bottom of the hierarchy. The most complex cognitive systems, such as attention, memory, language, and problem solving, are located at the top of the hierarchy. Thus any level other than the lowest will be a more specific description than the one below it. Any level other than the highest will be less specific than the one above it. Information can flow both from the bottom of the hierarchy to the top of the hierarchy and from the top of the hierarchy to the bottom of the hierarchy. Moving between levels is a form of information processing.

> *"Men ought to know that from the brain, and from the brain only, arise our pleasures, joys, laughter, and jests, as well as our sorrows, pains, griefs, and tears. Through it, in particular, we think, see and hear, and distinguish the ugly from the beautiful, the bad from the good, the pleasant from the unpleasant."*
> —*Hippocrates, 400 B.C.*

read a whole book in one second even if it were possible to see all the pages at once. Your "reading program" has neither the speed nor the capacity to do so. Doing too many things at once makes us clumsy and

> *"Science may be described as the art of oversimplification."*
> —*Sir Karl Popper, 1982*

ineffective. The limits of speed and capacity are important components of psychological theories in the information-processing approach.

Bottom-up and top-down processing on the telephone. Your response to the ring is bottom-up: You hear the telephone ring, symbolize it, and identify that someone wants to talk to you. Answering the call is top-down: You realize that the telephone must be answered and so pick up the receiver.

When information flows from the bottom of the hierarchy to the top of the hierarchy, it is known as bottom-up processing. Lower-level systems categorize and describe incoming perceptual information and pass it onto higher levels for more complex information processing. Using our example of vision: The bottom-up processing would be how light gets processed by the retina, moves along the optic nerve and visual pathways, and then activates the cells in the visual cortex.

When information flows from the top of the hierarchy to the bottom of the hierarchy, it is known as top-down processing. Top-down processing is concept driven. Perceptual information coming into the system can be influenced by what the individual has stored in the higher levels of the system, for example, information about past experiences. One often used example of top-down processing can be shown by looking at the Rubin vase (*see* right). If our memories of faces have been triggered by a series of previous exposures to outlines of faces, we will spontaneously interpret and thus perceive the Rubin vase as two black faces staring at one another. In the same way, if we have instead been recently exposed to pictures of outlines of vases, we will perceive the vase instead. Since we are looking at exactly the same picture, the bottom-up processing of the picture is the same. Any perception is therefore composed of interpretations that the mind imposes onto the physiological act of seeing. This is the extreme version of top-down processing—all information coming into the system is affected by what is already known about the world.

In 1988 the American psychologist and philosopher Jerry Fodor proposed an alternative "theory of modularity" for top-down processing. Fodor argued that top-down processing occurs only in some parts of the cognitive system at certain times. Fodor rejects the idea that all stored information can potentially affect all incoming information.

Three groups

Information-processing approaches are used by different types of scientists. There are three loosely defined groups: Experimental cognitive psychologists, cognitive scientists, and cognitive neuropsychologists. Although they all have their own areas of expertise and interest, they may occupy some of the same ground as researchers in artificial intelligence, linguistics, neuroscience, and cognitive anthropology.

As a result of top-down processing the Rubin vase can be perceived either as a white vase or two black faces looking at each other, but not both at the same time. The illusion was made famous by the Danish psychologist Edgar Rubin in 1915.

Experimental cognitive psychologists often concentrate on gathering empirical data in order to determine how memories are stored. They usually test theories in the laboratory by, for example, giving people lists of words to memorize under various conditions. If it turns out that people tend to remember words at the beginning and end of a list more easily than those in the middle, then the cognitive psychologist will ask how the

lists have been processed, where in the brain they are stored, and then how they are retrieved from memory.

Cognitive scientists build computational models based on programs and symbols. The major difference between a model and a theory is that the former is a more tightly specified version of the latter. The theoretical work of cognitive psychologists often helps cognitive

David Hume argued that the knowledge of cause and effect in a relationship was based on the accumulation of subjective experiences. Thus science, which looks to explain events in terms of cause and effect, is based on the weaknesses of subjectivity.

scientists develop these models, but the exchange of information works in both directions. For example, the computational model of the memory phenomenon previously described might consist of a program written in a computer language such as C or BASIC. When given a list of words, the program may generate a human response. Models are useful because they help generate predictions and can be manipulated in ways that would be unethical if used on a human being.

Cognitive neuropsychologists concentrate their studies on the brain itself, especially those people whose brains have been damaged in some way. For example, if a patient shows a specific problem when reading—they cannot read construction words such as "and" and "the"—and other patients show the opposite—they can read only construction words—then the cognitive neuropsychologist will suggest that construction words and other types of words are processed in separate areas of the brain. Therefore cognitive neuropsychologists believe that the processing of certain types of information is linked to specific areas of the brain. Though real-world examples are seldom so clear-cut, cognitive neuropsychologists have used this kind of evidence to evaluate the theories of cognitive psychologists and, of course, to propose theories of their own.

A science of the mind

The key difference between psychology and other scientific disciplines lies in the object of study. Traditionally, scientists study physical objects—atoms, electrons, cells, and planets—and the processes that affect them. Scientists then draw conclusions and propose theories based on their observations. Cognitive studies center around a nonphysical object—the mind. The information-processing approach allows psychologists to study the effects of the mind as a physical quantity and therefore more scientifically. The analogies of computer as brain and computer program as mind mean that psychologists can look at mental processing from a completely different perspective than, say, behavioral psychologists. Using computer programs, they can test hypotheses about how the mind works and even try to specify the individual processing steps. Indeed, many new discoveries have been made by describing the function of the brain and mind using computer terminology.

The modern science of psychology developed from the philosophers of the late 19th century. In 1879 the so-called father of modern psychology, Wilhelm Wundt (1832–1920), set up the first psychology laboratory in Leipzig, Germany (*see* Vol. 1, pp. 30–39). Wundt relied on introspection as a method of studying mental processes. He set up complex experiments and encouraged people to look at how their conscious experiences changed as a result of the experiment. In this way Wundt believed he could find out how the mind works. Researchers relied on people to report their own observations—the researchers could not observe them directly.

> *"Psychology as the behaviorist views it is a purely objective experimental branch of natural science. Introspection forms no essential part of its methods."*
> —John B. Watson, 1913

Psychologists soon grew impatient with introspection since the results of such experiments were flawed in two important ways. First, if people report their experiences after the experiment has taken place, they rely on memory. Memory is a constructive, fallible, and occasionally fictional process. Second, people find it difficult to observe their own conscious experiences. They do not have access to the inner workings of

mental processes, such as recognition and categorization, and hence cannot be expected to explain them. Last, introspection produces subjective, not objective, observations.

Imagine an apple on a table. The objective information about the apple consists of its weight, its age, and any other measurable characteristic. Subjective information would be what it tastes like, what memories it triggers, ideas about what apples can be used for, and so on. Subjective information is biased, personal interpretation, while objective information is impartial. So objective information is more likely to reflect the actual state of the apple. For this reason modern psychologists rely on objectivity when carrying out their experiments.

Innate concepts

Psychologists cannot look at the mind in the same way as they would an apple. The mind does not exist in a physical sense. So how can they study the mind objectively? The cognitive approach looks at the effect of the mind rather than the mind itself. For example, a fear of spiders is a subjective experience, but the enlargement of the pupils and the increase in heart and breathing rate are measurable, physical manifestations of this fear. From there a scientist can work backward to subjective cause or causes in the mind. Cognitive psychologists looked to eliminate the weaknesses of theories such as Wundt's introspection and later schools of psychology. They were influenced by a number of prominent thinkers, among them the French mathematician and philosopher René Descartes (1596–1650), the English philosophers John Locke (1632–1704) and David Hume (1711–1776) (*see* opposite), and most importantly the German philosopher Immanuel Kant (1724–1804).

Locke and Hume argued that all human knowledge resulted from an accumulation of sensory experiences. The human mind at birth was *tabula rasa* (a "blank slate"). The mind then becomes populated with

IMMANUEL KANT

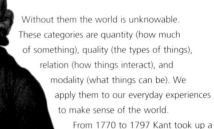

Immanuel Kant (1724-1804) is often described as the most influential human thinker. Kant was born in Königsberg, Prussia (modern Kaliningrad, Russia), and educated at the Collegium Fredericianum and later the University of Königsberg. He studied classics, physics, and mathematics until he was forced to abandon his studies following the death of his father and earn money through private tutoring. In 1755 Kant returned to his studies and obtained a doctorate. He remained at the university for 15 years, teaching science, mathematics, geography, and philosophy.

Kant's philosophy centered on epistemology, which is usually defined as "the possibility, origins, nature, and extent of human knowledge." He believed that the human conception of reality was partly due to innate (preexisting) ideas that people have about the world.

Immanuel Kant developed a theory of reasoning known as the transcendental method, or induction.

Without them the world is unknowable. These categories are quantity (how much of something), quality (the types of things), relation (how things interact), and modality (what things can be). We apply them to our everyday experiences to make sense of the world.

From 1770 to 1797 Kant took up a professorship of metaphysics and logic at the University of Königsberg. Some of his teachings embarrassed the government of Prussia, mainly his views on rationalism. (Kant theorized that knowledge is acquired by reason without resort to experience, rather than through religious revelations.) Accordingly, Kant was banned by the king of Prussia, Frederick William II, from speaking or writing on religious topics. Kant obeyed this royal decree for five years until the king died in 1794, whereupon he resumed his teaching and writing. Ten years later Kant himself died.

ideas taken from our everyday experiences. Life teaches us everything, including concepts of identity, relationship, causality, and so on. Hume was troubled briefly by the concept of causality. A causal relationship is a cause-and-effect relationship. Kick a ball, and it moves; punch a wall, and you will hurt.

To take another example, you know that clapping near the ear of a sleeping parent will elicit an energetic response. In Hume's view your knowledge of the relationship between the clapping (cause) and the parent's annoyance (effect) should result from an internal combination of the two ideas "clap" and "parent." But if it exists neither in the impression of "clap" nor in the impression of "parent," where does "causal" knowledge come from? For Hume it came from the subjective experience of the individual and was based on nothing more than the timely coincidence of events. The implication of Hume's idea is that cause-and-effect relationships might not be

correctly identified due to weaknesses of subjectivity. Science relies on objectivity, but it is also based on observations of cause-and-effect relationships. Science is therefore also based on the weaknesses of subjectivity, which can introduce bias.

Kant disagreed with the blank slate model of the mind. He suggested that some concepts, such as causality, logic, substance, space, and time, were innate—present in all of us from birth. In modern terms they are programmed into our genes. The mind builds knowledge out of these innate concepts as well as from the accumulation of sensory experiences. These concepts are said to be *a priori* ("from what is before"). The human mind needs *a priori* concepts just as much as a closet needs hangers to hold clothes.

The transcendental method
Like modern cognitive psychologists, Kant wanted to study these subjective *a priori* concepts objectively. This presents a problem. Kant recognized that subjective

things would remain subjective, just as objective things would remain objective. Anybody who wants to find out the truth about anything must have a preference for objective, unbiased information, because it is naturally closer to the truth. But Kant found a way out of the fix. He proposed a method of reasoning that, unlike the deductive logic of Aristotle, provided a probable as opposed to a definitive conclusion. By sacrificing definiteness, Kant found a way of harnessing subjective data to arrive at an objective conclusion. Kant called this method of reasoning the transcendental method.

The transcendental method is also called induction because the observations come before the explanations. (In the deductive logic of Aristotle explanations come before the expected observations.) Sherlock Holmes, the fictional detective created by Sir Arthur Conan Doyle, used this method in *The Adventure of Watson's Watch* (*see* box p. 16).

Imagine you are Holmes. Using the transcendental method, you start with a fact or a new set of facts, such as receiving a pocket watch from your friend Dr. Watson. The watch has several distinguishing features, such as it is (a) engraved with the initial *W,* (b) has a 50-year-old manufacturer's date, (c) has several small numbers scratched on the inside of the case, (d) has small indentations around the keyhole, and (e) is scored all over.

Now, ask yourself how these things might have got there. Examine each observation and deduce, using existing knowledge of the subject, an appropriate explanation. For example, combine fact (a), the watch is engraved with a *W* (which, since Watson presents us with the watch, we presume stands for Watson) and fact (b), the watch is 50 years old. Inference: The watch belonged to Watson's father. However, Watson's father is dead. Inference: It was bequeathed to his eldest son. For fact (c) these numbers are likely to have been scratched by a pawnbroker. Inference: The brother had

Sherlock Holmes and his friend Dr. Watson in a railway carriage. The transcendental method is the kind of reasoning used by Sir Arthur Conan Doyle's fictional detective Sherlock Holmes in The Adventure of Watson's Watch (see *box p. 16).*

bouts of prosperity and poverty. In each case, we see how the observable facts influence the speculative solution.

If the solution and the facts fit very well, then stop. If they do not, continue. At any time, new facts can be added that lead to further deductions. For example, new fact (d): Watson's exercised facial expression. Inference: You were correct.

Like Kant, cognitive psychologists also want to work with objective data. Given a set of facts, the cognitive psychologist can work backward, using the transcendental method, to propose a sequence of information-processing events to explain the facts. These events can then be tested. The methods used are scientific, which means they offer reliability (others can replicate an experiment and obtain the same results) and validity (safeguards prove the test is measuring what was intended and not another phenomenon).

As with any information-gathering process, the end product is constrained by the quality of the information-gathering tools. You cannot understand and predict

THE ADVENTURE OF WATSON'S WATCH BY J. H. WATSON

Adapted from *The Sign of Four* by Sir Arthur Conan Doyle, published in *Strand Magazine*, 1891.

Never was there a more worthy subject of the Crown than my dear friend, Mr. Sherlock Holmes. As I reach my final years, I wonder what more I can convey of this singular private-consulting detective. Glancing back through the Holmes canon, I find that, alas, many episodes are of a somewhat titillating nature. Therefore, I have resolved to redress this balance with what I shall call *The Adventure of Watson's Watch*. Uniquely, it illustrates his ingenious method without recourse to London's villainous criminal underclass.

It was a gray March evening, and I had called at my friend's Baker Street lodgings. We had dined handsomely on Mrs. Hudson's finest offerings. Soon the night drew in, and the room grew quiet but for the fall of distant hooves.

"Holmes, I have here a watch," said I. He regarded my announcement with some amusement, for it interrupted a turn at his chemical apparatus. "Would you have the kindness to let me have an opinion upon the character of the late owner as a test of your deductive powers."

"My dear Watson, my methods are primarily inductive in the mode of that great philosopher Immanuel Kant. But, pray, let me see the watch."

I handed him the watch with some amusement of my own. He balanced it in his hand, gazed hard at the dial, opened the back, and examined the works, first with his naked eyes and then with a powerful convex lens.

"Now. This watch belonged to your elder brother. He inherited it from your father. Observe, the initial *W* suggests your own name, and the date of the watch is nearly 50 years back, and the initials are as old as the watch. So it was made for the last generation, and jewelry usually descends to the eldest son, and he is most likely to have the same name as the father. Your father has, if I remember right, been dead many years. It has, therefore, been in the hands of your eldest brother. Moreover, he was a man of untidy habits, and careless."

"How so?" I admit I was exercised at his frankness.

"He was left with good prospects, but he threw away his chances, lived for some time in poverty with occasional short intervals of prosperity, and finally, taking to drink, he died. That is all I can gather." He passed me the watch.

"By Jove, you are precisely correct! But you cannot know this from the watch alone." His analysis pained me.

"You understand," said he, "I could only say what was the balance of probability. I did not at all expect to be so accurate." He reached for a pipe and began to fill it. "I began by stating that your brother was careless. When you observe the lower part of that watchcase, you notice that it is not only dented in two places, but it is cut and marked all over from the habit of keeping other hard objects, such as coins or keys, in the same pocket. Surely it is no great feat to assume that a man who treats a 50-guinea watch so cavalierly must be a careless man. Neither is it a very far-fetched inference that a man who inherits one article of such value is pretty well provided for in other respects."

I nodded, to show that I followed his reasoning.

"It is very customary for pawnbrokers in England, when they take a watch, to scratch the ticket number with a pin-point upon the inside of the case. It is more handy than a label, as there is no risk of the number being lost or transposed. There are no less than four such numbers visible to my lens on the inside of this case. First inference: Your brother was often at low water. Second inference: He had occasional bursts of prosperity, or he could not have redeemed the pledge. Finally, I ask you to look at the inner plate, which contains the keyhole. Look at the thousands of scratches all round the hole, marks where the key has slipped. What sober man's key could have scored those grooves? But you will never see a drunkard's watch without them." Holmes drew on the pipe.

I was subdued. "I admit that it is an accurate portrait of my unhappy brother."

"It is often said that a man's possessions retain a lasting impression of their owner."

"But the process of reading those impressions is extraordinary!" I ejaculated.

"Not so. The process is simple. Only the inferences, once divorced from their chain of reasoning, appear extraordinary." He fetched a book and gave it to me. The cover read *The Critique of Pure Reason*, by Mr. Kant.

I thumbed through this dense volume. "Why, Holmes, your method is detailed here—yet you have mentioned neither this book nor man prior to this conversation."

Holmes smiled in a conspiratorial manner, but then there came a knock at the door. It was a telegram from Inspector Lestrade. Before long, we rang for our boots and a cab, bound for an adventure of the most singular kind. As for Mr. Kant, I did not hear his name again.

the weather with a wet finger held in the air. And the mind is different from the weather because it is not a physical object. The brain, of course, is a physical object, but the mind lives in quite another realm. All the psychologist can do is study the effect of the mind to make educated guesses, never the mind itself. Here we are in the same predicament as physicists attempting to discover the nature of subatomic particles. This means that tools to explore and to measure must be clear, effective, and occasionally ingenious.

Comparing the mind to a machine using the transcendental method has generated a more complete picture of the mind than any other scientific method. In the 21st century, when we are tempted to look only ahead, it is worth remembering that the roots of comparison extend back as far as the philosophers of ancient Greece (*see* Vol. 1, pp. 10–15). It can also be noted that cognitive science would produce little without its researchers and their ingenious tools.

Reaction times

One of the most commonly used measurements in cognitive studies is reaction time. For example, a researcher could show you a particular word on a computer screen and ask you to press a key as soon as you have made a decision about it. What kind of decision? The researcher might show you a series of words like "oxen," "rout," "wont," and so on, and then a series containing "game," "hello," "take," and so on. The first series are all legitimate English words, but they are uncommon. The second series are English, too, but they are more common. If you had to decide if an individual word was a real word or a nonsense word, you would make your decision quicker with the common words than with the odder ones. Likewise, if I showed you nonsense words such as "gont," "faln," and "yert," you would be slower to dismiss them as nonwords in comparison with "hlut," "pryn," and "trah." Again this stems from how frequent things are. The former

Is this picture of a railroad track three-dimensional? Why? How do you think someone who had never seen any kind of picture before would react to it? Visual illusions such as this are used by researchers to measure reaction times in studies on perception.

series has nonsense words that conform to highly frequent English letter combinations ("nt," "ln," and "rt"). The second sequence does not ("hl," "yn," and "ah"). This frequency effect is one of the commonly confirmed facts in cognitive psychology. It forms the basis of a number of theories. You might be surprised by the range of competing theories that make different claims about how fast people should process different types of stimuli. Reaction-time measurement has been a linchpin of cognitive psychology since its beginnings and is likely to remain so for the foreseeable future.

> *"To think is to see."*
> *— Honoré de Balzac, 1834*

Vision

Seeing seems so breathtakingly easy that it comes as a shock to the uninitiated that psychologists bother to study it at all. Surely the eyes are like cameras? And the picture is viewed somewhere in the brain?

WINDOWS ON THE BRAIN

Some researchers think that the mind can be understood by examining brain activity under controlled conditions. There is much support for this approach. We know that when the brain is damaged, the mind is damaged. Often if the brain is damaged specifically, the mind is damaged specifically. Brain-activity measurements have another advantage. Cognitive theories may take a vast number of forms. "Lower-level" physiological evidence may help cast light on "higher-level" cognitive functions, such as memory and problem solving, in which there is more range for error. Thus although we would have some difficulty explaining mental phenomena at the level of the brain itself, collecting data from the brain will undoubtedly help explain some of these higher-level cognitive functions.

Single unit recording

Neurons are the "business cells" of the brain, responsible for all nervous activity. They are the subjects of single unit recording in which a tiny electrode touches a single cell. Neurons pass on information as electrical impulses. At rest a neuron will "fire" several times a minute. When a cell processes information, the firing rate increases. By varying a stimulus—say, a visual one—and varying the neurons studied, researchers can map out which parts of brain become "active" for different visual tasks. This is what the Canadian neurobiologist David Hubel (born 1926) and the Swedish neurophysiologist Torsten Wiesel (born 1924) did together in 1962 to uncover the breathtaking complexity of the visual cortex. This discovery has underpinned, and constrained, theories of low-level perception.

EEG studies

The electroencephalogram (EEG) is a device that measures electrical activity at the surface of the brain. The movement of impulses along neurons causes this activity. In terms of overall brain functioning EEGs have provided invaluable information about the stages of sleep and other basic physiological processes. However, with respect to the mind the EEG is a little unwieldy. First, electrical activity may vary spontaneously. Second, this activity is specific to the brain's surface and does not necessarily reflect activity deep within. Little can be done about the second problem, but the first can be countered using "averaged evoked response potentials." In an experiment the subject is presented with a series of similar stimuli, and the EEG activity recorded. This activity is averaged over the period of presentation time. This "blurs" the effect of spontaneous activity, leaving only the activity "evoked" by the stimuli. Some researchers compare EEG readings to eavesdropping on a conversation in an adjacent room by putting your ear to the wall. However, it may be used to differentiate between processes that concentrate in separate brain areas.

PET scans

The brain needs fuel—oxygen, sugar, and other nutrients—to do its job. This fuel is carried by the blood. When any part of the brain is engaged in a task, this part needs more fuel. For any specified task we can begin to see which areas work harder by monitoring the blood flow. This helps identify the functions of different brain areas. A scanning procedure called positron emission tomography (PET) uses radioactive isotopes to measure blood flow. Following injection, the isotope crosses the barrier between the blood and the brain, and enters the neural tissue. Since the isotopes are radioactive, they soon become unstable and emit a particle called a positron. When a positron collides with a particle called an electron, two light particles, called photons, form. Crucially, the two photons fly off in exactly opposite directions. A detector around your skull registers these photons. A straight line between the two impact points will show where the photons came from. In turn, this indicates the position of positrons and therefore the blood. More photons means more blood. PET is not very precise because the positron may travel a short distance before colliding with an electron. Also, the timescale of PET is minutes in duration, so short-lived changes may go unnoticed.

Positron emission tomography (PET) identifies areas of increased blood flow in the brain. It is a very accurate way of measuring regional cerebral blood flow.

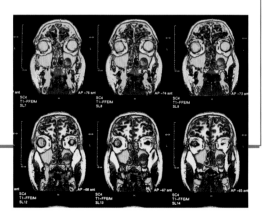

The information-processing approach suggests that the mind can be likened to a computer program that works using symbols. When artificial intelligence researchers attempted to write programs to instruct machines to "see" like people, problems soon emerged (*see* Vol. 2, pp. 140–163). The machines could be designed to avoid collisions and look for fuel, for example, without having experience of these processes. However, the research indicated that such a machine would need many sensory subsystems to maintain itself in a complex world like our own. Any computer program written to link the machine's sensory inputs to the mysterious "understanding" of a scene would need to be fast, adaptive, and complex. Even detecting the edges of a simple geometric figure on a blank background requires complicated

math. More than anywhere else, cognitive psychology has made major advances in our understanding of perception. The studies have shown that the human visual processing system is extremely complex and compartmentalized.

Attention

Our world is a cacophony of feelings, sights, smells, sounds, and tastes. You may be reading this passage, but your mind may be on any number of different things, all of which are conspiring to distract you from the words on the page. Attention provides us with the ability to concentrate on individual bands of incoming information and is therefore an important field of study in cognitive psychology. One of the most influential researchers into attention was the British psychologist Colin Cherry who, in 1953,

Not paying attention in class. This girl may be daydreaming about her boyfriend, a night out with friends on the weekend, tomorrow's hockey game, and anything else other than the task she has in front of her. Our ability to process the information at hand is limited, since many other thoughts are equally important to us.

FOCUS ON CONNECTIONISM

One approach to modeling the physiology of the brain is known as connectionism (see Vol. 1, pp. 126–133, and Vol. 3, pp. 64–87). It uses models composed of connected units. The process is noteworthy because, as we will see, it may not technically fall under the banner of our traditional conception of information processing.

Neural networks were first proposed in a paper published in 1943 by the American neuroscientist Warren S. McCulloch and the American logician Walter Pitts. They tried to explain how the brain could produce highly complex patterns by using a system of simple, connected neurons. McCulloch and Pitts suggested that groups of connected neurons worked together as a network. The McCulloch and Pitts model gave a highly simplified model of a neuron, but it was very important in describing the function of the brain.

One of the most important points about connectionist networks is that the neurons do not start out as good information processors. They learn this ability as a group over time. The first

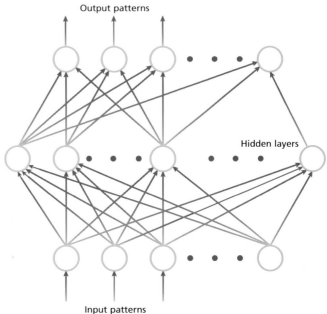

This multilayered neural network has an input layer, a hidden layer, and an output layer. Each neuron receives an input from the environment or the preceding layer and sends an output to the next layer. The input to the neuron may be either excitatory or inhibitory, and these signals are analyzed to determine the strength of the output. In turn, this becomes the input in the next layer. Neural networks are very good at learning the relationship between a stimulus and a response. After the network has been trained, it is ready to perform the task. An example is changing verbs from the present tense (stimulus) to the past tense form (response).

artificial network was built by Frank Rosenblatt in 1957. His machine—the Perceptron—had one input layer and one output layer only, but it impressed scientists with its ability to recognize simple patterns. Later, Marvin Minsky and Seymour Papert showed that the Perceptron was limited by the number of layers it contained. In the 1960s cognitive psychologists developed models that contained multiple "layers" of artificial neurons and could solve simple mathematical problems. This made the networks more powerful and biologically plausible.

Such networks are composed of artificial neurons arranged in layers. One neuron may excite or inhibit any other neuron it is connected to, though these connections

are typically one-way. Any stimulus that is presented to the network for processing is encoded as a pattern of activation (neurons are either switched on or off). When the network is working, any represented information becomes a pattern of activation distributed throughout the entire network. (This runs counter to the traditional conception of information processing because the representations are not separate symbols.) Many representations may be stored within a network even if it contains a relatively small number of neurons. Finally, the behavior of a network is determined by the number of artificial neurons and how they are arranged, its learning procedure, and the stimuli it experiences.

became interested in the "cocktail party effect" (*see* box p. 26). This effect is illustrated when you have a conversation

> *"Everyone knows what attention is. It is the taking possession of the mind, in clear and vivid form, of one out of what seem several simultaneously possible objects or trains of thought. Focalization, concentration of consciousness are of its essence."*
> —*William James, 1890*

in a crowded room, and the background noise is a meaningless babble. When somebody says your name, however, even

Finding the ball may be easy with three shells and a keen eye, but what about four, five, or six shells? To improve the speed and efficiency of our memory, there is a limit to how much we can remember.

though it is part of the background noise, you hear it quite distinctly. The cocktail party effect suggests that attention is an active process in which sensations are filtered out unless they are considered important enough to attend to. Information-processing research has gone a long way to explain some of the mechanisms that underlie attention. One theory suggests that because information processing is limited in capacity, areas of the brain may slow processing down, forcing us to focus on the information being processed.

Memory

In one sense we are defined by our memories. Memories of our life experiences are called episodic memories. Our ability to recall facts relies on

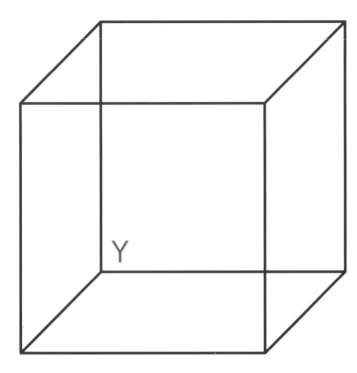

Mental representation

Mental representations—the inner representations the mind holds of external objects or ideas—have long puzzled philosophers and cognitive researchers. This huge topic underpins many other areas of psychology, including vision, memory, language, and problem solving. Ideas about mental representations are changing thanks in large part to connectionist models of brain function (*see* box p. 20). These models suggest that mental representations could be distributed as patterns of activation across neural networks rather than discrete, separate packages of data. However, some researchers argue that they are the same thing described from two viewpoints. One important notion is intentionality (*see* pp. 136–163). This theory proposes a distinction between physical objects and mental representations. For some philosophers intentionality is a defining characteristic of a cognitive system like the human mind.

Problem solving

Most human behaviors involve problem solving: finding a sock in a drawer, multiplying two numbers, deciding whether to take the train or the bus. Problem solving and decision making include all mental processes—perception, memory, attention, language, etc.—and form part of what people call thinking. Problem solving involves manipulations of either mental representations or the physical things around you, or both, to achieve a particular goal.

Gestalt psychologists (*see* Vol. 1, pp. 46–51) believed that insight and prior experience were crucial in solving problems. Gestalt psychology is notable because it rallied resistance to the prevailing behaviorist perspective. Behaviorists argued that problem solving was merely a trial-and-error process in which a successful solution was reinforced and stored in memory. Later, the mathematician Allen Newell and the

semantic memory. And memory for complicated, learned behaviors is called procedural memory. A further distinction identifies three types of storage. The first type is a kind of transitional memory. It refers to relatively unprocessed visual and audio information from the sense organs. The second is the more familiar short-term, or working, memory, which stores a limited amount of data for a few seconds. The third type of storage is long-term memory, which is stored permanently (*see* pp. 88–113).

Many cognitive psychologists think that information is transferred from working memory into long-term memory through the process of examining the information for meaning, the more deeply, the better. Others think that storage occurs as the mind compares new information with data already held in long-term memory. Vital questions remain: Are memories inaccurate or accurate, unchangeable or changeable? And what are the mechanisms by which working memories are processed into long-term memories?

In the perception of illusions such as the Necker cube the corner marked "Y" sometimes appears to be at the front of the cube and other times at the back. Gestalt psychologists suggested that the viewer restructures the cube to perceive it one way or the other.

economist Herbert A. Simon developed the influential General Problem Solver (GPS; *see* pp. 136–163), which is based on the assumption that human thought processes are comparable to the functioning of digital computers. Others have shown that task-specific knowledge has a profound effect on performance in, for example, chess problems, physics puzzles, and computer programming. The modern view of the nature of problem solving includes both nativist (innate) and empiricist (learned) elements.

Language processing

Like sensory perception, language processing appears simple. From an information-processing perspective, however, it is very hard work. Just to convert raw sound waves into speech, then segment that speech, categorize it, and identify its grammar is beyond the most complex computer programs. But a human may hear up to 100,000 words a day and understand nearly all of them. Most people cannot understand a phrase-marker diagram of a sentence, which maps out the grammatical relationships between words. But that is what you do easily every time you hear a sentence, thousands of times of day. Grammar makes human language distinct from, say, the sign language produced by trained apes. If you read the sentence "Colorless green ideas slept furiously," you know that it is nonsense, but also that it is better formed than "Furiously slept ideas green colorless."

One role of the cognitive psychologist is to try to understand the processes by which people speak and understand speech (*see* pp. 114–135 and Vol. 1, pp. 118–125). Most psychologists think that there are several distinct steps involved in speech. First, the brain organizes what you want to say, then grammar is laid out, and then the individual words are put into a mental map.

Understanding speech follows a similar pattern of discrete steps. Although different psychologists suggest that the

steps differ in number and complexity, the experiments they have used to test their theories show that people do plan their speech. The experiments have also shown that context plays an important role in speaking and understanding speech.

Summing up

As we have seen, the information-processing approach has a number of research frontiers. In each the goal is to figure out the representations or symbols involved as well as the programs that operate on them. Critics point to our limited knowledge of artistic ability, the emotions, creativity, genius, and so on to suggest that the approach is forever restricted. A related criticism points to the transience of the computer metaphor. Variously, the workings of the human mind have been compared to oceans, clocks, puppets, steam engines, telegraph exchanges, and computers as technology has progressed. Will our computer view of the mind be replaced by the next technological advance, the next wonder machine? It is possible but seems unlikely because the comparison between people and machines is a commonplace analogy, and people's brains are frequently compared with computers and their minds with computer programs. Although there are obvious differences, this comparison has proved useful in cognitive psychology and has generated theories in areas such as perception, attention, memory, and problem solving.

CONNECTIONS

- Attention and Information Processing: pp. 24–43
- Representing Information: pp. 64–87
- Storing Information: pp. 88–113
- Language Processing: pp. 114–135
- Cognitive Psychology: Volume 1, pp. 104–117
- The Mind: Volume 2, pp. 40–61
- Perception: Volume 2, pp. 62–85
- Consciousness: Volume 2, pp. 110–139
- Artificial Minds: Volume 2, pp. 140–163

Attention and Information Processing

"Whoever treats of interest inevitably treats of attention."

William James

What are you doing at the moment? Reading these words. But even as you read, your senses are receiving information from all around you. Try and think about everything you can see, hear, smell, and feel right now. Can you still concentrate on what you are reading? Your attention has been diverted, and you find it difficult to carry on reading successfully. This shows the importance of attention and information processing in performing day-to-day tasks.

KEY POINTS

- The mind may concentrate on a single input, but it remains alert to other things: Some it may ignore; others may distract its attention.
- According to filter theory, the brain processes the information it wants and leaves the rest behind.
- Attenuation theory states that all available information enters the brain, but data that are regarded as unimportant are paid less attention than more pressing matters. However, this pecking order is under constant review, thus enabling attention to shift when necessary from its current focus to a new concern.
- Both filter theory and attenuation theory assume that information is processed before it enters the brain. Not all psychologists agree: some believe that it is all processed and selected according to need.
- Psychologists are especially interested in the ability to concentrate on more than one thing at a time. The problem is defining the nature of a single task—virtually everything can be seen as a series of subtasks.
- Cognitive neuropsychology uses scanning and imaging to observe changes in the brain as it pays attention and processes information.

Consider a busy intersection during the rush hour. It cannot cope with the volume of traffic, and lines quickly build up. Traffic moves freely when only one car approaches from each direction. It is the same with your mind. Right now you choose to pay attention to the words on the page. Your brain can easily process this single source of information, enabling you to understand the text. That becomes more difficult if you try to think about the other pieces of information your senses are receiving. You are unable to

"The distinction between active and passive attention is made in all books on psychology, and connects itself with deeper aspects."
—William James, 1899

cope with all this information at the same time. Like the intersection, your brain has a limited capacity.

Motorists often speak of a situation such as our intersection as a "bottleneck." Psychologists use the same term to describe the brain's limited capacity to consciously process information. How do we deal with this limitation?

You probably consider many of the things around you to be irrelevant, even distracting, as you read this chapter. Therefore you simply ignore them. That is, you use attention to select just the relevant information from what is stacked up behind the attentional bottleneck and choose to ignore everything else.

The American philosopher William James (1842–1910) (*see* Vol. 1, pp. 30–39) described attention as "Taking possession by the mind . . . of one out of what seem several simultaneous possible . . . trains of thought." But how do we choose what to pay attention to and what to ignore? Do we have enough resources to divide our attention, or is it limited in a fashion that forces us to select just one thing?

Imagine you are watching your favorite television program. At the same time, someone is trying to tell you about his or her day. You have chosen to pay attention to what is showing on the screen; and although you may pretend to be listening

Talking while watching television—the two activities, though similar in nature (they both involve looking and listening to words), can be carried out at the same time, but neither person is fully concentrating on either activity.

and partially take in some of the words, you cannot really fully concentrate on what the other person is telling you.

Focusing on one thing and ignoring everything else around you involves selective attention. Selective attention enables you to choose a single thing to occupy your mind. But what happens to your attention if it is diverted away from the television to register interest in something interesting someone else suddenly has to say, such as an offer of money? You may well have found yourself in a similar position and been accused of selective deafness. This suggests that the mind is capable, in certain circumstances, of attending to more than one source of data, but that it may choose not to do so.

Auditory attention

Many questions about how we focus our attention have been answered by research exploring selective hearing. Our busy lives are filled with hundreds of sounds. It would be impossible for us to interpret and make use of any of them were it not for our selective attention.

To explain more about this, most researchers use the dichotic listening task. Participants wear headphones and listen to two different messages at the same time, one in each ear. Participants are asked to attend and respond to only one of these messages, ignoring the other. Colin Cherry's shadowing experiments (*see* box p. 26) are good examples of a typical dichotic listening task.

The results of Cherry's experiments address an important question about focusing attention. When does the brain choose which information it will attend to? Does the brain process all the information it receives before selecting what to focus on, or is the information selected first, leaving everything else unprocessed in the data bottleneck?

Dichotic listening studies suggest that the information is selected before it has undergone a great deal of processing. In Cherry's experiments participants knew very little about the unattended message.

THE COCKTAIL PARTY PHENOMENON

Imagine you have arrived at a party. There are many groups of people, all having different conversations, so at first you hear an incomprehensible mix of different voices. Later, when you have been at the party for a while and are engaged in a conversation with friends, you no longer hear the other conversations around you. Despite being in close physical contact with others engaged in their own conversations, you hear only the participants in your own. Your attention is focused on those you are talking to. The other sounds your ears detect remain ignored behind the attentional bottleneck. This ability to focus on one conversation and ignore others talking around you is called the "cocktail party phenomenon" and was first identified by Colin Cherry in 1953.

Colin Cherry was an electronics researcher at the Massachusetts Institute of Technology. He found that our ability to focus our attention on one conversation involves making use of the physical differences in the messages we hear to select the one we are interested in. They include the pitch (for example, women tend to have higher voices than men) and the location of the speaker.

Cherry examined the cocktail party phenomenon using a dichotic shadowing task. People wore headphones and heard a different message in each ear, one of which they had to shadow—that is, repeat back as soon as they heard it. He found that people did not hear any of the messages that they were not asked to shadow. Indeed, participants rarely noticed if this message was presented backward or in a foreign language. However, they were able to detect physical changes in the subordinate message, such as speech being replaced by a musical tone or changes in the gender of the speaker.

Cherry's work is a good example of how a simple observation—that we are able to focus attention on one conversation out of many—was developed into a hypothesis and explored within a focused laboratory study. The move into the laboratory and the use of headphones can be criticized as being far more artificial than the original social setting. However, the experiment was very influential in helping us understand attention and prompted other researchers, such as Donald Broadbent, to explore further how we select and attend to the sensory information we receive from around us.

People at parties concentrate exclusively on the conversations in which they are themselves engaged and hear nothing else—until, that is, someone mentions their name or something that grabs their attention.

This suggests that information is selected for attention very early in its processing.

Based on such evidence, in 1958 the British psychologist Donald Broadbent (*see* box p. 27) developed a theory of early attentional selection. He called it the filter theory. The basic idea is that when information from the senses reaches the bottleneck, a choice has to be made as to which message to process. Up until this point nothing has been processed at all.

Broadbent proposed that a sensory filter selects a message for further processing based on its physical characteristics, such as pitch or location. Just as coffee passing through a paper filter leaves behind dregs, so the chosen message then passes through the filter, leaving everything else behind the bottleneck, where it receives no further processing. Broadbent's filter theory accounts for the findings of dichotic listening task experiments. In the shadowing task, for example, both messages reach the sensory filter, where the target message is chosen on the basis

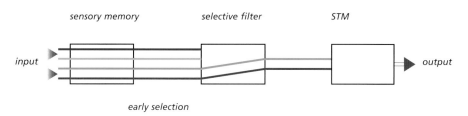

A diagrammatic representation of Broadbent's filter theory of selective attention. STM stands for short-term memory.

sensory memory   selective filter   STM

input   output

early selection

of its location. The theory also accounts for Cherry's experiments on focusing on one conversation among many.

Taking a name check

However, imagine now that you are at a party and have focused what you think is your whole attention on the conversation in which you are presently involved. Suddenly, someone across the room mentions your name. Your attention is immediately redirected, in the same way as in our earlier example of the mention of money while you were watching television. You changed the focus of your attention not because of how you heard

the information but because of what that information was about. Broadbent proposed that no information is processed at all until it reaches the sensory filter. If this is indeed the case, how can we shift our attention in response to meaning in another, subsequent message?

Broadbent's claim was based on the observation that participants have no conscious awareness of the meaning of the unattended message. But could meaning be processed outside our conscious awareness? In 1975 psychologists Elsa von Wright, Paul Anderson, and Evald Stenman presented participants with a list of words, and mild electric shocks were

---

DONALD BROADBENT

BIOGRAPHY

Donald Broadbent, sometimes known as the father of cognition, was born in 1926 in Birmingham, England. It was not his original intention to become a psychologist. In 1944 he joined the British Royal Air Force with the aim of becoming a pilot. However, he soon realized that the equipment he was using was poorly designed given the cognitive processes involved in flying. He also became interested in the effects of practice on flying ability. He decided to study these issues further at the University of Cambridge's department of psychology, where he worked under Sir Frederic Bartlett. Broadbent graduated in 1949 and remained in Cambridge to work at the Medical Research Council's Applied Psychology Unit (APU).

Broadbent's early thinking was greatly influenced by Bartlett and also by Kenneth Craik. Bartlett strongly supported the idea that people played an active role in their mind's processing capabilities, while Craik pioneered an approach whereby theories about the brain and behavior were developed in the same way as an engineer would develop a theory about a complex machine.

Such ideas formed the background to Broadbent's early work, including his 1969 filter theory of selective attention (see above). Broadbent's filter theory was the first systematic model of a number of cognitive processes linked together. This type of model is termed an information-processing system. Filter theory formed the basis for the many other information-processing system models of human cognition, including memory, language processing, and problem solving, as well as subsequent models of attention. Broadbent's theory of selective attention has been one of the most influential models of human cognition.

As director of the APU from 1958 to 1974, Broadbent helped make the unit one of the world's most important psychology research institutions. Throughout his career he strove to develop psychological theories that could be of benefit and practical use to people. He is best known for his work on attention. All subsequent theories have been compared with his work in this area. Donald Broadbent died in 1993.

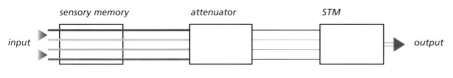

attenuated selection

Diagrammatic representation of Anne Treisman's theory of attenuated selection, according to which the level of processing applied to input information is increased or reduced by the receiver's view of its importance. (STM stands for short-term memory.)

given in conjunction with some of these words. Participants were found to show an unconscious physiological reaction to the words associated with the shocks when they were later presented in the unattended message during a shadowing task. The inference from this experiment is clear: Despite not being consciously aware of hearing these words, the participants were obviously interpreting their meaning somewhere in their minds.

Central to Broadbent's theory was the idea that only the piece of information selected by the filter is processed—everything else remains ignored. However, we know that it is often possible for us to redirect our attention on the basis of meaning, such as when we hear our own names or the mention of money. Experiments by von Wright and others have also shown that the brain must be processing the unattended information to some extent, despite the lack of conscious awareness that it is happening.

Cognitive links

Broadbent's filter theory was enormously influential in the development of cognitive psychology. However, it suffered because it was too inflexible. We can redirect our attention depending on the meaning of the message, and we can process the message even when it is outside our consciousness. For all its merits, Broadbent's theory fails to take account of these facts.

Attenuation theory

Such limitations led Anne Treisman, professor of psychology at Princeton University, to develop a new attenuation theory of selective attention. Treisman retained the idea of a sensory filter at the attention bottleneck. However, in her account the filter is more flexible and relies on both physical characteristics and meaning to focus attention. Moreover, she rejected Broadbent's idea that unattended information is simply ignored. Instead, she proposed that unattended messages are attenuated, or weakened, and thus receive a reduced level of processing. However, this processing is so reduced that the participant has no conscious awareness of it unless the meaning takes on some significance.

Treisman's theory can account not only for the findings of von Wright and others, but also for our ability to redirect attention on the basis of meaning.

Broadbent's and Treisman's theories both state that our attentional bottleneck occurs as soon as sensory information enters our brain, before processing occurs. An alternative hypothesis is that all the information we receive is fully processed before selection occurs. Psychologists J. and D. Deutsch suggested this idea in 1963, saying that it is only after complete processing that we select which piece of information to become aware of.

This "late theory" of selective attention can also account for von Wright's findings

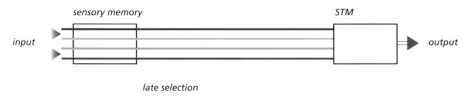

late selection

Diagrammatic representation of Deutsch and Deutsch's late theory of selective attention. Input information is selected only after having reached the short-term memory (STM).

Try and find the letter T. When you have done that, look at the diagram below.

and information your eyes are receiving to find your friend or relative? What problems do you overcome in doing so?

Psychologists have addressed such questions using "visual search" experiments. Try the two visual search exercises on this page before reading any further. You will no doubt reach the conclusion that it is easier to find the O than it is to find the T. Why is this? It is because T and L share the same features—a horizontal line and a vertical line—the only difference is in where the two lines meet. O, on the other hand, shares no features with L and so is easy to spot.

Feature integration theory
In problems such as this the target letter is said to "pop out" from the surrounding letters. The main theory used to explain these and other findings about visual search was developed in 1986 by Anne Treisman and is known as feature integration theory (FIT).

Treisman's theory states that when you look at a visual scene, you create a series of "maps" that describe it. For example, when you looked at the letter diagrams, you created one map showing where all the horizontal lines were, another where all vertical lines were, and so on. In a scene

and our ability to redirect attention, and so rivals Treisman's theory. Subsequent research has suggested, however, that this contrast between early and late selection may need to be recast. That is because the way in which attention operates may be flexible, so that the manner of selection depends on the particular circumstance. Late selection may be more likely, for example, when the available inputs are all familiar, relatively slow paced, or involve few decisions about the nature or direction of processing. Early selection may be more likely in the absence of these factors.

Searching for something
So far our discussion of how we focus our attention has explored the manner in which we select what to spend our brain's limited processing resources on out of the huge amount of information our senses are constantly receiving. But what if you want to search for something specific—to scan your environment for a particular item that you are not quite sure where to find, for example, a relative you are supposed to be meeting at a busy airport or a friend you have arranged to get together with at a very crowded party? How do you sift through all the people

Try and find the letter O. You should find this task easier than the one above because the shape of the letter O contrasts more strongly than the letter T with the surrounding letters L.

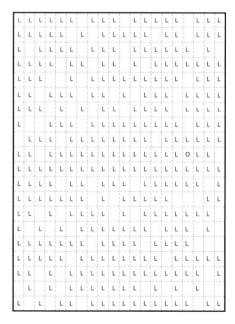

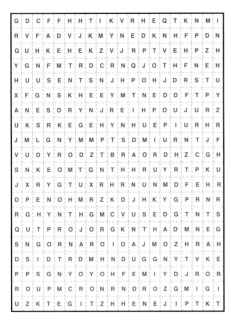

Try and find the letter B among these capital letters, then look at the diagram below.

can be wrongly perceived as a white car. Treisman's theory has inspired research, such as experiments on the perception of texture or features of shapes, that is still being carried out today.

Similarity theory

Treisman's theory has been rivaled by the much simpler similarity theory. It was proposed by John Duncan and Glyn Humphreys in 1992. The results of research carried out by Humphreys and P. T. Quinlan in 1987 could not be explained by Treisman's theory. They proposed that the amount of time it took to identify a feature might depend on the number of items of information required to identify it. Similarity theory states that the ease of any visual search is determined by how similar the target is to the other images competing for attention—the distracters. So in the two visual search exercises, T is harder to find than O because its shape bears a closer resemblance to that of the distracters. As the similarity between the target letter and distracter increases, so the difficulty in detecting the target increases.

Similarity theory also says that a visual search becomes more difficult as the distracters become more similar to each

such as the T among the Ls you must then mentally search through these maps, combining the horizontal and vertical lines in each position until you find the one that is different. But with the O among the Ls, because no features are shared, there is no need for this effortful, attention-demanding feature integration stage, and so the search is faster. The T and the O are target elements since they are the ones the observer has to identify in a field of background elements.

In support of her theory Treisman described a phenomenon known as illusory conjunction. If you look out onto a street, FIT states that you create many mental maps, one describing where all the horizontal lines are, another describing where all the red objects are, and so on. You then need to integrate these maps so that instead of separate features, you see a red car. This demands attention, and in busy scenes there are only enough attentional resources available to integrate the features in part of it. Outside this part the integration happens in a fairly random manner, and sometimes features can be incorrectly integrated. For example, a red car passing a white store on the edge of your vision

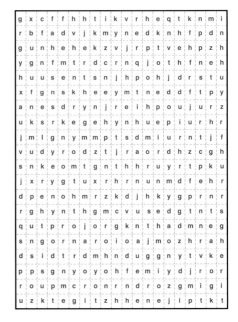

Try and find the letter b among these lower case letters. This task is easier than the one above because the shapes of lower case letters are more clearly differentiated than those of capitals.

CHANGE BLINDNESS

EXPERIMENT

Observers seem to have an inability to detect changes in scenes such as pictures. This is known as change blindness. It is change blindness that makes "spot-the-difference" puzzles so tricky. In 1997 cognitive scientists Ronald Rensink, Kevin O'Regan, and James Clark showed participants pairs of pictures that were identical except for one detail—for example, a man wearing a hat in one picture and not in the other. Despite the fact that participants knew that their task was to find the difference between the pictures, they found it very difficult to do so and sometimes had to look between the pictures more than 20 times to find it.

Also in 1997, Daniel Levin of Kent State University, Ohio, and Daniel Simons of Harvard University explored change blindness in moving images. They showed participants a movie of two women having a conversation. The camera followed the two women during the conversation, and every time the camera changed its focus, details of the scene changed. For example, at one point the camera was pointing at woman A. Red plates could be seen on a table. Seconds later the camera changed its focus onto woman B. The plates suddenly became white. When the camera returned to woman A, the food changed position on the plates. Most participants failed to notice any of the changes. Even when asked to watch the film again having been told to look out for the changes, the participants noticed an average of only two out of the nine changes.

What does change blindness tell us about attention? We believe that we see our world completely. Change blindness shows us that there are, in fact, gaps in our perception. We fail to see objects unless purposefully focusing our attention on them and often fail to notice any changes in their position.

other, as you can see in the tasks shown on p. 30. It is easier to find the b among lower case letters than the B among capital letters (*opposite*) because capital letters have more features in common. Search performance is a function of the similarity among the distracters. So, according to this theory, visual search is all a question of similarity, and there is no feature integration process. The main criticism of this explanation is that similarity is a vague concept and there is no agreed measure of what similarity is.

Sometimes we want to do more than one thing at once such as drive a car and hold a conversation. However, it is nearly impossible to figure out, for example, a difficult math problem at the same time as reciting a poem.

When we try to do more than one thing at once, we divide the brain's limited processing resources between each task. This is easier for some tasks than others and depends on two main things: How similar the two tasks are, and how good we are at each of them individually. Although the brain has a limited capacity, it can do two tasks simultaneously for as long as neither exceeds the limits of its general and specific resources.

Divided and undivided attention
Before considering the significance of task similarity for divided attention, let us look a little bit more closely at our processing

Most drivers maintain that they are capable of driving and talking to someone at the same time. They think about what they are hearing and saying, and pay attention to the road ahead. Less experienced drivers have to concentrate their attention solely on driving and cannot hold a conversation at the same time.

resources and how they are allocated. Do all tasks compete for the same limited amount of attention, or do different types of tasks use different mental resources? If all tasks involve the same general resources, the nature of the task would not matter; all tasks would compete equally for a share of the resources available, and we would be able to do as many things as our supplies of attention allowed. However, if our processing resources are specific to each task, it will be easier to combine tasks if they are different (for example, driving and talking) than if they use similar mental resources (for example, reading a book and talking).

Many studies have shown that divided attention is more difficult if the tasks are similar. Consider the experiment described in the box below. None of the tasks is entirely straightforward, but you will definitely find it harder to count vowels while following a conversation because both tasks involve processing language. In an experiment published in 1972 in the *Quarterly Journal of Experimental Psychology* D. A. Allport, B. Antonis, and P. Reynolds asked participants to repeat a passage of text. At the same time, they asked them to memorize either a list of words presented through headphones or a set of pictures. Participants had a poor recollection of the list of words. However, they were able to repeat the text and remember the pictures. Tasks that are similar are more likely to interfere with each other as they compete for our attention.

DIVIDING ATTENTION

FOCUS ON

Below is a nursery rhyme. Your task is to count how many vowels it contains. You must do this in complete silence and as quickly as possible.

"Twinkle, twinkle little star
How I wonder what you are
Up above the world so high
Like a diamond in the sky
Twinkle, twinkle little star
How I wonder what you are."

The correct answer is 48 vowels. Did you get it right? How easy did you find it?

Here is a second nursery rhyme. Again, count the vowels, only this time listen to some music at the same time. Make sure the music you choose is only instrumental, with no words.

"Jack and Jill went up the hill to fetch a pail of water.
Jack fell down and broke his crown,
And Jill came tumbling after.
Up Jack got and home did trot as fast as he could caper.
He went to bed to mend his head
With vinegar and brown paper."

How did you find the task this time? Was it any more difficult? Were you consciously aware of the music all the time? (The correct answer is 64.)

Here is one last nursery rhyme. Again, count the vowels, but to make it more interesting, listen to a conversation on the radio or television while you count.

"Oh, the grand old Duke of York.
He had ten thousand men.
He marched them up to the top of the hill
And he marched them down again.
And when they were up, they were up.
And when they were down, they were down.
And when they were only half way up,
They were neither up nor down."

How did you find the task this time? Could you follow the conversation at the same time as counting the vowels? Were you able to divide your attention between the two tasks? (The number of vowels is 73.)

You should have found the task easiest when you did it in silence. You may have been able to divide your attention between counting the vowels and listening to the music, although it may have been harder and taken you longer. You probably found it harder to do this at the same time as following a conversation. Your brain struggled to process the information about the text and the conversation at the same time because these two tasks are similar—they both involve processing language. (The fact that there are an increasing number of vowels in each of the rhymes can be shown to have no effect on the outcome of the experiment.)

CELL PHONES AND DRIVING: A LETHAL COMBINATION

PSYCHOLOGY & SOCIETY

There are now over 100 million cell phones in use in the United States. People use them everywhere: at home, in schools, in the street, on buses and trains, and even in the car while driving. But is it safe to use a cell phone and drive at the same time? You may think so: after all, we know that we are capable of driving and talking at the same time—why not chat on the phone? A recent survey revealed that 85 percent of cell phone users admitted to, at least occasionally, using the phone while driving. If driving is an automatic task, that should still not pose a problem. Our conscious attention can be focused on the conversation while our automatic processing takes care of driving. However, research shows a more worrying picture.

Research carried out in 1998 by J. M. Violanti found that people who use a cell phone while driving are nine times more at risk of a fatal accident than those who don't use the phone in the car. In fact, simply having a phone switched on in the car doubled the risk of a fatal accident. Why is it so dangerous to use a cell phone while driving? Violanti examined reports of all traffic accidents in the state of Oklahoma between 1992 and 1995. Drivers who had been using cell phones were found to be more likely to pay less attention to the road, drive at unsafe speeds, drive on the wrong side of the road, crash into a stationary object, overturn their vehicle, and swerve prior to the accident than those who had not been using phones at the time of the accident. Another study published in 1999 showed that controlling speed and keeping in lane are less accurate when dialing numbers on a cell phone than in normal driving.

Such disturbing evidence has led some countries, such as Brazil, Israel, Italy, and some states in Australia to make it illegal to use phones while driving. Some U.S. states have adopted such legislative action. Washington has imposed a law that cell phones can only be used with a state-approved "hands-free kit."

In 1999 David Lamble of the University of Helsinki, Finland, explored the ability of drivers to detect a car ahead decelerating. He compared drivers who remained looking ahead, undistracted, with drivers dialing random numbers on a keypad (divided visual attention) and with drivers doing simple memory tasks that required nonvisual attention. You can predict that the divided visual attention group would experience the greatest difficulty in reacting. However, drivers doing both tasks were slower to react than those paying full attention to the road. A hands-free kit does not remove the safety problems associated with using cell phones while driving.

The fact that two similar tasks are difficult to perform together supports the idea that our processing resources are task-specific. That is why we are able to drive and talk or write and listen to music at the same time. However, consider what happens when we are approaching a busy intersection. Can we still process the information we need to negotiate it safely at the same time as holding an important conversation? Even if they are dissimilar, we are unable to do difficult tasks at the same time, which suggests that some of our processing resources are general to all tasks. This has implications for the use of cell phones while driving where task-general attentional resources are diverted away from the task of driving the car.

If you play a musical instrument, dance, play sports, or have any other such skill, you will have been told time and again,

"Practice makes perfect!" We all know that when we practice something, we become better at it. How does this relate to dividing attention?

We have already discussed how easy it is to hold conversations while driving. But that is true only for experienced drivers; learner drivers generally find it almost impossible to talk while they are at the controls. Thus we can see that it is easier to divide attention between two tasks we are good at. To see why this is so, we have to look more closely at exactly what tasks such as driving a car or holding a conversation involve.

So far we have considered tasks such as driving as only one task. Is it really that simple? Consider what the task of driving involves. You have to pay attention to traffic in front of and behind you, your speed, the course of the road, steering, any

potential hazards such as children on the sidewalk, and so on. Can this really be described as a single task? Perhaps driving itself is an example of divided attention. Likewise, to hold a conversation, you have to control the movements of your mouth, process the information your ears receive, and decide what to say in response. Virtually any task can be seen as a collection of smaller subtasks.

> "We can only perceive things we are attending to; we can only attend to things we perceive."
> —William Greene and Gail Hicks, 1984

Learning to drive does, indeed, feel like dividing attention. When you learn to drive, all the subtasks seem truly separate. You have to think individually about the curvature of the road and how to move the steering wheel accordingly, using your mirrors, how fast you are going, and so on. When novice drivers are paying attention to a difficult part of road, such as an intersection, they may forget how much pressure needs to be on the gas and stall the car. Thinking about all these subtasks uses up all their attentional resources. Once the skill of driving has been mastered, it can become one single, organized task. The experienced driver is able to handle all the subtasks at the same time without allowing them to interfere with each other. That is why many longtime motorists speak of driving as having become second nature to them.

Every time you learn a new task, you initially have to divide your attention more or less consciously among its subtasks. That demands a large amount of your processing resources. Consider learning to play the violin. Playing the note C involves:
• reading the correct note from the written music;
• using the correct string;

A young girl having a violin lesson. At the start of her studies she will play every note deliberately; as she gains confidence and expertise, many of her movements will become natural, and she will no longer think about them.

• putting a finger correctly on the neck;
• and bowing the string.

The novice violinist has to think about each of these steps. After much practice the experienced player simply sees the note C on the music and produces the sound with no conscious awareness of the subtasks involved. That uses only a tiny proportion of attention, leaving plenty for other tasks. The pianist Liberace often combined playing the piano with chatting to the audience during his performances.

So when we have practiced a task so much that we have become expert at it, we no longer need to use up attentional resources when we do it again—it ceases to be a consciously controlled action and instead becomes automatically controlled. You used to have to think about every subtask involved in walking or riding a bicycle: Now these actions occur automatically; you do them without thinking. Indeed, it is often hard to stop doing things that have become automatic even if you want to. This is central to the "Stroop effect," a task used in research into automaticity (*see* box p. 36).

The human autopilot

Have you ever walked out of your house on the weekend only to find yourself beginning to go to school or work the same as you do every weekday? When we do such things automatically, we often describe it as being on autopilot. We no longer need to control our actions consciously in the same way that pilots no longer need to control their planes manually when they fly on autopilot. That can be useful since such tasks no longer need to compete for our limited attentional resources. The table on page 36 highlights

PRACTICE, PRACTICE, PRACTICE!

EXPERIMENT

In 1976 three American academics—Elizabeth Spelke, William Hirst, and Ulric Neisser—conducted an interesting and influential study demonstrating the importance of practice in enabling more than one task to be done at the same time. The study involved two students, Dianne and John. Dianne and John had to perform two tasks at the same time—read a short story for comprehension and write down words dictated by the experimenter. At first they found it very hard to do the two tasks at the same time and found themselves reading much more slowly than usual. The tasks are similar—they both involve processing language and so draw on the same task-specific attentional resources.

Dianne and John spent two hours a week practicing doing the two tasks at the same time. After six weeks they found it easy to do the two tasks and were able to read as fast and with as much comprehension while having words dictated to them as they could when they were only reading. Reading at the same time as writing the dictated words had become no more difficult than reading while tapping a foot. Many of us have found ourselves in a library asking someone to stop tapping or humming, only to be told, "I didn't know I was!" Tapping a foot at the same time as reading may be something that is done outside the conscious attention of the reader. Spelke, Hirst, and Neisser found that Dianne and John could remember only about 35 out of thousands of words they had written in the dictations during the study. They had become so expert at taking dictation that it no longer demanded their conscious attention.

When two complex tasks, such as reading and writing, can be performed well together, it is usually because the skills involved have been highly practiced. In 1972 psychologist Floyd Allport found that expert pianists can play a piece from a sheet of music at the same time as listening to messages. This can be done only after years of practice. Novice musicians often find it impossible to listen to their teacher's instructions while playing pieces. After years of practice the task of reproducing the piece of music coded in the manuscript becomes automatic—the pianists no longer have to use conscious attention to read the music and play the tune; they can do it without thinking. In the same way, after six weeks of practice Dianne and John no longer had to think about writing their words. They automatically reproduced on paper the sounds they heard. That enabled them to direct all their attention to reading and comprehension, and the dual task became as easy as the dictation had been on its own.

CONTROLLED PROCESSES	AUTOMATIC PROCESSES
Require focused attention, so they can be hindered by limited processing resources.	Independent of focused attention, so not hindered by limited processing.
Occur serially (one step at a time), for example, turn key, remove brake, look in mirrors, etc.	Subtasks occur in parallel (at the same time or in no particular order).
Can easily be modified.	Difficult to modify once automatic, for example, changing from driving on the left-hand to the right-hand side of the road
You are consciously aware of the task.	Not always consciously aware of doing the task.
Relatively time consuming.	Relatively fast.
Tend to be more difficult or complex tasks.	Tend to be simpler tasks.

the differences between tasks that are controlled and demand attention and those that occur automatically.

How does automatization occur? John Anderson suggested in 1983 that during practice you become better and better at each of the task's various subcomponents. For example, when learning to drive, you become better at controlling the brake, better at using mirrors, and so on. Eventually these subtasks become combined into larger components of the task, so controlling the brake and using the mirrors occur simultaneously, without the need to think about them separately. These larger components are then

THE STROOP EFFECT

Quickly read aloud the following words:

red, blue, brown, green, .

Now quickly name aloud the colors you see in the sequence below:

green, **blue,** , **red, brown.**

Now, quickly name aloud the colors you see in the sequence below:

blue, green, , brown, **yellow.**

You probably found the first two tasks quite simple. In each the color of the ink corresponded with the word, and so it was easy to read the writing and name the colors. The third task was harder because the colors of the ink differed from the color name. The written words interfered with you naming the ink color. This is known as the Stroop effect.

Originally devised in 1935 by American psychologist John Ridley Stroop (1897–1973), the test has become one of the experiments used most frequently for the study of unconscious, automatic attention. The Stroop effect shows the strong tendency to read the printed word rather than name the color.

This happens because word recognition is a very well-practiced task, especially for schoolchildren and college students. Because word recognition is so highly practiced, it can proceed automatically (see box p. 35). When something is so well practiced that it occurs automatically, we find it difficult to ignore regardless of all conflicting information. People find it very hard to stop themselves from processing the written word because it is a reaction that occurs automatically and is beyond what is known as their attentional control. As soon as the brain receives the relevant information from the page, that is what it deals with; everything else is too complicated and cannot be processed without conscious effort.

combined until eventually the entire task becomes a single, integrated procedure rather than a collection of individual subtasks. Anderson argued that the task becomes automatic at the point at which it becomes fully integrated into one task. This occurs suddenly, rather like a switch in automobile gears.

Instance theory

In 1988 Gordon Logan, professor of psychology at Vanderbilt University, Nashville, Tennessee, disputed Anderson's idea that automatization occurs suddenly. His instance theory states that automatization occurs gradually, as the task is practiced over time.

When we learn a task, such as multiplication, we start by applying general responses, for example, counting four sets of five for 4 x 5, six sets of five for 6 x 5, and so on. With practice we gradually accumulate knowledge about our specific responses to specific stimuli, so we learn that 4 x 5 = 20 and 6 x 5 = 30 without the need to figure it out by counting. We have gradually learned a specific automatic response to each specific combination of numbers. Research suggests that Logan's instance

theory better explains responses to specific stimuli, such as mathematical calculations, while Anderson's theory provides a better general explanation of automaticity.

The use of EEGs

Until recently, psychologists had to rely mainly on experiments to develop their theories about attention. Technological advances now mean we can watch and record attention in action. Attention has been explored in studies recording the brain's electrical activity during tasks by means of electroencephalography (EEG). It has also been studied using techniques that have enabled researchers to watch the blood flow through the brain while participants carry out a task. Examples of this include positron emission tomography (PET) scans (*see* Vol. 6, pp. 118-141).

> *"I am interested in testing theories empirically, in studies of focused attention, divided attention, and dual-task situations."*
> —*Gordon Logan, 2002*

Cognitive neuroscience

Brain recording and imaging enable us to explore attention in a different way than behavioral experiments, allowing us to address different questions. This type of research is known as "cognitive neuroscience" (*see* Vol. 1, pp. 104–117). For example, is there one single center in the brain that controls all our attentional resources, or are there different, task-related resource allocation centers? Can any physical or psychological disorders affect our attentional abilities; and if so, what can we learn from them about attention in general? Such studies exploring the effect of biological disorders on cognition are examples of "cognitive neuropsychology." So, what lessons about attention can we learn from the study of cognitive neuroscience and cognitive neuropsychology?

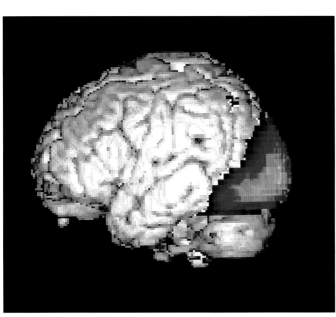

A positron emission tomography (PET) scan of activity in the human brain while seeing words or pictures. The left side of the brain is shown, with the front at the left. The stimuli have activated the visual area in the occipital cortex (colored red–orange).

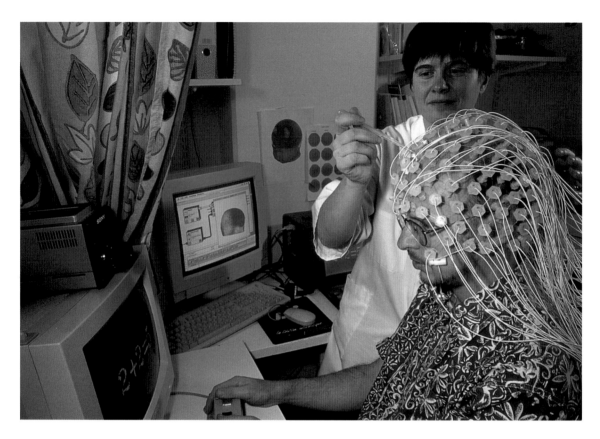

Do we focus our attention by enhancing our perception of the target above that of everything else around us; do we suppress our perception of everything but the target; or does selective attention occur as a result of both enhanced processing of the target and suppression of its competitors?

In 1994 Michael Posner, professor of psychology at the University of Oregon, and Stanislas Dehaene answered these questions as follows—it depends! All three possibilities may occur depending on the nature of the task and the area of the brain involved. The task then is to determine which attentional processes occur in which areas of the brain.

Cognitive neuroscience has enabled such studies. In a 1993 study using PET scans, Maurizio Corbetta of Washington University in St. Louis, Missouri, and colleagues found that the regions of the brain associated with perceiving relevant physical attributes were activated during visual search tasks. For example, when the task involved motion, the brain regions associated with motion perception were activated; when the task involved color, the region associated with color perception was activated.

In addition, Corbetta and colleagues found that different regions of the brain are associated with selective attention, divided attention, and searching. Such findings support the view of Posner and Dehaene that the mechanisms involved in attention vary according to the specific requirements of the task.

Event-related potentials

An alternative way of studying attention is by the use of electroencephalograms (EEGs), with which psychologists record the brain's electrical activity as it changes over time. Sometimes these recordings are made immediately after the person sees or

A participant undergoing an electroencephalogram (EEG) to examine his mental activity while solving math problems. Tests such as this have provided researchers with illuminating new insights into the physiological basis of attention and information processing.

NEGLECT SYNDROME—A PARTIAL VIEW OF THE WORLD

A man sits up in bed in his hospital room. We will call him Bill. Bill has had a stroke in the right parietal (top) lobe of his brain. His doctor walks in and approaches him from the left. Bill doesn't see her or react to her being there; and as she moves to the right of him, he greets her as if she had just arrived. The doctor asks Bill to clap his hands together. He lifts up only his right hand and gestures as if clapping. "What about your left hand?" the doctor asks. "Can you try and move it for me?" Bill replies that he is doing so, despite the fact that his left arm remains motionless on his knee. The doctor then holds up two objects, one to the left of Bill and one to the right. She asks Bill what she is holding; he mentions only the key she is holding to his right side. He is apparently unaware of the pen that she is holding in her other hand.

The doctor shows Bill a picture of a house. He is able to tell her what it is. She then asks him if there is anything unusual. "No" he replies, failing to see that the house is actually on fire. The flames and smoke are on the left of the drawing. Next the doctor asks Bill to draw a clock. In his drawing only half of the clock is shown. The doctor then gives Bill a sheet of paper containing horizontal lines

and asks him to draw a vertical line exactly in the middle of each. Bill draws his lines to the right of each line. The doctor also notices that he has missed the lines to the left of the paper—he has not drawn any lines of his own on them. She asks him if he has finished the task, and he replies that he has crossed all the lines on the paper. He has failed to notice those on the left of the sheet.

One of the neurological tests given to patients to assess for neglect syndrome is a sheet of paper containing horizontal lines. The patient is asked to bisect the lines exactly in the middle with a vertical line. Patients with left-hand side neglect tend to bisect to the right of center since they cannot attend to the far left of the lines. Patients also tend to fail to respond to the lines on the left of the page.

At lunch time Bill complains that his meal was too small. His nurse observes that he has only eaten the food on the right side of his plate. He has ignored the food to the left. Bill's stroke has left him with left-hand neglect syndrome. He is unable to attend to anything in the left half of his visual field. He is not blind on that side, and he notices nothing odd about his behavior. To him anything that occurs to the left of his vision no longer exists.

hears something. Such recordings are called event-related potentials (ERPs), since they are the brain's electrical responses to some particular occurrence.

Between 1988 and 1992 the cognitive neuroscientist Risto Näätänen of the University of Helsinki, Finland, conducted many studies using ERPs to explore attention. Näätänen has shown that we do respond to stimuli, such as very brief changes in the unattended message during a shadowing task. However, this has no effect on the controlled shadowing task and often occurs with no conscious awareness. These findings support the view that some automatic, superficial processing can occur without requiring our attentional resources.

We can learn a great deal about attention from imaging and recording "normal" participants. We can also learn from studying people who do not show normal attentional processes. As we have

seen, attention is central to our performance of all cognitive tasks. We need it to perceive sensory information in order to focus on a particular thought and to avoid distraction from a task. It is no surprise, then, that attention is affected with many disorders of the brain. How do such conditions affect attention and what lessons can we learn from situations such as brain damage in which attentional processes are impaired?

Imagine a fictitious character called Bill with a real condition (*see* box above). Bill's case study is typical of patients who experience neglect syndrome following a stroke. A stroke or other damage to the brain can cause damage to one side of the brain, generally the right-hand side as in Bill's case, leaving patients unable to respond to or have any awareness of objects that occur in their visual field on the opposite side. Bill demonstrates all the main characteristics of neglect syndrome.

The tendency to ignore the left side of space is linked to the patient's failure to use the left side of his body. Bill was sure he was lifting his left hand to clap. His inability to do so was not due to physical paralysis. People with neglect syndrome simply fail to attend to their left side; they forget about its existence. This is not caused by a physical motor deficit, just as their inability to attend to visual stimuli to their left is not linked to any sensory deficit. Neglect syndrome is not a disorder of seeing or moving but of experiencing and responding. It is not a perceptual disorder but an attentional one. People with neglect syndrome have a "selective inattention" to the left of their world.

What is striking about people with neglect syndrome is that they do not seem to have any idea that they have no awareness of that side. They don't think, "I can't see to my left"; their left just does not exist as something to think about.

Anosognosia

This refusal to admit to something being wrong is symptomatic of a condition known as anosognosia, meaning a lack of knowledge about an illness. It is because neglect syndrome is a disorder of attention that anosognosia is such a strong feature. You can't miss what you are not aware of.

Posner and his colleagues have studied attention in people with neglect syndrome. They have found that these people can be instructed to attend to their neglected side during attention tasks. From their studies of neglect syndrome they suggested a three-stage model of attention. To attend to a stimulus we have to:
• disengage from our current focus of attention;
• shift our attention to the new location; and
• engage our attention with the new task.

People with neglect syndrome have problems with the first stage of attention—they are unable to disengage from the right-hand side of their visual field in order to focus their attention to their left-hand side.

Attention deficit disorder

People with neglect syndrome are unable to disengage from their right in order to shift their attention to a stimulus on their left. Attention deficit disorder (ADD), however, involves the third stage of the Posner model: People with ADD find it difficult to engage their attention with any one task.

Approximately 4–6 percent of children in the United States have a form of ADD (*see* Vol. 6, pp. 68–91). It is caused by immaturity or dysfunction in the attentional control of information processing. In many cases this immaturity improves with time, but around half of those with the disorder will continue to experience problems in adulthood. ADD is characterized by difficulties in

Neglect syndrome is not confined to humans. This dog has suffered brain damage and eats only from the left side of its bowl.

concentration and focusing attention on any task or stimulus. This leads to those affected being easily distracted, impulsive, and hyperactive. Their attentional problems also result in a tendency to find it hard to see a "big picture" linking their world, their thoughts, and their feelings to their actions. This results in fragmented behavior. A child with ADD finds it difficult to concentrate at school, and the behavioral aspects of the disorder can lead to social problems and family difficulties. It has been proposed that attention deficit disorder occurs when the areas of the brain that control and direct attention are immature or not fully "on line." PET studies have shown that there is decreased activity in the right hemisphere of the brain in people with ADD, in particular in the anterior cingulate cortex—the part of the brain associated with fixing attention. Decreased activity has also been observed in the frontal lobes of the brain—a region associated with awareness—and the "upper auditory cortex," where integration of thoughts and

"RITALIN TIME!"

PSYCHOLOGY & SOCIETY

An increasingly familiar sight in schools across the United States is that of children lining up to be given their Ritalin dose. The increased use of Ritalin has created a "double-edged sword." Many children have received and benefitted from the drug. However, many people have argued that the increased awareness of ADD that has accompanied the media coverage of Ritalin has led to overdiagnosis of the disorder and overuse of Ritalin. This has led to hot debate about the use of the drugs.

Research has shown that Ritalin increases attention and concentration in children with ADD and also improves their ability to shut out distractions during tasks. Such findings have arisen from clinical trials of the drug, in which its performance has been compared with that of a placebo (a dummy drug that does nothing). Between 1984 and 1994 Ritalin was the focus of 45 such trials, making it the most researched psychotropic drug used in the treatment of children. All 45 trials showed Ritalin to be more effective than the placebo in focusing attention and increasing persistence to a task. The drug was also found to help control many of the behavioral aspects of ADD.

These positive findings concerning the use of Ritalin have led to its widespread acceptance in the community and have contributed to the rapid increase in its use. In 1999 American physician John J. Ratey argued that the use of Ritalin and other stimulant drugs is the easiest and most effective treatment for ADD and crucial to its management. However, this opinion is not shared by all the doctors, teachers, and families involved with children who suffer from this condition. There are two main arguments against the use of Ritalin—first, that the drug has too many worrying side effects, and second, that it is prescribed too widely. The side effects associated with Ritalin include loss of appetite, difficulty in getting to sleep, and stunted growth. Proponents of the drug's use acknowledge these effects but argue that the benefits outweigh the disadvantages. There is also some concern that children using amphetamines will go on to abuse other, similar drugs. So far, research has shown this not to be the case. However, widespread use of Ritalin is still in its early days, and long-term research following children currently on Ritalin into adulthood is necessary to investigate these concerns further.

The rapid increase in the use of Ritalin has provoked many people to express concern that its popularity is leading to many children being too quickly labeled as having ADD and being treated with the drug. Treatment is cheaper than lengthy investigations. Recent reports have expressed concern that children who may have temporary behavioral disturbances are being given snap diagnoses and prescribed Ritalin to make them more controllable in school. A study in 2000 by Peter R. Breggin, a practicing psychiatrist in Bethesda, Maryland, suggested that up to 20 percent of fifth-grade boys in Virginia are being prescribed the drug. There are no compelling reasons to believe that such widespread prescription is justified.

Ratey has described Ritalin as "a happy intersection of neuroscience and availability of a drug to fit the supposed problem." That is certainly a point of view, but skeptics question whether the increasingly widespread use of the drug reflects a society that is overanxious to seek a drug to fix all its problems. The debate about the use of Ritalin seems likely to continue.

THE P300 POTENTIAL: AN ERP MEASURE OF ATTENTION

The brain continually produces large amounts of electrical activity that can be measured using EEGs (electroencephalographs). However, using special techniques, researchers can eliminate this background activity to examine the tiny electrical responses that are produced when the brain sees an image or hears a sound. They are called event-related potentials (ERPs) since they are the signals generated in response to a particular occurrence. Some ERPs are so consistent that they can be used as indicators of mental processes. In particular, your brain produces a positive electrical signal 300 milliseconds (thousandths of a second) after something grabs your attention. This signal is known as the P300.

One interesting application of the P300 attention marker is its use in enabling completely paralyzed people to communicate. The patient faces a computer screen on which the letters of the alphabet are displayed, as shown in the diagram (left). She then focuses her attention on one of these letters. The computer highlights the various letters one at a time, simultaneously examining the patient's EEG signals to see whether a P300 is produced. If so, the computer knows that the patient was focusing her attention on that letter and so registers it and moves on to the next letter in the sequence. For example, the patient may want to communicate the word "pain" in response to discomfort. The patient would attend to the letter p. A P300 will occur as her attention is alerted to the computer highlighting the third letter of the fourth row. That will occur every time the letter p is highlighted until eventually the computer determines that p is the first letter of the word. The patient is then asked to attend to the second letter and so on.

A computer highlights each letter in turn at the same time as the patient's EEG recording is scrutinized for the P300 attention marker. Although slow and difficult (it can take 15 minutes to communicate a single sentence), this method can provide a means of communication to people who otherwise would have none. With further developments in this method and the technology it relies on it is hoped that a more efficient and less cumbersome device can be developed to enable completely paralyzed people to communicate.

A	G	M	S	Y
B	H	N	T	Z
C	I	O	U	
D	J	P	V	
E	K	Q	W	
F	L	R	X	

A computer highlights each letter in turn at the same time as the participant's EEG recording is scrutinized for the P300 attention marker.

perceptions occurs. These patterns result in the attentional and behavioral characteristics of ADD. There are numerous thoughts, feelings, and pieces of information all vying for attention, and the mechanisms to deal with them are faulty.

Many children are prescribed drugs such as Ritalin to control the symptoms of the disorder. These are basically the same as amphetamines ("speed"). In the late 1990s the number of children prescribed Ritalin in the United States increased by 150 percent. The United States now uses five times more Ritalin than the rest of the world. Ritalin works by increasing the amount of certain neurotransmitters, particularly dopamine (associated with attentional control), in the brain's cortex. The increased action of these neurotransmitters stimulates the activity of the cortex, including the regions that are underactive, in people with ADD. This

Pain can to some extent be managed (controlled) by an act of conscious will. This child demonstrates the fact by controlling the pain from lying on a bed of nails.

enables the brain to focus attention and piece together sensory information, thoughts, and actions, resulting in more focused behavior, better concentration, and less distraction (*see* box p. 41).

Attending to pain

While we have largely looked at attention in relation to how we see and hear the world, it also plays a big role with other senses—particularly in our perception of pain. We all experience physical pain from time to time, and PET studies have shown that the anterior cingulate cortex, the area of the brain associated with focusing attention, is highly active when we are in pain. We tend to direct too much attention to the area of our body affected by pain, and knowledge of this tendency can be used beneficially in managing it. Studies have shown that by trying to distract yourself and direct more of your attention elsewhere, you can effectively

reduce the awareness of pain. Some people have developed such an ability to control their conscious will like this that they can overcome great pain (*see* picture above).

Conclusions

What can we conclude from our discussion of attention? One thing that is clear is that it plays a critical role in our lives, and that we experience many problems when it is dysfunctional. Cognitive neuroscience and neuropsychology have identified the main regions of the brain associated with attention—the frontal lobes and the anterior cingulate cortex—and research has shown that attention can often be improved with mental training or with drugs like Ritalin. A feature throughout is that attention is central to our conscious existence. It directs and orchestrates our perceptions, thoughts, and feelings, and enables us to carry out the tasks we need to do to live our lives.

CONNECTIONS

• Storing Information: pp. 88–113
• Beginnings of Scientific Psychology: Volume 1, pp. 30–39

• Cognitive Psychology: Volume 1, pp. 104–117
• The Mind: Volume 2, pp. 40–61
• Perception: Volume 2, pp. 62–85
• Physical Therapies: Volume 6, pp. 118–141

Learning by Association

—— *Association is one of the most important aids to acquiring knowledge.* ——

Much of what we learn is the result of conditioning. There are two major types of conditioning: Pavlovian and operant. Conditioning was first observed in experiments on dogs, but is now known to be present in people and has been observed in other animals.

Learning does not exist in isolation in the brain—nearly every piece of information in the human mind is associated with something else. When we learn a new concept, fact, or skill, we habitually link it with, and lock it onto, things we know already. Occasionally we may do this deliberately as an aid to memory, but it happens all the time with or without conscious effort. Psychologists have made a detailed study of the various stimuli that cause this to happen and the responses they evoke.

Say you are a contestant on a quiz show, and the question master asks you: "How many symphonies did Beethoven write?" "Nine," you reply and score a point. But then instead of congratulating yourself, you may find that your mind has skipped to other links between quizzes and the number you just thought of such as: "How many planets are there in the Solar System?" or "How many Muses were there in Greek mythology?" As soon as the question master read out what was on the back of his or her card, you might have

Anne Robinson, quizmaster of the show The Weakest Link. *One way in which the mind works is by associating one fact with another. If the contestants on this quiz show hear an answer, that could trigger memories of other questions to which it could be the answer. This process is, however, usually highly structured and goal-directed, and not a random stumbling from one association to another.*

thought, "That's the same number of symphonies as the number of letters in the composer's name." Some knowledge can be acquired through a series of associations, and conditioning involves the process of association.

The mind does not just progress from one association to another, however, and the structure of knowledge cannot be understood solely in terms of simple associations. Learning—the acquisition and retention of knowledge—is a complex process. Many of the early psychologists who set out to understand it hoped to discover general laws by studying animals in laboratories. Although they did not find a single principle that underlies the whole of learning, their experiments and discoveries form the basis of some modern theories of learning.

From experiments on animals psychologists identified two main types of conditioning—classical and operant. Researchers built on the theory of classical conditioning to develop instrumental (*see* p. 51) and operant conditioning (*see* p. 52), which are both based on the same principles of learning.

CLASSICAL CONDITIONING

One of the pioneer students of learning was Russian physiologist Ivan Pavlov (1849–1936) (*see* Vol. 1, pp. 74–89). He was originally interested in digestion but broadened his area of study after noticing

KEY TERMS

- **US—*unconditioned stimulus***, for example, food that makes a dog salivate in anticipation of a meal.
- **UR—*unconditioned response***, for example, the salivation of a dog in response to the sight or smell of food.
- **CS—*conditioned stimulus***, for example, when the ringing of a bell just before a meal comes to be associated with the imminent arrival of food.
- **CR—*conditioned response***, for example, the salivation that occurs as a response to the ringing of the bell that has become associated with food.

that dogs would salivate not only when food was set in front of them but also when they anticipated it was going to be. So he and his assistants studied what has been termed "mental reflexes" to try and quantify the exact relationship between the presentation of food and the salivation response by the dogs. They did so by experimenting with different variables, such as the temporal pattern, and measuring the salivation response in each case. The dogs lived in cages and

> *"I am an experimenter from head to foot. My whole life has been given to experiment."*
> —Ivan Pavlov, 1949

experienced about one hour of testing a day. During testing the dogs were restrained on a platform in a contraption now known as the Pavlovian harness.

Whenever Pavlov's team used dogs that had no previous experience of what was going to happen or not happen, all the results were exactly as the scientists expected—the animals salivated when the food was presented to them and not before. But once the dogs gained experience in the laboratory, they began to respond to cues associated with food. One dog would start to salivate as soon as it was brought into the testing room and saw the experimental apparatus. Another dog salivated when a laboratory assistant

KEY FACTS

- An unconditioned stimulus leads to an unconditioned response.
- After conditioning, a conditioned stimulus results in a conditioned response.
- Behavior therapy or modification is the practical application of operant and classical conditioning to change problem behavior.
- Positive reinforcement is achieved by providing a person with a reward, such as praise, for certain behavior.

in a white coat walked past its cage. In neither case had food yet been presented. Pavlov then realized that he had discovered a form of simple associative learning. The dogs had mentally linked the laboratory platform or the appearance of the man in a white coat with the delivery of food. This type of learning is termed classical conditioning.

One of Pavlov's experiments. The dog eats the food, but it goes through an opening made in its gullet and does not reach the stomach. The stomach still excretes juices in anticipation, showing a conditioned reflex.

> *"While you are experimenting . . . Don't become a mere recorder of facts, but try to penetrate the mystery of their origin."*
> —*Ivan Pavlov, 1927*

Pavlov redirected his laboratory work away from the study of digestion to further investigate his new discoveries. He and his assistants published many scientific papers on classical conditioning and in 1927 a book, *Conditioned Reflexes*.

US and UR, CS and CR

In his experiments with dogs Pavlov called food the unconditioned stimulus (US) and salivation the unconditioned response (UR). The word *unconditioned* is used in both cases to emphasize that the relationship between the two things has not been learned.

Pavlov then conducted learning trials on the dogs. Each trial typically consisted of the presentation of a further stimulus, such as a tone, followed by presentation of the US (food). The trials were brief; for example, the tone would be presented for ten seconds, and then the food would be brought in. The time between each trial was usually several minutes.

In the first few trials the dog had little reaction to the tone but salivated in response to the arrival of the food. This was the unconditioned stimulus-response relationship. Later though, the dog salivated when it heard the tone. The tone had thus become the learned, or conditioned, stimulus (CS), and salivation was the conditioned response (CR) to hearing it. The word "conditioned" is used for both stimulus-response relationships: the CS and the CR (tone and salivation), and the CS and US (tone and food). Pavlov found that once the CR has appeared in response to the CS, it grows in strength over a number of trials.

Extinction and generalization

The CR will continue only if both the CS and the US keep being applied. The dogs will salivate when they see the man in the white coat only for as long as they associate his appearance with food. But if they see the man repeatedly, and no food is presented, the conditioned response

PAIRING THE CS AND THE US

EXPERIMENT

There are a number of different ways to pair the conditioned stimulus (CS) and the unconditioned stimulus (US). In delayed conditioning the CS occurs first, and the US occurs at the end of the CS presentation. There is an overlap in the presentation of the CS and the US. The time difference can either be short or long. In trace conditioning the CS presentation occurs first. The CS comes on and lasts a period of time and then goes off. Then, after some time, the US occurs. In simultaneous conditioning the CS and US are presented and terminated at the same time, that is, simultaneously.

For these reasons delayed conditioning offers the most superior type of classical conditioning, especially when the delay is short, and thus tends to be the most often used classical conditioning procedure in experimental situations.

will diminish and eventually disappear altogether—this is known as extinction.

When Pavlov used tones to condition the dogs, he noticed that they responded to similar sounds as well as to the exact sound itself. The frequency of tones is measured in hertz (Hz), the number of vibrations per second. Tones with similar frequencies sound similar, and apart from octave gaps, tones with completely different frequencies sound completely different. If salivary conditioning is accomplished with a tone of 1,000 Hz, the dog will also salivate when it hears frequencies of 950 Hz and 1,050 Hz, for example. The salivation response will not be as strong, but it will be present. The dogs will salivate when they hear tones of 900 Hz and 1,100 Hz, but not as much as when they hear tones of 950 Hz or 1,050 Hz. This is generalization of the CR.

Despite this tendency to generalize, dogs can also be trained to differentiate between very similar tones. If a dog experiences a series of trials in which a tone of frequency 1,000 Hz is paired with food, and yet a tone of frequency 950 Hz is never followed by food, the dog will learn to salivate when it hears the 1,000 Hz tone, but not when it hears the 950 Hz tone. This capacity to learn to tell the difference is termed discrimination.

General laws of learning

Through his investigation of salivary conditioning in dogs Pavlov identified and defined the general principles of acquisition, generalization, discrimination, and extinction. Later investigators found these same phenomena using different procedures. Through being repeated successfully in different experimental situations these principles thus became laws of learning.

Pavlov's research demonstrated that learning can be the result of classical conditioning. Research has shown that there are many other types of learning.

By experimenting on dogs, Pavlov established four general principles of learning: acquisition, generalization, discrimination, and extinction. Using different tones, he found that the dogs generalized their response to the stimulus and that they could discriminate between tones.

IT MUST BE SOMETHING I ATE

In the 1960s John Garcia and his colleagues at the University of California, Los Angeles, discovered taste-aversion conditioning. It stresses the individual's role in making associations, particularly the built-in predisposition to associate two stimuli such as taste with illness. The subjects were laboratory rats, and the response system was gastrointestinal illness. The rats were fed a new food they had never eaten before. Then they were made ill with X-ray radiation or an injection of lithium chloride. Later, after recovering, the rats avoided the food they had eaten just before the illness. In this case the conditioned stimulus (CS) is the taste of the new food, and the unconditioned stimulus (US) is the illness-inducing radiation or chemical.

In other classical conditioning procedures repeated pairings of the CS (such as the man in a white coat) and the US (for example, food) must occur close together in time before the subject (a dog) makes a conditioned response (CR). With taste aversion, however, the CR occurs with just one pairing of the CS and the US, even though they may be presented minutes or even hours apart.

A similar effect can be seen in people who suffer food poisoning. Say on your first trip to Santa Barbara, California, you try mussels, a shellfish you have never tasted before. Six hours later you are very sick, and you spend the next three days in bed on your back. The likely result of this experience is that you will never want to eat mussels again. This will probably happen even if the malady that struck you was not gastroenteritis at all, but merely a bout of influenza that was entirely unconnected with what you ate.

Taste-aversion conditioning occurs when you associate a food with being ill and never eat that food again, even if it was not the cause of your illness. People often make this association between seafood and food poisoning.

Understanding the procedure

To understand any classical conditioning procedure, you first need to identify the relationship that exists between the stimulus and the response before the procedure is carried out. In Pavlov's work the unconditioned stimulus was food, and the unconditioned response, salivation—in other words, dogs naturally slobber when they are going to be fed.

Thus for a conditioned response to merit the name, it must be related to the unconditioned response. The CR may happen before or at the same time as the UR. In the case of Pavlov's dogs the conditioned response is the creatures' anticipation of food, which is triggered when they hear or see the associated

stimuli; the unconditioned response is salivation, which always occurs when the dogs see or smell food.

Pavlov's study of salivary responses in dogs established classical conditioning as an important laboratory procedure for the investigation of associative learning. Later investigators developed different classical conditioning procedures, studying other species and response systems. To give just one example, many laboratories have studied the eye-blink response system in adults. Here the unconditioned stimulus-response relationship is that between a puff of air delivered to the eye (the US) and blinking (the UR). The conditioning procedure involves pairing another stimulus, for example, showing a dim

MORPHINE AS AN UNCONDITIONED STIMULUS

CASE STUDY

The drug morphine is an analgesic—it relieves pain. However, with repeated doses the drug loses some of its effect. This gradual resistance is called tolerance.

In the 1970s and 1980s Shepard Siegel of McMaster University, Ontario, Canada, wondered if classical conditioning was the basis of this tolerance. He reasoned that the unconditioned stimulus (US) was morphine, and the unconditoned response (UR) was the painkilling effect. He believed the conditioned stimuli (CS) were the events surrounding the injection, including the sight of the needle. According to his theory, the conditioned response (CR) should be the opposite of the UR, as in the case of heart-rate classical conditioning (*see* p. 50). So, the CR should be increased sensitivity to pain, which explains tolerance to morphine.

To test this theory, Siegel performed a series of laboratory experiments with rats. First, he placed the animals on a hot metal plate and measured the rate at which they licked their paws with and without them first having had a dose of the painkiller. Low pain sensitivity would mean slow paw licking, and high pain sensitivity would mean fast paw licking. After several injections of morphine, which reduced the rate of licking, Siegel gave the rats an injection of saline, an inert substance. When he placed the animals back on the hot plate, they showed fast paw licking and therefore high pain sensitivity. This was in accordance with his prediction.

By inference, it appears that if the human body knows it is going to get a painkiller, in its effort to maintain homeostasis (equilibrium) it tries to counter the pain-

killing effect of the drug with a learned, compensatory, "opponent response" to "cancel out" the UR. Thus it becomes more sensitive to pain in anticipation of a drug that is meant to reduce it. Thanks to this compensation for the drug's effects we observe drug tolerance.

Siegel proposed that heroin addicts also experience classical conditioning. The US is the heroin, and the UR is the painkilling effect of heroin. The CS is the setting in which the heroin is injected. Like morphine, the CR would be the opposite of the UR. Siegel then reasoned that if an addict were to inject heroin in a new environmental setting, then the CR would be minimal and therefore the effects of the heroin intense.

To test this theory, Siegel conducted the following experiment. He gave rats daily intravenous injections for 30 days. The injections were either a placebo (a dummy) or heroin and were given either in the animal colony or a different room where there was constant white noise. The drug and the placebo were given on alternate days, and the drug was always administered in a particular environment: some rats were always given heroin in the white-noise room and the placebo in the colony; others were always given heroin in the colony and the placebo in the white-noise room. Another group of rats served as a control; they were also injected, but only with the placebo in different rooms on alternate dates.

All the rats were then injected with a large dose of heroin. Of the experimental group, some rats (group one) were given the heroin in the same room as they had been given it before, while the others (group two) were given it in the room in which they had previously been injected with the placebo. Of the control group, 96 percent died, showing the lethal effect of the heroin in nontolerant animals. Rats in group two were partially tolerant to heroin, and only 64 percent died. But only 32 percent of the rats in group one died, showing that tolerance to heroin was even greater when the large dose was given in the same environment as that in which the drug had previously been administered.

Siegel suggested that one reason addicts suddenly lose their tolerance could be because they take the drug in a different environment. Surveys of heroin addicts admitted to hospitals suffering from the effects of an overdose tend to support this conclusion. Many addicts report that they had taken the near-fatal dose in an unusual circumstance or that their normal pattern was different on that day.

A tube of morphine. Studies on rats show that if the body thinks it is getting a painkiller, sensitivity levels will rise. Further studies showed that tolerance of the morphine-based drug heroin drops in unfamiliar surroundings.

yellow light on a screen (the CS), followed by the puff of air to the eye. After several trials the person displays the CR (blinks) when the dim yellow light appears on the screen before the puff of air. If an electric shock is the US, the UR will be a feeling of pain followed immediately by a jerk away from the source of the current. This reaction is automatic, predictable, and invariable. Much research has been carried

> "If the environment, learning or otherwise, could be controlled to provide the proper stimulus, then the proper response can be elicited."
> —John B. Watson, 1914

out into whether or not animals can anticipate the shock. Anticipation allows the animals to either avoid the shock or prepare for it, minimizing the effects. This phenomenon is known as fear classical conditioning. In experiments on rats they were first trained to press a lever in order to reach their food, then given electric shocks almost immediately after a light had been flashed in their line of vision. The light thus became a conditioned stimulus—whenever the rats saw it, they recoiled, expecting the electric shock. Later, the same light was shone just as they were about to press the food lever. The result is that they did not press it, implying that the rats do experience fear and anticipate the shock. As a response to the fear they tensed their muscles, which interrupts all physical activity.

Mary Cover Jones used classical conditioning to help a child, Peter, overcome his fear of rabbits. A rabbit was brought closer and closer to Peter as he was eating his favorite desserts. Gradually the rabbit came to have pleasant and satisfying associations, and Peter overcame his phobia.

Here the unconditioned response is very different from the conditioned response. The UR is an escape reaction, and the CR is the result of fear. Using the same experimental methods, researchers have also studied heart-rate classical conditioning in rats and people. The US is a mild shock, and the UR is a heart-rate increase in response to the US. A CS such as a tone is then paired with the mild shock. The CR is a heart-rate decrease. Once individuals learn that a shock is to follow the CS, they adapt by having a heart-rate decrease. This is in anticipation of the heart-rate increase that will occur when the shock is presented.

Desensitization of phobias

Phobias are irrational fears. They can be learned by classical conditioning. In 1920 John Broadus Watson (1878–1958) and his second wife, Rosalie Rayner, published a report about their work with an 11-month-old named Little Albert (*see* Vol. 1, pp. 74–89). Watson and Rayner said that before Albert was conditioned, he was an outgoing and curious child with few fears. He was interested in the people and animals, even the rats, in Watson's laboratory. However, the child did have a strong fear reaction to loud noises: For Albert loud noise (the US) caused a fear response (the UR). Once a day Watson and Rayner showed a white laboratory rat (the CS) to Albert and followed it with a loud noise (the US). Within a few days Albert was afraid of the rat (the CR). Little Albert had been conditioned to associate the white rat with his fear of the loud noise.

In 1924 Mary Cover Jones (1896–1987) of Ohio University reported that by using classical conditioning techniques, she was able to help a phobic child named Peter. His irrational fear was of rabbits. Jones allowed Peter to eat his favorite desserts and then brought a rabbit gradually closer to him. Over time he began to associate the appearance of the rabbit with the pleasure of enjoying his favorite food. The conditioned stimulus of food and habituation to expect the food with the rabbit canceled out the fear of the rabbit.

Wolpe's treatment

In 1958 the clinical psychologist Joseph Wolpe (born 1915) published his work concerning the systematic desensitization of human phobias. Wolpe assumed that human phobias were learned by classical conditioning, just as Albert had learned to fear the white laboratory rat. Wolpe used Jones' work with Peter as the basis for his contention that phobias could be removed. The therapeutic treatment developed by Wolpe has three steps. First, the therapist and the patient engage in a lengthy conversation about the latter's fears. Together they rank the fears into a hierarchy from the least to the most feared things or situations. Next, the therapist teaches the patient a variety of relaxation techniques. They include breathing exercises, muscle stretching, and relaxing, and imagery about tranquil places. Most patients learn to become deeply relaxed as a result of these techniques. Finally, while deeply relaxed, the patient is prompted to imagine confronting the fear situations. This starts with the items on the list that cause the least fear and progresses to those that they find the most terrifying.

Wolpe found that more than 90 percent of the people with phobias he treated achieved a good or excellent therapeutic result from systematic desensitization. The treatment is effective and much quicker than other therapies used to treat phobias—it can be successfully completed in 20 hour-long sessions over a period of one month.

INSTRUMENTAL CONDITIONING

Classical conditioning is a type of learning that explains a range of behaviors based on innate responses such as emotional reactions (especially fears and phobias) and food aversions. The unconditional response has to be automatic and involuntary. The U.S. psychologist Edward Lee Thorndike (1874–1949) (*see* Vol. 1, pp. 74–89) identified instrumental conditioning, a learning procedure in which there does not need to be an inborn response to start with, and the animal's behavior is voluntary, that is, it operates on its environment.

To demonstrate the instrumental conditioning theory of learning, Thorndike built a series of puzzle boxes

> *"The development of human mental life could be likened to that of the animal kingdom as a whole."*
> —Edward Lee Thorndike, 1905

to test a variety of species, most famously cats. These boxes were made of wood and metal, and contained several devices, such as bolts, buttons, latches, levers, and rings. A cat was shut inside the box. If it manipulated the right gadget, it could escape. Thorndike tested 13 cats, each within its own box. Each box had an escape mechanism different from the others. Thorndike observed the behavior of the cats and recorded the time it took them to escape, trial by trial.

On the first trial each cat would engage in a number of different behaviors that were ineffective for getting out of the box. These behaviors included hissing, spitting, pacing, and clawing. Eventually—perhaps after several minutes—the cat would manage by a process of trial and error to escape. Then trial by trial each cat would make progress: The ineffective responses would decrease in frequency, and the effective escape response would occur sooner. But progress was very slow—the cats did not learn the way out through flashes of insight, but they gained this knowledge over a period of time, learning by trial and error and gradually dropping the unsuccessful responses. This was, however, an important finding. Thorndike's results suggested that the cats learned neither through insight nor by applying their problem-solving abilities. After the initial blind groping the good efforts were rewarded and were, therefore, more likely to be repeated in the future. Thorndike's first explanation of this result was that "Responses are connected to situations simply because they occur

---

> *"A scientific analysis of behavior must, I believe, assume that a person's behavior is controlled by his genetic and environmental histories rather than by the person himself as an initiating, creative agent."*
>
> —*B. F. Skinner, 1974*

---

frequently in those situations." This became known as the law of exercise. Later, however, he changed his notion of why a bond would develop between stimulus and response. His new idea was that when a response occurs in a stimulus situation and leads to a "satisfying state of affairs," the response gradually becomes imprinted as a habit. In this way repeated successes (such as escapes from the puzzle box) lead to stronger and stronger stimulus-response bonds. Also, as trials go on, the ineffective behaviors gradually become weakened. That is because only effective behaviors are rewarded, and the ineffective behaviors are not rewarded.

This explanation was formalized by Thorndike as the law of effect, which states: "Of several responses made to the same situation, those which are accompanied, or closely followed, by satisfaction to the animal will, other things being equal, be more firmly connected with the situation, so that, when it recurs,

they will be more likely to recur; those which are accompanied or closely followed by discomfort to the animal will, other things being equal, have their connections with that situation weakened, so that, when it recurs, they will be less likely to recur." This general law of learning applies to many different species in many different situations.

B. F. Skinner

Thorndike's discovery—that responses that are instrumental in producing good outcomes produce associative learning—influenced many psychologists, especially B. F. Skinner (1904–1990) (*see* Vol. 1, pp. 74–89). Skinner spent many years elaborating Thorndike's learning theories through carrying out further experiments on conditioning of animals in boxes.

Charles Darwin's theory of evolution (*see* Vol. 1, pp. 134–143) persuaded both Thorndike and Skinner that there is a continuity of species, and so general laws of learning that are applicable to humans can be determined through the study of nonhuman animals. Pavlov's research on classical conditioning convinced Skinner that reliable and valid laboratory data could reveal facts about conditioning and learning. Skinner was also influenced by the writings of John B. Watson on behaviorism (*see* Vol. 1, pp. 74–89), stressing that rigorous psychology should focus on observable behavior. Although behaviorism is largely rejected by psychologists today, the findings do still have some practical applications. But the greatest influence on Skinner's work was Thorndike's research with cats.

OPERANT CONDITIONING
Skinner developed a procedure similar to Thorndike's, which he called operant conditioning. In this context "operant" means that the behavior of the animal "operates" on the environment. In the 1930s at Harvard and the University of Minnesota he constructed a special box to use for experiments studying the behavior of rats. The device is sometimes known as

the "Skinner Box," a term first used by the behavioral psychologist Clark L. Hull. But Skinner himself disliked this name, and he always referred to it as the operant conditioning chamber.

The operant conditioning chamber is illuminated by a light in the ceiling. The

> *"The reinforcements characteristic of industry and education are almost always intermittent because it is not feasible to control behavior by reinforcing every response."*
> —B. F. Skinner, 1953

floor is a series of tightly packed stainless steel rods. There is a front panel with a metal lever that can be depressed by the rat and a pellet dispenser that can drop small food pellets into a dish. The chamber has several lightbulbs on the front panel that can be turned on and off by the experimenter and speakers to present auditory stimuli such as tones. The earliest operant conditioning chambers were automated by

electromechanical or solid-state switching circuitry; modern examples are automated by computers.

In scientific terms the basis of operant conditioning is a contingency between responding and its consequence. If the rat presses the lever in the operant chamber, then it is likely to be given a food pellet—the animal performs the operant, and the probability of reinforcement increases. Since prior to conditioning the rat was kept hungry, the result of the contingency is that the rat presses the lever to obtain a high rate of response in the form of food pellets. Skinner labeled this "reinforcement of the lever-press response." The concept of reinforcement refers to the strengthening of the response, as shown by the increasing frequency with which the rat performs it.

Later, Skinner developed a similar operant conditioning chamber to study the behavior of pigeons. Unlike rats, pigeons have excellent eyesight, including color vision, and Skinner wanted to study visual discrimination in learning. So his chamber for this purpose contained an illuminated disk that the pigeon was trained to peck in return for food.

A pigeon taking part in one of Skinner's experiments in 1950. The pigeon must match a colored light with the corresponding colored panel in order to be rewarded with food.

Positive reinforcement

Skinner also studied an operant conditioning contingency that weakens a response. The contingency is that if the rat presses the lever, then the animal receives a painful electric shock to its paw. The result is that the rat's response of pressing the lever decreases and may stop altogether. Skinner termed this "result punishment." He was a consistent advocate of the use of reinforcement rather than punishment. He thought that the effects of reinforcement were permanent, while the effects of punishment were temporary.

Skinner advocated positive reinforcement for good behavior. Positive reinforcement encourages people and animals to repeat good behavior. This dog's owner should reward his pet for bringing the paper.

Positive reinforcement is achieved simply by providing the subject with something it likes or enjoys. It encourages

> *"When a bit of behavior has the kind of consequence called reinforcement, it is more likely to occur again. A positive reinforcer strengthens any behavior that produces it."*
> — *B. F. Skinner, 1974*

the animal to repeat a behavior that seems to cause that consequence. There are many examples: The sea lion gets a fish for balancing a ball on the end of its nose, the dog gets a biscuit for bringing its owner's slippers, or a child receives lots of praise and attention from his or her parents for behaving well.

Within this broad category are two subdivisions—primary and secondary. A primary positive reinforcer is something that the animal likes instinctively and does not have to learn about. Such reinforcers include food and the chance to mate. A secondary positive reinforcer is something that the animal has to learn to like. The learning can be accomplished by classical conditioning or by some other method. Money, for example, is a secondary reinforcer—it is, as it were, an acquired taste. Adult people may pursue it eagerly, but it would be no good offering a three-year-old $10 to stay in her own bed all night rather than move into her parents'—she has not yet been conditioned to realize that money can be a desirable commodity.

Schedules of reinforcement

A schedule of reinforcement is the timetable that determines when a reinforcement will be available for the next response, and how often a behavior will result in a reward. There are many

REINFORCED BRIDGES

FOCUS ON

Animal trainers may create special secondary reinforcers known as bridges. For example, when trainers reward a horse with a sugar lump (the primary reinforcer), they might also pat it. That is the bridge. The horse may enjoy the pat almost as much as the food reward. This process creates a conditioned positive reinforcer also known as a conditioned reinforcer. Some animals that have learned a bridge may react to the reinforcer as positively as to the reward itself.

This horse may come to enjoy being patted as much as the carrot it is being given. This association between the primary and secondary reinforcers, known as a bridge, is used in animal training.

kinds, including: fixed interval, variable interval, fixed ratio, variable ratio, and random. A fixed interval means that a reward will be given after a certain time. A variable interval schedule means that reinforcers will be put into operation after different lengths of time.

In a fixed ratio schedule the reward or reinforcement will be available only after a certain number of repetitions of the required task. A fixed ratio of 1:1 means that every correct performance of a behavior will be rewarded. But if, for example, the fixed ratio is 1:3, every third behavior will be rewarded. Some people are paid on this basis, which is known as piecework: a typist may get $10 for every 100 address labels typed, but nothing for doing only 99 (a ratio of 1:100). This type of schedule may work well, but is not always effective. In some cases removal of the reinforcer will lead quickly to the extinction of the behavior—in other words, if the rewards are not frequent enough to elicit a response from the

person or animal, then they will give up doing it altogether. In other cases the subjects alter their behavior once they have figured out that the first two performances will not be rewarded, and that the third one will be no matter what.

> *"A science of behavior which concerns only the behavior of groups is not likely to be of help in our understanding of the particular case."*
> — *B. F. Skinner, 1953*

In a variable ratio schedule reinforcers are distributed on the basis of an average number of correct behaviors. A variable ratio of 1:5 means that on average one out of every five behaviors will be rewarded. But it might be any one of the five, as long as it averages out at one in five over a period. Finally, in a random schedule

there is no correlation between the behavior and the consequence. This is how fate and chance operate.

If a behavior that has been reinforced in the past stops being reinforced, then that behavior might be extinguished. In order to avoid this, you should find a secondary reinforcer. For example, although you might not give your dog a treat every time it sits on command, you should nevertheless reward it with some praise ("Good boy!"). In some cases a variable ratio schedule of reinforcement tends to slow down the rate of extinction or make the behavior less vulnerable to extinction. If people expect to gain a reward at some point, but not necessarily every time they do something, they are not likely to stop after the first few times their action fails to generate the desired result. This is the

Variable reinforcement of a behavior does not necessarily mean that it is extinguished. The gambling halls of Las Vegas are full of people who think they might hit the jackpot eventually, so they do not stop playing just because they do not win every time.

principle that underlies the popularity of slot machines. Although statistically the odds against a payout may be astronomical, people keep playing the one-armed bandit because they think, "Maybe I didn't win last time, but next time I'm sure to be lucky."

When a behavior that has been strongly reinforced in the past no longer gains a reinforcement, animals might experience what is known as an extinction burst. That is when they perform the behavior over and over again in a frenzied burst of activity. It then disappears, but there may be a spontaneous recovery in which the seemingly extinguished behavior returns.

There are many other things to be aware of when operating a schedule of reinforcement. If the animal is acting out of fear, you may be rewarding the fear response rather than discouraging the undesired behavior. If, for example, you cuddle a shy dog, it may think you are rewarding it for the very behavior you want to eliminate. Timing is also of the essence. If the animal stayed for as long as you wanted, and you give it a chocolate as a reward after you have then said, "Come," it may think that you are rewarding it for the latter behavior rather than the former. Also, the reward must be sufficient to motivate a repetition. Mild praise is not enough for some animals. Another potential problem is that reinforcements may become associated with the person

> "Operant conditioning is selection in progress. It resembles a hundred million years of natural selection or a thousand years of the evolution of a culture compressed into a very short time."
> —B. F. Skinner, 1981

giving them rather than any behavior by the animal. If the animal realizes that it will not get any rewards without you being present, it may not be motivated to act when you are not there. Animals may become sated with the reward you are offering—when they have had enough, it will no longer be motivating.

An important and unresolved debate about operant conditioning centers on whether or not motivation for certain behavior is extrinsic (for example, money or food) or intrinsic ("just for fun" with no material gain). One group of researchers argues that the two types of reward are the same, which means that operant conditioning is the broad study of how rewards maintain behavior. The opposing view is that intrinsic and extrinsic rewards are very different; for example, people may paint or write purely for enjoyment, which means that operant conditioning is the study of how certain rewards maintain certain behavior.

Positive punishment

Positive punishment aims to reduce behavior by taking away a pleasant treat or something good. If a person or animal enjoys or depends on rewards of this type, they will work to avoid losing them and are less likely to repeat behavior that results in their withdrawal. If, for example, two children have their allowances decreased when they keep fighting, that will give them an incentive to stop fighting and make sure peace is kept.

Positive punishment, when applied correctly, is the most effective way to stop unwanted behaviors. Its main flaw is that it does not teach specific alternative behaviors. Yet it is not always the punishment itself that reduces the

Positive punishment, such as the threat of pocket money not being paid, may be sufficient to persuade these brothers to share their toys. The threat of withdrawing the allowance may be enough to stop their bad behavior, with no need to carry it out.

behavior—the threat of it may be enough. Such stimuli are known as secondary positive punishers. If, for example, a puppy becomes conditioned to expect a tap on the nose every time it soils the carpet, it may learn to regard the raised hand as enough of a cue to go outside to relieve itself; the warring brothers may calm down as soon as the parent mentions the possibility of withholding their pocket money. But they are not always successful. A dog may be called to heel so often when

THE BABY IN THE BOX

BIOGRAPHY

B. F. Skinner and his wife Eve had two daughters, their firstborn Julie, and then Deborah. When Eve became pregnant with Deborah, she asked her husband if he could come up with some ideas to make baby care easier. So Skinner built a baby-care chamber. It was a temperature-controlled box where Deborah could play and be clothing-free for hours each day. Contrary to some reports, Deborah was a very happy and healthy infant who became a well-adjusted adult. Skinner published a report about this in *Ladies' Home Journal*. He attempted to market the baby chamber, but with no success.

Unfortunately, the story about the baby in the box has been often told, and told in an inaccurate way. Of course, Skinner is famous for his work with operant conditioning with rats, pigeons, and other animals in boxes. So some have written that Deborah was the subject of various experiments in her box. This is simply untrue.

Deborah's older sister Julie cared for her infants in baby-care chambers very similar to those used for Deborah. The sisters have been always clear about the warm and loving environment they shared with their parents. Both were close with both their parents throughout their lives.

There have, however, been rumors about both of Skinner's daughters. The rumors have included reports that they committed suicide or were psychotic. The truth is, however, that Julie is a successful professor of educational psychology, and Deborah is an artist whose work has been shown at London's Royal Academy.

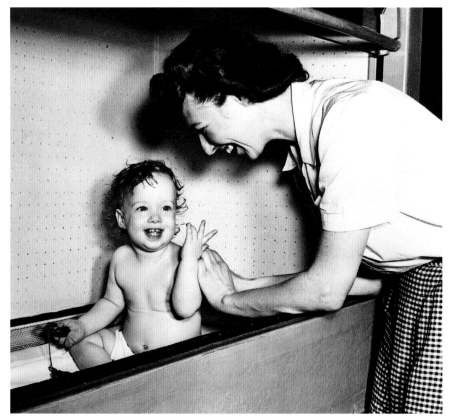

Deborah Skinner with her mother playing in the baby-care chamber designed by her father. It was a safe environment where temperature and humidity were carefully controlled.

it is enjoying itself that it starts to associate its own name with a punishment and will cease to come when called. This is known as a conditioned negative punisher. To be effective, a positive punisher must follow a behavior immediately or be clearly connected to the behavior. Many dog trainers actively condition the word "No!" with some punisher to form an association between the word and the consequence. The conditioned punisher is an important part of training certain behaviors in operant conditioning.

Behaviors are usually motivated by the expectation of a reward. Even with a punishment the motivation of the reward is often still there. For example, a child may enjoy attention from an adult even though it takes the form of nagging. Or the rat might risk an electric shock if there is the possibility of the reward of food.

As with positive reinforcers, the imposition of positive punishments must be carefully timed to correspond exactly

One problem with punishment is that the rewards of the deviant behavior usually outweigh the disadvantages of the punishment. These young boys drinking alcohol together may find the experience rewarding enough to risk being banned from going out or seeing each other.

with the unwanted behavior for it to have an effect. Say you want your dog to stop chasing sheep—if you call the dog and hit it when it arrives, it may fail to make the connection with the sheep and think it is being punished for coming to you.

The more experience the animal has of receiving rewards for its behavior, the greater the punishment has to be to stop or decrease the unwanted behavior—a teenager may find that the pleasure of drinking alcohol or smoking outweighs the parental punishment of being "grounded." Another problem is that punishments may become associated with the person supplying them. The dog that was hit for worrying sheep may still chase them, but only when you are not around.

Stimulus control
Once a rat has been trained to press a lever for food, its lever-pressing behavior can be brought under stimulus control. Suppose a tone is introduced and every

few minutes switches from on to off and from off to on, and the rat's lever-pressing response is reinforced only while the tone is on. The rat will learn to press the lever only while it hears the tone. The tone serves as a discriminative stimulus, and the rat's lever-pressing behavior is controlled by the stimulus of the tone.

Discriminative stimuli such as the on-off tone acquire reinforcing properties. They can be revealed in the operant conditioning chamber. Once the rat has learned that the tone is a discriminative stimulus, it will engage in behavior that produces the tone. For example, suppose the tone is kept off until the rat jumps in the air. When it jumps in the air, the tone comes on, and the rat might press the lever for a food reinforcer, and the tone would turn off again. The sequence or chain of behavior is now: jump–tone on–press lever–food. There are two behaviors and two reinforcers in this

chain. The first response is the jump, and the first reinforcer is the start of the tone. The second behavior is the lever press, and the second reinforcer is the food pellet. Food is a natural reinforcer. The tone is a conditioned reinforcer in that the reinforcing property of the tone was acquired through conditioning.

> *"Of course, behaviorism 'works.' So does torture."*
> —*W. H. Auden, 1970*

Notice that this chain of behavior is built with the terminal behavior first. The rat was first taught to press the lever for food. Then a discriminative stimulus was introduced, and it became a conditioned reinforcer. Then another response must occur before the conditioned reinforcer is delivered. Long chains of behavior can be

Shaping is an important technique in training animals to perform a complex series of actions. At first, very approximate actions are rewarded, but gradually rewards are only given for behavior closest to the desired response. This is known as successive approximations, and the technique has been used to successfully train animals such as this dolphin to perform a complicated sequence of behaviors.

built in this way using conditioned reinforcers and natural reinforcers. Complex behaviors are also taught by shaping. It involves approximate behavior being reinforced initially and gradually increasing the demands made on the animal to gain a reward until the exact behavior is achieved. This technique has been used to train animals to perform in circuses or on television.

BEHAVIOR THERAPY

B. F. Skinner was greatly interested in behavior therapy and behavior modification—the application of operant conditioning to the modification of problem behaviors. In 1948, while at Indiana University, he inspired fellow graduate student Linda Fuller to apply operant principles to an institutionalized

> *"If we do end up acting just like rats or Pavlov's dogs, it will be largely because behaviorism has conditioned us to do so."*
> — *Richard Dean Rosen, 1977*

18-year-old who had been diagnosed as feebleminded and spent his time lying in bed, not moving. The man never made a sound and, since he refused to eat or drink, was force-fed. Fuller treated him with a milk reinforcer, which was directly injected into his mouth. Using continuous reinforcement, she succeeded in training him to make movements with various parts of his body.

In the 1950s, again at Harvard University, Skinner inspired Ogden Lindsley, another graduate student, to work with psychotic patients at Boston Massachusetts State Hospital. Lindsley modified their behavior using candy and cigarette reinforcers. In 1963 a psychologist named Teodoro Ayllon, also under Skinner's tutelage, worked with an institutionalized psychotic woman who had a nine-year history of stealing and hoarding towels. Following Ayllon's

instructions, the staff gave her many towels whenever she stole one. She eventually had a total of 650 in her small room! Then she started removing the ones she already had from her room. The reinforcing value of the towels had been reduced by providing her with so many. In 1968 Ayllon and Nathan Azrin established what they called a token economy at Illinois State Hospital, a facility for female schizophrenics. The women earned plastic tokens for engaging in desirable behaviors, such as making their beds and eating properly. The tokens were then exchanged for privileges, such as being able to take a long walk in the grounds, and for desired items, such as candy. Using Skinner's definition, the tokens were conditioned reinforcers. Ayllon and Azrin found that desirable behaviors increased dramatically. When the tokens were removed, the desirable behaviors decreased. Finally, when the tokens were reintroduced, the desirable behavior increased dramatically once again.

Operant conditioning was also used in 1969 by W. Isaacs, J. Thomas, and I. Goldiamond to treat a schizophrenic man who had been mute for 21 years. They used chewing gum as a reinforcer. To earn it, the man had to make lip and eye movements, make a sound, and so on. After five weeks the man spoke and continued to do so.

Another technique is to measure physical functions such as heart rate or blood pressure, amplify them, and show them to the person as a sound or in some other form of representation. This has been successful in helping people control a particular reaction, for example, in stressful or frightening situations.

Current applications

Skinner's contingencies of reinforcement have had dramatic success in modifying various undesirable behaviors, such as overeating, smoking, shyness, speech problems, and autism. Many residential programs for the mentally retarded employ operant conditioning principles as part of the treatment. Although some people applying Skinner's work have used punishment and aversive procedures, Skinner was against such practices and always advocated reinforcement. He argued that although punishment teaches individuals that a certain behavior is inappropriate, it does not show them the correct way to behave. It may also be effective in the short term; but as soon as the punishment is stopped, the undesired response is likely to return.

Applications in education

Reinforcement can be used in a classroom. For example, children might earn tokens for obeying certain well-defined rules. The tokens are secondary reinforcers since they are exchanged for a desired activity such as running around outside or reading a favorite book. Teacher approval can be a powerful positive reinforcer in schools.

Punishment, if it is used, can take the form of verbal warnings or being denied a favorite activity. If the behavior is not damaging to the child or others, then extinction or ignoring the problem behavior is a possible solution.

Objections

Some people object to behavior therapy on ethical grounds. First are the objections to the use of unpleasant stimuli, for example, in aversion therapy. The reply to this criticism is that the end result justifies the method. For the person to benefit they may have to suffer confronting what they are afraid of and may find the experience painful but will benefit in the long-term.

Second are concerns about depriving people of the right to choose how they behave. The argument against this criticism is that nobody is free to choose how to behave, and people are already subject to reinforcement and punishment

Children having fun learning mathematics. It helps the learning process if every correct response is positively rewarded, for example, by gaining stars or points. Operant and classical conditioning theories have been effectively applied to classroom learning.

in everyday life. The therapist controls these stimuli for the benefit of the person. Another objection is that the effects of this mode of therapy or learning are short-lived. That is because it treats the immediate behavior rather than the underlying problem.

The central proposal of both Pavlovian and operant conditioning is that there are general principles of learning covering a wide range of species in various situations. Most of the theories of learning are derived from experiments conducted on animals in a laboratory. Skinner, for example, wrote a book solely about key-pecking in pigeons but was convinced that the findings could be generalized, so he entitled it *The Behavior of Organisms*. Critics say that these results cannot be automatically transferred to people, who have more complex nervous systems, and who are capable of thought. Skinner's assumption could be wrong since certain forms of learning are specific to a particular species or depend on what is being learned—language learning in humans, for example. Some learning principles cannot be universally applied.

In spite of these criticisms and the fact that few psychologists totally accept these techniques today, the legacy of the behaviorists has been to contribute significantly to the development of learning theory and therapy.

Summary

Behaviorism is often regarded as the most scientific approach in psychology because it focuses on behavior that can be directly observed and measured. The range of behaviors it can be used to explain is very wide, and practical applications can be very powerful and effective. Critics argue, however, that the findings from research on animals cannot be directly transferred to the behavior of people. Another criticism is that its explanations for how people learn are too simple—individuals are more complex than the theories of Pavlov, Thorndike, Skinner, and Watson allow. This reduction of learning behavior

to simple responses of reinforcement and punishment is also regarded by some critics as dehumanizing. Finally, critics attack the superficiality of this approach to learning. A problem behavior is eliminated or changed, but the underlying difficulties are not tackled. The behavorist response is that if these techniques are successful in treating problem behavior, there is no need to analyze further.

> *"The control of behavior is an intricate science, into which the average mother could not be initiated without years of training."*
> —B. F. Skinner, 1948

Pavlovian and operant conditioning are both types of learning by association with the central belief that behavior is elicited by certain stimuli. One stimulus reminds us of another and thus influences our next action. The main difference between the two theories is that operational conditioning regards learning as a more active process, and the person "operates" on their environment. Much of our behavior, our actions in everyday life, is influenced by conditioning. Although the workings of the mind and how we learn are still—and will probably always remain—incompletely understood, it seems clear that much of our behavior is due to some form of association. The challenge for psychology is to harness this insight and put it to practical use.

CONNECTIONS

- Nature and Nurture: Volume 1, pp. 22–29
- Behaviorism: Volume 1, pp. 74–89
- Emotion and Motivation: Volume 2, pp. 88–109
- Problem Solving: Volume 3, pp. 136–163
- Stages of Development: Volume 4, pp. 58–77
- Intelligence: Volume 5, pp. 118–141
- Physical Therapies: Volume 6, pp. 118–141

Representing Information

———— *"To be a smell is one thing, to be known as a smell, another."* ————
John Dewey

Our brains can hold an enormous amount of information: Most people know how to read, write, and say thousands of words; we know how to get from our homes to dozens of different places; psychologists have shown that we can remember thousands of different pictures. A great deal of research into the brain focuses on how it stores and represents this wealth of data.

In the modern world all sorts of devices represent information. Some, like books and maps, have been around for thousands of years. At the other extreme the World Wide Web did not exist until 1993, although the Internet has been around for several years longer. However, even the oldest book is a newcomer compared to the brain. The human brain has been representing information for millions of years.

For thousands of years philosophers have been trying to figure out how the mind stores and represents information. About a hundred years ago psychologists began conducting experiments to answer this question. To do an experiment, you have to have some idea of what you will find. Scientists call such an idea a hypothesis. As psychologists experimented, they searched for suitable hypotheses to express how the mind

If this city street were mapped, not every detail would be shown—maps are external representations that omit unnecessary information.

KEY DATES

1883 Francis Galton investigates mental imagery.
1892 Gottlob Frege writes *On Concept and Object*.
1932 Frederick Bartlett publishes *Remembering*.
1958 Ludwig Wittgenstein publishes *Philosophical Investigations*.
1966 Ross Quillian submits his Ph.D thesis on semantic hierarchies.
1969 Brent Berlin and Paul Kay publish their findings on color terms in different languages.
1973 Researchers show that people can remember a minimum of several thousand images.
1973 Eleanor Rosch shows that categories have typical and atypical members.

1977 Roger Schank and Robert Abelson propose script theory.
1981 James McClelland publishes a network theory of concept representation.
1983 Stephen M. Kosslyn writes *Ghosts in the Mind's Machine*.
1985 James McClelland and David Rumelhart propose a network model of category learning.
1986 David Rumelhart and colleagues write *Parallel Distributed Processing*.
1993 Denis le Bihan and colleagues show that the parts of the brain used for imagining pictures are the same as those used for seeing them.

might represent information. Was the process of committing something to memory like drawing a picture inside your head? Were the stories people knew by heart stored in the mental equivalents of books? Did the brain represent our understanding of different words in the same way that a dictionary does?

People share information in many different ways. Books are written, pictures are painted, and maps are drawn. However, books, pictures, and maps are not the same as the things they stand for. A map of New York is not New York, for example. Maps, books, and pictures are representations. Representations are objects that give us useful information about the world. They also omit useless information. For example, a tourist map of New York does not mark the position of manhole covers. Tourists do not need to know where the city's manhole covers are. The inclusion of unnecessary information on a map makes it harder to read and less useful.

> *"I found that the great majority of the men of science . . . protested that mental imagery was unknown to them."*
> —*Francis Galton, 1880*

Psychologists describe maps, books, and pictures as external representations. They are distinguished from internal representations, which are the ways that the brain stores and displays potentially useful information.

PICTURES IN THE BRAIN

People have theorized about internal representations for centuries. The Greek philosopher Aristotle (384–322 B.C.) argued that memory was like storing pictures in the head. Philosophers have debated this point ever since, but scientists only joined the debate around 120 years ago. In 1883 the English scientist Francis Galton (1822–1911) investigated the

KEY POINTS

- Maps, books, and pictures are external representations. They give us useful information about the world and deliberately leave out unimportant information.
- Internal representations are the way the brain stores potentially useful information.
- When we imagine a picture, we use some of the same parts of the brain as when we see the picture.
- Imagined pictures (or mental images) are similar in some ways to photographs.
- Our memory for pictures is affected by the way that we interpret them.
- Although we can remember thousands of pictures, our memory for detail fades fast.
- Mental maps can take months of experience to establish.
- Categories are groups of objects that may include nouns, verbs, or abstract concepts.
- The defining attribute view of concepts states that all concepts can be described by a list of attributes. Each attribute is necessary, and together they define the concept.
- Category membership is not all-or-none, and members differ in their typicality. Psychological research has revealed, for example, that people classify a robin as a typical bird, but not a penguin.
- When people think about a category, they tend to think of its typical members.
- The brain may store information about categories in a feature-associative network. An alternative theory suggests that information is stored in a network of specific examples.
- Human brains contain general information about the usual events that occur in particular situations. Roger Schank and Robert Abelson referred to this information as scripts.
- Stories are classed by people according to their broad themes, or schemata.
- Our expectations about what generally happens in a situation affect our memory for what actually happened.
- Our ability to remember stories is influenced by their meaningfulness to us.
- Connectionism is a way of thinking about the mind that takes into account biological knowledge of the brain.

imagery used by the brain by asking a number of eminent friends to imagine the way their breakfast table had looked that morning. Quite a few said they had no mental picture of their breakfast table. They could remember what they had eaten, but did not think they had a picture of the table in their heads.

MENTAL ROTATION

Imagine you are looking at two pictures of the same object, but from different angles. People are usually able to deduce that the object is the same in each picture, but how do they come to this conclusion? Many people feel as if they are turning one object in their mind's eye until it is the same way up as the other. They can then tell that the two objects are the same.

Do people really turn objects in their mind's eye to compare them? In 1971 psychologists Roger Shepard and Jacqueline Metzler conducted a series of experiments to find out. They produced a number of drawings of a pair of objects. In some drawings the objects were identical; some were drawn at the same angle, but others were drawn at angles varying between 20 and 180

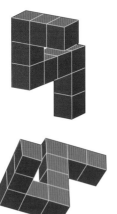

Shepard and Metzler showed images like these to subjects and asked whether or not they represented the same object at different angles. The researchers found a close link between the angle of rotation between the images and the time people took to decide whether or not the objects were identical.

degrees to each other. A second set of pictures also showed a pair of objects at various angles, but one was the mirror image of the other.

The researchers showed the drawings to a group of people and timed how long they took to decide whether the two objects were the same. When they looked at the resulting data, Shepard and Metzler noticed that for every extra degree the object had been rotated through, people took a little longer to decide whether they were the same. It seemed that people were able to turn the images in their minds at a rate of about 50 degrees a second.

In a later experiment the scientists added an arrow to the drawings that indicated which way to mentally turn the objects. Most of the time the arrow told the truth. If it pointed in a clockwise direction, then it was more efficient to go clockwise rather than counterclockwise. However, a small number of the arrows pointed in the wrong direction. This misled the subjects into mentally rotating the objects the wrong way. Again, the researchers found a close link between the angle the image was rotated (and therefore the effective distance) and the time taken to recognize the image.

Shepard and Metzler's work on mental rotation sparked many interesting research projects. In 1982 Juan Hollard and Valerie Delius performed a similar experiment with pigeons. In contrast to the human subjects of Shepard and Metzler, the pigeons did not seem to mentally rotate the images. The time the birds took to decide whether images showed the same objects was not affected by differences in the angles between them.

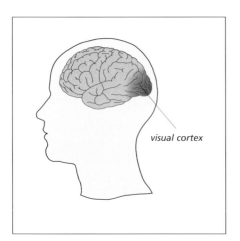

The visual cortex lies toward the rear of the brain. It is connected via the optic nerves to the retina, a structure at the back of the eyeball that translates light into electrical nerve impulses. The activity of the visual cortex is high both when looking at an image and when remembering it later on.

Psychologists now know that people can generate mental images. Techniques that map brain function, such as fMRI (*see* Vol. 2, pp. 20–39), show which parts of a person's brain are most active. When people look at pictures, a part of the brain called the primary visual cortex starts working hard. When you take the picture away, the primary visual cortex relaxes. When you ask people to imagine the picture they have just seen, the primary visual cortex starts working hard again. In fact, it works almost as hard as when the picture was present. This research shows that the same regions of the brain are highly active both when we see a picture and when we are are imagining it.

If imagining a picture we have just seen is just like seeing it, what about pictures we have never seen? People are good at forming mental images. Imagine a robin hopping across the ground. Now imagine that there is a cow standing behind it. The cow is bending its neck to look at the robin. Many people experience the same sequence of events as they imagine these pictures. First, they see a robin. The robin is large in their mental image, perhaps taking up half the picture. When they have to include the cow, they "zoom out" from the robin, or they make it smaller so there is enough space to fit the cow into the image.

> *"A word is like a key. When a word unlocks the correct stored memories, it is meaningful."*
> —*Stephen Kosslyn, 1999*

In 1975 the American psychologist Stephen Kosslyn asked people to imagine a particular animal with another one standing next to it. For example, he asked someone to imagine a rabbit sitting next to an elephant. He then asked a question about the rabbit, such as "Does the rabbit have a pointed nose?" Kosslyn then asked a different person to imagine a rabbit, but this time with a fly sitting next to it. He asked that person the same question. Kosslyn found that people took longer to answer questions about the rabbit if it was standing next to the elephant.

When the subjects in the experiment made mental images, they had to "zoom in" or "zoom out" to fit both the animals in. The mental image of the rabbit is larger when the animal is next to a fly than when it is next to an elephant. Kosslyn showed that the time taken to answer questions about mental images was closely related to the amount of "zoom" required to bring details into view.

If people are presented with large and small photographs of the same rabbit, they can spot whether the rabbit's nose is pointed more quickly when looking at the larger image. Kosslyn showed that the same was true for mental images. Just like photographs, the images we form in our minds have a limited size, and closer views are needed to determine small details.

It is tempting to describe mental images as photographs in the head. However, mental images do not represent what we have seen; rather, they represent our interpretation of what we have seen. In 1985 psychologists Deborah Chambers and Daniel Reisberg demonstrated this point in an elegant yet simple experiment. Show the image below to a friend very quickly before closing the book. Ask your friend what the picture showed, and whether there was anything else it could be. Next, ask your friend to draw the image as they remember it on a piece of paper, and then ask the questions again.

Most people think that the original picture shows either a duck or a rabbit. In fact, the picture is ambiguous. No one in the experiments could "see" both the duck and the rabbit in their mental image. However, almost all people could see the

Is this a duck, or is it a rabbit? The duck–rabbit experiment works best if the subject has never seen the object before, so why not try showing it to friends to see how they interpret it.

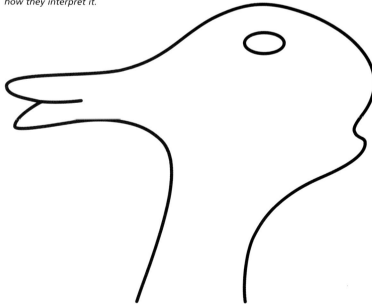

An experiment by Morton Gernsbacher provided an excellent demonstration of this. Gernsbacher showed one of a pair of similar pictures, such as the ones on the left, to a subject. Ten seconds later she showed both pictures and asked which of the two was seen previously.

Gernsbacher showed one of a pair of images like these to subjects. She later showed them both images together and asked them which they had already seen. This research helped illustrate the short-term nature of mental pictures.

other animal once they had translated their mental image onto paper.

Mental images tend to have a fixed interpretation, while pictures and photographs in the outside world do not. The images that appear in our minds cannot be described simply as internal photographs. These pictures are internal representations, and meaning is an important part of that representation. Mental pictures are also short-lived.

> *"Perception must, it seems, be a matter of seeing the present with stored objects from the past."*
> —Richard Gregory, 1970

After a gap of 10 seconds most got the question correct, but after 10 minutes the number of people getting the right answer did not differ statistically from guesswork alone (that is, 50 percent). The experiment worked best when the subjects did not know in advance what questions they were

---

DROODLES

Look at the pictures on the right. If you closed the book, do you think you could draw them accurately from memory? What if there were 28 pictures? Researcher Gordon Bower and his colleagues conducted an experiment using images like these in 1975. They showed people 28 different pictures and asked them to redraw as many as they could from memory.

People found this task tough. On average, they managed to reproduce about half of these nonsensical pictures. A second group of subjects, however, was shown the pictures with the addition of a series of short captions. For example, the caption for the picture on the left was *a midget playing a trombone in a telephone booth*. The caption for the picture on the right was *an early bird who*

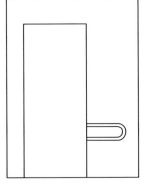
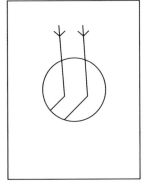

Two of the 28 droodles used by Bower and his team. People find these nonsensical images easier to remember and redraw when associated with contextual captions.

caught *a very strong worm*. When the pictures had captions that made them meaningful, the subjects found it significantly easier to remember and draw them.

Bower and his team showed that memories can be triggered by contextual cues. Bower described his pictures as droodles because without captions they were just doodles, but with captions they became drawings.

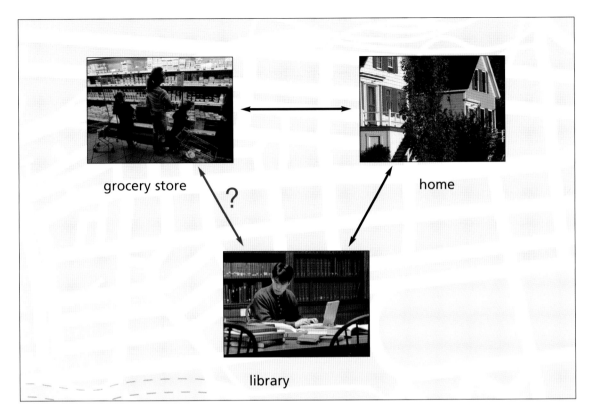

grocery store

home

?

library

to be asked. It demonstrated that in the longer term people do not store photographlike images in their heads. They may do so initially but detail is soon lost. Some experiments suggest that mental images lose some of the information presented by a photograph within around two seconds.

> *"People remember nonsensical pictures much better if they can comprehend what they are about."*
> —*Gordon Bower, 1975*

People are good at saying whether they have seen a picture before, as long as the options they get to choose between represent different scenes or events. Later research showed that people who were shown 10,000 images could later correctly identify about 8,300 of them as pictures they had seen before.

Mental maps

Maps differ from photographs in many ways. The main difference is that they are less naturalistic. Maps tend to represent the minimum amount of information required by the user. As we have seen, mental images tend to lack fine detail in a similar way. Also, maps use false colors to aid interpretation. For example, wide and narrow roads are generally both gray in photographs, but they might be blue and green on a road map.

As we have seen, mental images are also as much about interpretation as photographic accuracy. So, if our brains represent photographs like maps, do they represent the information provided by external maps in a similar way? People are normally pretty good at remembering how to get from A to B. For example, you may know that to get from home to the subway station, you need to go down the hill, turn left at the corner, and the station is on the right. You may also know that

With instructions you know how to get from home to the grocery store and from the library back home, but could you point in the direction of the library from the grocery store? Without the help of a map the answer is "probably not."

LUDWIG WITTGENSTEIN

BIOGRAPHY

Ludwig Wittgenstein (1889–1951) was one of the most influential philosophers of the 20th century. He was born in Vienna, Austria, and originally trained as an engineer. In 1908 he moved to Manchester, England, where he was paid to experiment with kites. Later, he met the philosopher Gottlob Frege (1848–1925), who suggested he should study with the famous British philosopher Bertrand Russell (1872–1970). In 1922 Wittgenstein published *Tractatus Logico-Philosophicus*, a work that was to have a profound influence on many philosophers and psychologists. Feeling that his book had answered all the important philosophical questions, Wittgenstein gave up philosophy to become an elementary school teacher in Austria. In 1929 he returned to Cambridge University, England, to teach, and in 1939 he was

awarded a chair in philosophy. As well as teaching, Wittgenstein wrote extensively. The summit of his achievements was *Philosophical Investigations*, which according to his wishes was published after his death.

Philosophical Investigations made a major contribution to our understanding of mental representation. Before its publication psychologists thought that all concepts could be represented by a set of defining attributes. A bachelor was "adult," "single," and "male." In the same way there were defining attributes for birds, chairs, and democracy. In *Philosophical Investigations* Wittgenstein challenged this idea. He wrote: "Consider for example the proceedings we call 'games.' I mean board games, card games, Olympic games, and so on. What is common to them all? Don't say: 'There must be something in common, or they would not be called games' but look and see whether there is anything common to all. For if you look at them you will not see something that is common to all, but similarities, relationships, and a whole series of them at that . . . I can think of no better expression to characterize these similarities than 'family resemblances.'"

Wittgenstein was saying that many concepts do not have defining attributes. Even if you can think of a defining attribute, then there is often the problem of "overinclusion." Games tend to involve an element of competition (even if it is with yourself), but there are all manner of things in life that involve a degree of competition that people would not normally refer to as a game.

Wittgenstein's way of thinking about concepts opened up a whole new area of psychological research. The work of a number of later researchers, such as Eleanor Rosch, can be seen as developments of the ideas of Ludwig Wittgenstein.

Although trained in engineering, Ludwig Wittgenstein's fascination with the philosophy of mathematics led him to study with Bertrand Russell in Cambridge. He served as an officer in the Austrian army during World War I (1914–1918) and wrote the bulk of his doctoral dissertation in an Italian prisoner-of-war camp. This work was later published as Tractatus Logico-Philosophicus.

to get from the swimming pool to your house, you go over a bridge, up the hill, follow the street around, and turn right at the corner. People remember and use this sort of information every day.

It is tempting to think that the brain holds these sets of memories as a series of mental maps. Maps, however, contain a lot more information than a set of

directions and landmarks. If you were at a friend's house, you would be able to follow their directions and make your way to the grocery store. If you were at the library, you would be able to get to your friend's house. However, if you were at the library, would you be able to point in the direction of the grocery store? The answer is "probably not" unless you had a map. In most cases only people with considerable experience of a town or those who have studied a map beforehand have a good memory for such information.

In 1982 Perry Thorndyke and Barbara Hayes-Roth demonstrated the inaccuracy of most people's mental maps. They interviewed secretaries working in a particularly large and complex office building. They found that secretaries who had recently arrived could accurately describe how to get from A to B. For example, they had no difficulty giving directions from the coffee room to the computer center.

However, the new secretaries were often unable to indicate the straight-line direction of the coffee room from the computer center. Generally speaking, only secretaries who had worked in the building for several years could do this.

> *"Concept is a vague concept."*
> *—Ludwig Wittgenstein, 1958*

Even people who have had years of experience with an external map often make errors unless they have the map in front of them. If you live in the United States or Canada, ask yourself whether Montreal is farther north than Seattle. If you live in Europe, ask yourself whether London is farther north than Berlin. The answer to both questions is no, but most people would answer yes. Canada is north of the United States, but the Canadian border reaches farther south in the east of the United States than in the west of the country. Most of the United Kingdom lies north of Germany, but southern England is on the same latitude as the north of Germany.

People often make these sorts of mistakes, suggesting that the brain does not represent locations in a truly maplike way. People seem to reason about where cities are, for example, from the location of the broader regions that contain them. This often leads to mistakes.

DICTIONARIES IN THE BRAIN

Dictionaries store information about the properties of objects. They also store information about actions (verbs) and abstract concepts like democracy. People also store much of this information in the brain. Does the brain represent this information in the same way that dictionaries do? Psychologists usually focus on objects such as cats, shoes, or hammers. They may also look at ill-defined categories—"patients suffering from a mental disorder," for example.

Writers of dictionary entries aim to present a list of defining attributes or features. For example, the *Cambridge*

A dictionary definition of an elephant would probably include the terms "large," "gray," "mammal," and "tusks." They are all necessary defining attributes. Put them together, and they become sufficient to define the animal.

English Dictionary defines an elephant as "a very large gray mammal which has a long nose (trunk) with which it can pick things up." Gottlob Frege (1848–1925) was the first to suggest that all concepts could be described with a set of defining attributes. The "defining attributes" theory is best explained by example. Think of the word *bachelor*. The defining attributes of this concept are "male," "single," and "adult." Each attribute is "necessary." If any is missing, the person cannot be a bachelor. Together the three attributes are "sufficient." If you know someone is an adult single male, you can be sure that he is a bachelor—no further information is required. The idea that all visible objects and all concepts could be represented by defining attributes came to dominate philosophical and psychological thinking for a time but was strongly opposed by Ludwig Wittgenstein (*see* box p. 70).

Psychologists describe groups of objects that share certain defining characteristics as "categories." The objects that make up categories are called "members." The views of Frege led to the conclusion that all objects must either be classified as members or nonmembers of a category.

For example, all objects either are or are not members of the category "furniture." Membership in a category is all-or-nothing; there are no shades of gray. However, the decisions people make when allocating objects to categories do not seem to follow this rule. Psychologists

Michael McClosky and Sam Glucksberg asked people whether certain objects belonged to the category "furniture." Everyone agreed that chairs were furniture and that cucumbers were not. When they came to bookends, however, some people thought that they were classed as furniture, while others did not. In addition, people were inconsistent about their definitions. The researchers asked people about objects like bookends on a number of occasions. Some people said that bookends were furniture the first time they were asked but not the second, or on the second time but not the first.

If peoples' mental dictionaries contained lists of defining attributes, the results of the experiment should have provided complete agreement about whether bookends were furniture or not. We would expect decisions about common categories to remain constant from one day to the next.

The research of Eleanor Rosch revealed further problems with the defining attribute view. If the mental dictionary is simply a list of defining attributes, there should be no such thing as a good or a bad example of something, such as a bird. All objects should either be birds or not birds. Rosch asked people to rate how typical they thought various members of categories were. People generally agreed on typical

A robin and a penguin—which is the more "typical" bird? The work of Eleanor Rosch suggests that most people think of a robin as an example of a typical bird, but do not think the same of a penguin. This is despite the fact that penguins have feathers, and their females lay eggs—zoologically, they are as much birds as robins are.

ARE SOME NUMBERS ODDER THAN OTHERS?

EXPERIMENT

When people are asked to think about categories, they tend to think about typical members. If you are asked to think of a sport, you are more likely to think of football than of weight lifting. This depends on how quickly we categorize things—typical category members are categorized more quickly and therefore more easily.

Are all categories like this? What about odd numbers? Odd numbers are those that leave a remainder when divided by two. The number 106 is even because when it is divided by two, the answer is a whole number, 53. The number 23 is odd because when it is divided by two, the answer, 11.5, is not a whole number. All numbers are either odd or even. There is no doubt and no debate.

Anyone who can divide by two can tell whether a number is odd or even. Odd numbers seem to be a perfect example of a category that is defined by a clear rule. Does this mean there is no such thing as a typical odd number? Psychologist Sharon Armstrong and colleagues decided to investigate. They gave some people a list of odd numbers such as 501, 3, and 57. They then asked them to rate each number on the list for how "good" an odd number it was. People tended to agree that 3 and 7 were good examples of odd numbers. They also agreed that 501 and 447 were bad examples of odd numbers. The same sort of result was found for even numbers. The numbers 4, 8, and 10 were "good" even numbers, while the numbers 34 and 106 were "bad" even numbers. Psychologists disagree on why this should happen. One theory is that people do not really use the "any number that does not leave a whole number when divided by two" rule to decide whether a number is odd. For a start, most people know that 1, 3, 5, 7, and 9 are odd numbers without having to figure it out. They have learned this information by rote in math lessons. As a result, 1, 3, 5, 7, and 9 come to mind when we think about odd numbers. This leads us to rate them as "good" or typical odd numbers.

When we see a number like 501, we do not know immediately whether it is odd, but we can figure it out swiftly. If the final digit is odd, then the number is odd. Although we can see that 501 is odd, it is not typical because it is encountered relatively infrequently.

and atypical members. For example, people agreed that robins were typical birds but that penguins were not. If people's mental dictionaries were as Frege had suggested, there should be no such thing as a typical bird. The question should be meaningless, forcing people to guess. When people guess, they tend not to agree. The fact that people did agree suggested there was something more to their concepts than a series of defining attributes.

Rosch wanted to show that typicality was central to the way people thought about categories. She did so by showing sentences like this to college students:

- A robin is a bird.
- A chicken is a bird.

The students had to decide as quickly as possible whether each sentence was true or false. They made their decisions more quickly when the object was a typical example of its category. For example, they took less time to agree that "a robin is a bird" than to agree that "a chicken is a bird." Obviously, both of these questions are easy to answer, but people do take measurably longer to answer the second question, although the time difference is measured in fractions of a second.

> *"Most, if not all, categories do not have clear-cut boundaries."*
> *—Eleanor Rosch, 1978*

Rosch suggested that when people are asked to think about a category, they do not think of a list of defining attributes. Instead, they think of typical members of that category. If you are asked to think about "birds," you tend to think of some typical birds. Perhaps a robin comes to mind. If you are asked whether a robin

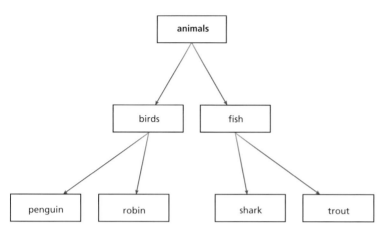

An example of a hierarchy. "Animals" sits at the top of the tree. "Birds" and "fish" are categories of animals, and they can be subdivided further into more specific examples, such as "trout" or "robin."

is a bird, the answer is easy because the term "bird" brings robins to mind. If you are asked whether a dolphin is a mammal, this takes longer because the word *mammal* is more likely to make you think of other more typical mammals.

Even when categories are easily defined by attributes, people still seem to be influenced by typicality. We have seen that "bachelor" can be defined by the attributes "single," "adult," and "male." Yet people tend to agree that some bachelors are more typical than others. For example, Tarzan is not a typical bachelor because he had no chance to marry when he lived in the jungle. Even concepts like numbers differ in typicality (*see* box p. 73).

Hierarchies

We have seen that a dictionary defines an elephant as "a very large gray mammal." In dictionary definitions words like *mammal* are quite common. Dictionary writers try to define objects as part of a "hierarchy." If you look at the diagram above, you will see that at the top of the hierarchy is the term "animals." Both birds and fish are types of animals, so they sit below "animals" on the hierarchy and are connected to it by downward arrows. Robins and penguins are both types of birds, so they are connected to "bird." In the same way "trout" and "shark"

Not all species of birds are able to sing melodious tunes, but among those that can are canaries. A dictionary definition will need to include the phrase "canaries can sing." However, the phrases "canaries have feathers" and "female canaries lay eggs" are redundant as long as the dictionary definition mentions that "canaries are birds."

are both "fish" and are connected to "fish." Dictionary writers use hierarchies because they help shorten definitions.

If the dictionary states that "a robin is a bird," the reader knows that a robin has feathers and wings, and that the female lays eggs. The dictionary does not need to include "a female robin lays eggs" in the definition because the phrase "a robin is a bird" already tells the reader that. Might the brain use the same trick to reduce the amount of information it has to store?

Allan Collins and Ross Quillian argued that the answer was "yes." They presented a series of sentences like this to students:

- Canaries can sing.
- Canaries have feathers.

The students were quick to agree that canaries could sing. They took longer to agree that canaries had feathers. If the brain were organized like a dictionary, that is exactly what you would expect to find. If you imagine you know nothing about birds, you will need a dictionary to check whether "canaries can sing." If you look up "canary," the dictionary will tell you that "canaries can sing." That is because not all birds can sing, so singing has to be part of the definition. However, the dictionary does not mention feathers.

Color in Different Cultures

How many different colors are there? One answer is "about seven million." That is the number of different colors that our eyes can detect. Modern computer screens can display at least 16 million different colors. Compare these huge numbers to the number of different words you know. Very few people know more than about 80,000 words in their native tongue. Most of us can see about 100 times more colors than we have words in our language. Even if every word in your language described a color, each word would have to represent about 100 different colors.

How many different color words are there? In some languages, like English, there are quite a lot. However, there are many we do not use very often. Magenta (a dark purple-red) is one example. There are also some that only apply to certain types of object. For example, "blond" is really only used to describe hair (and some types of beers). In a 1969 paper psychologists Brent Berlin and Paul Kay suggested that there were just 11 basic color terms. They are: black, white, red, green, yellow, blue, brown, purple, pink, orange, and gray.

These 11 basic color terms occur in most languages and mean basically the same thing in all of them. Berlin and Kay visited many different countries with many different languages. They showed people in these countries more than 300 little colored squares. They then asked them to pick out the best red, the best green, and so on. They asked this for all 11 basic color terms in 20 different languages. People from all over the world agreed on the best representatives of the basic colors.

The Dani people live in the highlands of Irian Jaya, New Guinea, where they grow sweet potatoes and raise pigs. The Dani language is unusual because it does not contain any color terms— there are words only for "light" and "dark."

But not all languages have color terms. The Dani people of Irian Jaya, New Guinea, have only two color-related words in their language. They have one word for dark things and another for light things. Eleanor Rosch used Berlin and Kay's colored squares technique to teach some of the Dani the names for some basic colors. The colors that people around the world had agreed were the best examples of basic colors were the ones that the Dani found easiest to learn.

Berlin and Kay argued that basic color terms seem to represent something common to all people. The brain is geared to select certain frequencies of light as typical examples of colors. This is mirrored in people around the world regardless of ethnic group or culture.

It tells you that a canary is a bird. If you look up "bird," the dictionary tells you that it has feathers. You have your answer, but only after looking in two different places, which has taken a measurably longer period of time.

Collins and Quillian believed that the human brain organizes information into dictionarylike hierarchies. Many psychologists liked this idea, and for a time it was popular. However, it soon became apparent that Collins and Quillian were wrong. Another group of psychologists—Edward Smith, Edward Shoben, and Lance Rips—gave students a slightly different series of sentences. Two of the sentences that the researchers used were:

- A chicken is a bird.
- A chicken is an animal.

If the brain was like a dictionary, it should take longer to check the second sentence than the first. To check that a chicken is a bird, you just need to look up the definition of "chicken." To check that a chicken is an animal, you also need to look up the definition of "bird." The researchers showed that the opposite

David E. Rumelhart

BIOGRAPHY

David Rumelhart remains an influential figure in many fields of psychological research. In the 1970s he worked on the interpretation of stories, publishing a major work in 1975 on the "grammar" of storytelling. He also wrote *Explorations in Cognition* in collaboration with Don Norman in 1975. This work had a great influence on many future developments in cognitive psychology.

In 1981 Rumelhart worked with James McClelland on a theory about how we read words. In 1985 they wrote about how the brain might learn and store information about categories. Both works are modern classics of cognitive psychology, and their influence is still felt today.

In 1986 Rumelhart and McClelland joined about a dozen other scientists to write a massive, two-volume book called *Parallel Distributed Processing: Explorations in the Microstructure of Cognition*. This book is often credited with taking mainstream psychology in a completely new direction. This new field became known as connectionism (*see* box p. 81). In the 1980s

and 1990s connectionism took cognitive psychology by storm. Many commentators consider it to be one of the most important developments in the history of psychology.

As well as being part of a team responsible for bringing connectionism into mainstream psychology, Rumelhart was an author of one of its best-known articles, "Learning Internal Representations by Error Propagation." This paper contained a mathematical equation called the back-prop algorithm without which many of today's connectionist theories would not exist.

In 1998 David Rumelhart developed a progressive neurodegenerative illness called Pick's disease. In 2000 an Internet multimillionaire called Robert Glushko set up a prize in his honor. Glushko had been one of Rumelhart's graduate students. Although he did not stay in research, he never forgot David Rumelhart. The David E. Rumelhart prize is a cash prize of $100,000 that is awarded annually to the team or person making the most important contribution to the study of cognition.

---

was true. People took longer to agree that a chicken was a bird than they took to agree that a chicken was an animal. Why should this happen?

> "The essence of memory organization is classification."
> —Bill Estes, 1994

Remember how Eleanor Rosch showed that some category members were more typical than others? According to her research, a robin is a typical bird, but a chicken is not. When asked to think about birds, people do not often think of chickens. As a result, checking the sentence "a chicken is a bird" takes longer.

Now look again at the second sentence, "A chicken is an animal." When asked to think about animals, chickens sometimes spring to mind. It therefore takes less time to check and agree with the sentence "A chicken is an animal." The same sort

of argument can be applied to the original results of Collins and Quillian. When you think about canaries, singing is probably one of the first things to come to mind. Having feathers is also part of being a canary, but that is probably not the first thing you think of. People are quicker to confirm that a canary sings than to confirm that it has feathers because singing is a more "typical" characteristic of canaries than are feathers.

Mental dictionaries

We are not sure how the brain stores information. One popular idea is that the brain's dictionary is pretty disorganized. Our mental dictionaries do not contain a long, neat list of definitions. Instead, our knowledge is held within a mass of connections between small chunks of information. Psychologists call these chunks features. Some of the features of being a dog might be "furry," "four-legged," and "having a wagging tail." We learn things like this about dogs when we are young. Our brains store this

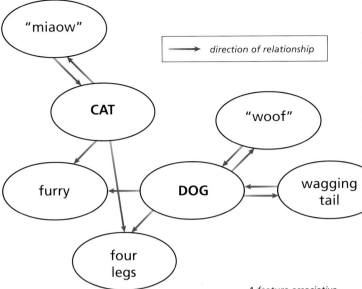

direction of relationship

is more like the cats than the dogs. You decide that it is a cat. The problem with this idea is that each time you see something, you have to cross-refer with a lot of examples. You cannot just look at cat examples because you do not yet know it is a cat. You need to look at all categories, comparing the object to dogs, cars, cucumbers, refrigerators, and so on. And yet we can decide whether an object is a cat in a fraction of a second. If the brain had to make all these comparisons one at a time, this decision would take

information by forming links between features like "wagging tail" and labels like "dog." The diagram above shows part of our mental dictionary. This sort of association is described by psychologists as a feature-associative network.

How do you "read" this sort of mental dictionary? The easiest explanation is to think of the circles in the diagram as lights. If you want to know whether a dog is furry, you light up "dog." There is a link from dog to furry, so "furry" also lights up. You have your answer—dogs are furry.

Another popular idea about our mental dictionary is that it is filled with examples. According to this theory, your dictionary entry for "dog" is just a collection of particular dogs you have met. It might include a description of your pet dog, Lassie, your neighbor's dog, and the guard dog you once saw at a factory. Your dictionary entry for "cat" is similar. It might contain a description of your grandmother's cat, a friend's cat, and a cat you have seen on a TV commercial.

Imagine you are walking down the street and see a four-legged animal coming toward you. Is it a cat or a dog? Quickly you compare the animal in front of you to the cats in your dictionary and the dogs in your dictionary. Overall it

A feature-associative network (above). "Dog" and "cat" are both linked to features common to each, such as "four legs," and to unique characteristics, such as "miaow."

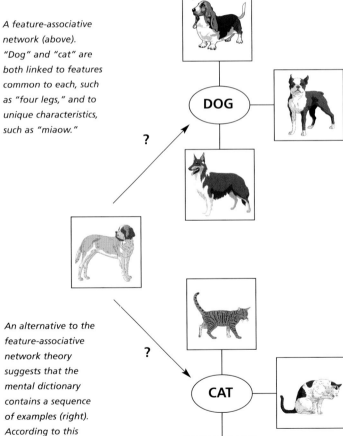

An alternative to the feature-associative network theory suggests that the mental dictionary contains a sequence of examples (right). According to this idea, the human brain must cross-refer with all the stored examples in order to identify an object.

77

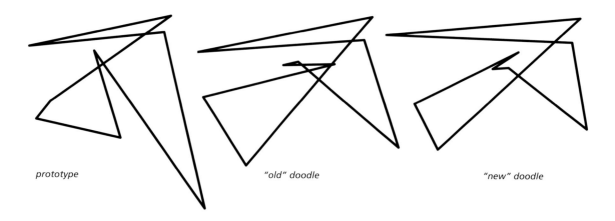

prototype   "old" doodle   "new" doodle

much longer. We know that the brain is very good at doing a lot of things at the same time. If the comparisons can be made contiguously, it is possible that our mental dictionaries are indeed simply a collection of examples. Research in this field is currently focused on deciding which of these ideas is correct.

Writing a mental dictionary

Dictionaries do not just come into existence; they have to be written. The same is true for our mental dictionaries. People are not born with a complete set of information about the objects around them, so they have to learn as they go along. We have already looked at how the information that is present in the mental dictionary is organized, but how does this information get there in the first place?

One way to study this is to teach adults new categories. To make sure the categories are new for everyone, psychologists often use made-up ones. Made-up categories allow us to answer questions that are difficult to answer with real categories. A 1981 experiment by Donald Homa, Sharon Sterling, and Lawrence Trepel provides a good example of this. The researchers invented some categories of doodles. Making each doodle category involved two steps.

First, they created a prototype doodle. The prototype was the most typical member of a category.

Second, they created other members of the category by moving the points of the doodle around a little. They were also part of the prototype doodle's category, but they were less typical than the prototype. The psychologists created three different doodle categories in this way. Homa and his colleagues took some of the doodles they had made and put them to one side. They showed the rest of the doodles to college students and taught them which category each came from. These doodles were termed "old" doodles.

> "To categorize is to . . . group the objects and events and people around us into classes."
> —Jerome S. Bruner, 1956

When the students had mastered this, the psychologists took the doodles they had put to one side and asked the students to decide which category each of these "new" doodles had come from. The college students were fairly good at doing this, but not as good as they were with the old doodles.

Homa and his colleagues designed different categories of doodles, each based on a different prototype. Subjects learned to associate "old" doodles with the correct prototype categories. Later, the subjects were presented with previously unseen "new" doodles. The subjects were good at categorizing the new doodles, but not as good as they were at categorizing the old ones. That is because the old doodles had been incorporated into the mental dictionaries of the subjects, while the new ones had not.

The students found the old doodles easier to deal with because they had information about them in their mental dictionaries. They had not seen the new doodles before, and so they had not been entered into their dictionaries. Many psychologists consider results like these to be good evidence that mental dictionaries are collections of specific examples. On the other hand, some psychologists argue that these results can be explained by feature-associative networks. The true answer remains unknown, but research in this area continues to progress rapidly.

SCRIPTS AND THEMES

A dictionary will tell you what eggs and flour are, but it will not tell you how to bake a cake. To find that out, you need to look in a cookbook. Cookbooks are just one example of the wide range of instruction manuals that people rely on. Home maintenance books and car repair manuals are two other common examples. Instruction manuals tell us, step by step, what we have to do to complete a task. When we are familiar with a task, we do not need to use an instruction manual—we can rely on our memory to tell us what to do. Few people, for example, need an instruction manual to tell them how to get dressed each morning.

Does the brain store information about everyday events in the same way that an instruction manual would? Roger Schank and Robert Abelson suggested that people use mental scripts for occasions such as going to a restaurant. Scripts are a list of the typical events that occur in a specific situation. For example, the script for a trip to a restaurant might be:

Enter restaurant. Go to table. Sit down. Get menu. Look at menu. Choose food. Give order. Wait and talk. Waiter delivers food. Eat and talk. Receive check. Pay check. Leave.

Obviously, not all restaurants are like this. In some restaurants, for example, you are asked to pay before you eat. A script does

Schank and Abelson suggested that people use mental scripts when dealing with everyday situations, such as going to a restaurant. Scripts allow people to have a good idea of what to expect from the experience.

not tell you for sure what will happen, but it does tell you what is likely to happen most of the time.

Scripts also help us communicate with other people more efficiently. If you ask someone what they did last night, and they reply, "I went to a restaurant," your restaurant script will provide you with an idea of the series of events the person experienced. Schank and Abelson thought that scripts were for specific events. For example, if you have visited a doctor, then you might have a "visit doctor" script and through that know roughly what to expect. If you have never visited a dentist, then you will not have a "visit dentist" script and will not know what to expect. The "visit doctor" script cannot help because you are not visiting a doctor.

However, it seems likely that our expectations about events are a little broader than this. When we visit any healthcare professional, there are a number of steps that we can expect. They include making an appointment, describing the problem, and receiving treatment. In some situations these steps also include writing a check. If we have visited a doctor, we can predict some of the things that will happen on a trip to a dentist's office, even if we have never

visited one ourselves. People certainly seem to have a great deal of shared knowledge about some events, such as going to a restaurant.

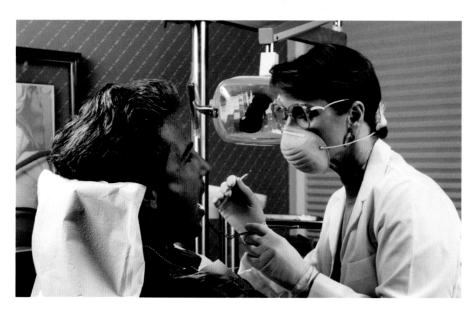

Someone visiting a dentist's office for the first time (below left) cannot rely on a script relating to a trip to the doctor (above). The specific details of a visit vary from one profession to the next. However, visits to healthcare professionals involve a number of steps that are usually common to all, such as making an appointment and describing symptoms. These steps can be incorporated into a general "healthcare" script that helps the patient anticipate the general sequence of events at such visits.

REMEMBERING STORIES

People have the ability to listen to stories, remember them, and then tell them to others. Long ago this was the only way we ever experienced stories. They would be told by one generation and learned by the next. These days we rely much more on books than on our memories. Most of us, though, know some stories. They may be tales we were read as a child or the plots of Hollywood blockbusters. Although it is not necessarily true that everyone has a novel within them, most of us have at least one story to tell.

Is remembering a story like writing a book in our heads? If it were, it would not matter whether the story made sense or not; we could still write it in our mental story book and read it back later. Read the story below to a friend, then ask your friend to recall the story without referring back to the text.

"If the balloons popped, the sound wouldn't be able to carry far, since everything would be too far away from the correct floor. A closed window would also prevent the sound from carrying, since most buildings tend to be well insulated. Since the whole operation depends on a steady flow of electricity, a break in the middle of the wire would also cause problems. Of course, the fellow could shout, but the human voice is not loud enough to carry that far. An additional problem is that a string could break on the instrument. There would be no accompaniment to the message. It is clear that the best solution would involve less distance. Then there would be fewer potential problems. With face-to-face contact the least number of things could go wrong."

Trying to remember this story without looking back is pretty difficult. Researchers John Bransford and Marcia Johnson found that people generally only remembered about three or four things from this story. The story does not make much sense, and so it is hard to remember. Now show your friend the illustration on the left, and try reading the story again. That time it should make a lot more sense. Bransford and Johnson found that people who saw the illustration first remembered about eight different things about the story. This is about twice as many as people who had not seen the picture. This shows that our memory for stories depends heavily on our ability to understand them.

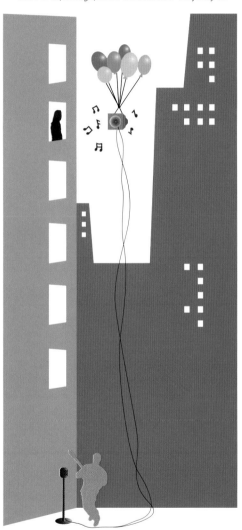

This diagram adds context to the odd little story above. When read in conjunction with the picture, more details of the tale can be remembered.

Psychologists Gordon Bower, John Black, and Terrance Turner asked people to list about 20 things that usually happened when they went to a restaurant. Almost three-quarters of the people included five key events. They were: looking at the menu, ordering, eating, paying the check, and leaving. Almost

half of the people asked included seven further events. They were: ordering drinks, discussing the menu, talking, eating a salad or soup, ordering dessert, eating dessert, and leaving a tip.

Peoples' memories of specific events are affected by their mental scripts. Bower's team gave people some stories to read. They were based on scripts like "going to a restaurant," but the psychologists had jumbled the order of some of the events. So, for example, one story might involve someone going to a restaurant, paying the bill, and then sitting down and ordering some food. Next, they eat their food and then look at the menu. Finally, they leave.

When people were asked to remember the stories, they often described what normally happens in a restaurant rather than what actually happened in the story. So the story would typically be remembered as someone going to a restaurant, sitting down, looking at the menu, ordering their food, paying the

Can testimony be fully trusted? Holst and Pezdek showed that scripts can affect memories of certain events. They gave subjects facts about a hypothetical robbery. A week later they asked the subjects for their version of events. Rather than detailing the facts as presented, the subjects' stories often fitted around a generic "robbery" script. This finding has wide-ranging legal implications, providing a psychological framework for false identification and recall on the witness stand.

check, and then leaving. Mental scripts help us anticipate what happens in certain situations; they may also color our recall of what happens in reality.

> **"We read for the gist, and very quickly forget the details"**
> **—Trevor Harley, 1995**

Valerie Holst and Kathy Pezdek showed that people who witness crimes can experience the same problem. They showed that when people try to remember what really happened in a crime they witnessed, they sometimes refer to a mental script and recall what typically happens instead. In another experiment Gordon Bower and colleagues gave people several different stories to read. Later, they gave the same people a different set of stories. Some stories were exactly the same as before; others were new. The researchers asked the volunteer readers to decide which stories were new. The volunteers were generally good at this, but a certain type of new story caused problems.

If a story was new but described an event similar to an old story, the subjects sometimes thought they had read it before. They became confused by stories that had the same script and were also nonplussed by stories that had different but related scripts. For example, one of the original stories involved a trip to the dentist. Later, the subjects read a new story about a visit to a doctor. The volunteers would often believe that they had read the story before. They had not,

Stills from the movies Romeo and Juliet *(1936), with Leslie Howard and Moira Shearer (below), and* West Side Story *(1961), starring Natalie Wood and Richard Beymer (right). Although set in different eras and places, they share many themes.*

but they had read a story with a similar theme. This suggests people remember stories in terms of general themes. These organizing themes are less tied to a specific situation than a script and can be very generalized. For example, most people would say that the 20th-century *West Side Story* is similar to William Shakespeare's *Romeo and Juliet*, despite the fact that they are set in different countries and in different

FREDERICK BARTLETT

Sir Frederick Bartlett (1886–1969) was one of the founding fathers of modern psychology. The Laboratory of Experimental Psychology at Cambridge University, England, had been open for about a year when Bartlett joined as an assistant in 1914. By 1931 Bartlett was a professor and head of the laboratory.

By the close of World War II (1939–1945) Bartlett's former students were running the majority of university psychology departments across the United Kingdom. Bartlett fought hard to get psychology recognized as a scientific subject. His success had a profound influence on 20th-century psychology.

Historians of science believe that no living psychologist will be able to have so great an influence on psychology as Bartlett. In the early 20th century psychology was still a new subject. Bartlett was at his most productive during a time of transition; psychology moved from being a relatively obscure discipline to a major scientific field.

Frederick Bartlett is probably best remembered for his ideas about schemata. A schema is a piece of general information stored in the brain that helps us understand the world around us. For example, the restaurant script (*see* p. 79) is a schema. Bartlett argued that people from different cultures can have different story schemata. A story schema provides information about the sort of general events that we expect to find in stories and the order in which we expect them to happen.

In perhaps his most famous experiment Bartlett translated a Native American folktale called "War of the Ghosts" into English. He then asked some of his students to memorize it. As shown by this excerpt, Native American folktales are very different from the stories that were familiar to 1930s Cambridge students:

> *"He told it all and then became quiet. When the sun rose, he fell down. Something black came out of his mouth. His face became contorted . . . . He was dead."*

When the students later had to retell the stories, they altered them to sound much more like English tales. Bartlett believed that remembering was not like writing things in a book and reading them out again. He saw memory as a process of reconstruction, and our expectations about how things normally are affect our memories of what happened. In 1932 he published his theories on memory in a book called *Remembering: A Study of Experimental and Social Psychology*.

Bartlett's ideas about schemata were largely ignored in the United States at the time but have subsequently been included in many textbooks. In 1952 he retired from university research, but he continued to theorize and write, and in 1958 Bartlett published another important book, *Thinking*.

Bartlett translated a Native American folktale and asked students to learn and recite it. The students altered details of the story to resemble their own cultural context more closely than the original version.

Action and
adventure

Social
dilemmas

Journeys
and voyages

Science
fiction

Murder
mystery

Triumph over
adversity

Wild
West

Love and
romance

Magic and
mystery

Gothic
horror

centuries. *West Side Story* is a musical, while *Romeo and Juliet*, which was written around 1595, is a play. (In fact, *West Side Story* was based on *Romeo and Juliet*.)

Roger Schank has argued that the stories share the common theme of "mutual goal pursuit against outside opposition." Romeo and Juliet love each other and so want to be together. Their togetherness is the mutual goal that they pursue. Their parents oppose the relationship, and so Romeo and Juliet pursue this goal against outside opposition. The theme of *West Side Story* is exactly the same.

Psychologist Colleen Seifert and colleagues showed people a series of stories that differed in many details, but all had the same general theme. Once the subjects had read the stories, the researchers asked them to write out similar stories. Most of the subjects wrote stories that contained different details but had the same general theme. Seifert's team also gave people a set of stories to sort into different piles. The

Seifert and her team conducted an experiment that showed that people categorize what they read into themes. People use such organizing themes to categorize much of the information that enters the mind.

subjects were allowed to do this in any way they wanted, but most sorted them into common themes.

"In order to observe one must learn how to compare."
—Bertolt Brecht, 1949

INFORMATION AND THE BRAIN
For most of the 20th century psychologists relied on metaphors to explain how the brain stores information. In literature metaphors are words that describe people and objects by likening them to things they are not. The phrase "the city is a jungle" is a metaphor. Cities are, of course, not jungles. A "born-again" Christian has not literally been born for a second time, and so on.

Psychologists have used objects constructed by people as metaphors for the minds that made them—the mind has been equated with a photograph album, a dictionary, and the script of a play. In the end, though, the mind is none of these things. It is simply the mind.

Many psychologists are now coming to the conclusion that the mind should be examined for what it is. One step in this direction is what some people have described as the "connectionist revolution." Connectionism is not so much a specific theory as a way of thinking about psychology (*see* box p. 76). Connectionists believe that theories about the mind should take into account how the brain really works. The brain does not contain dictionaries, maps, pictures, or instruction manuals.

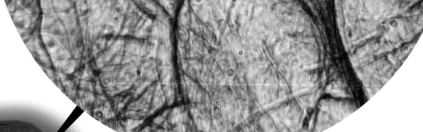

It contains nerve cells, called neurons, that communicate through electrical signals—the nerve impulse. We know quite a lot about how neurons interact and a little about how they store information. For example, we know that compared to modern computers, neurons work very, very slowly.

We also know that neurons work in a "massively parallel" way. When you look at a picture, some neurons detect horizontal lines, some detect vertical lines, and others look for diagonal lines. They all do this at the same time, as well as carrying out a multitude of other functions. Connectionist theory

The brain (left) contains a network of nerve cells, or neurons (above), of staggering complexity. Scientists are gradually uncovering the electrical and chemical interactions that allow these cells to communicate, and psychologists are using the results to revise many theories of the mind.

COGNITIVE SCIENCE

FOCUS ON

Throughout the 20th century psychologists conducted experiments to find out how the mind represents information. Philosophers, neuroscientists, and computer programmers have also explored the same issues. Some psychologists attempted to distance themselves from philosophy, but philosophers like Ludwi Wittgenstein (*see* p. 70) showed that philosophers have an importantpart to play in the search for an understanding of the mind.

The 20th century saw great advances in our understanding of the brain. We know much more about its composition and its connections, and neuroscientists continue to make important discoveries every year. The more we know about the brain, the better we will understand the mind. In the second half of the 20th century digital computers developed from clumsy devices that filled several rooms to very powerful tools that fit on a desk, a lap, or in a pocket. As computers became more powerful, people thought of more and more things they could do with them. However, psychologists and programmers alike soon realized that a two-year-old or a rat could do things that were beyond the most powerful of computers. If we better understood how people and other animals did things, we could build truly remarkable computers that would make today's machines obsolete. With the arrival of connectionist ideas theories of the mind began to use more equations and fewer words, involving mathematicians and physicists as well as psychologists. Over the last 20 years it has become obvious that psychologists, philosophers, neuroscientists, computer scientists, and mathematicians were all working on the same sorts of questions; but because they were from different disciplines, they seldom communicated. To solve this problem, universities began to set up a new subject called cognitive science. Cognitive science departments include people with different backgrounds and skills who are united by their desire to answer the sort of questions raised by this chapter. Cognitive science is now a popular degree course at a number of universities around the world.

Despite recent technological advances, a small child can perform feats of mental agility that remain far beyond the capabilities of the most powerful computers.

incorporates biological features of the brain. The theories often include mathematical principles to describe how neurons communicate with and learn from each other. Some of them include the concept of drawing a relationship between the working of the brain and a computer.

There are connectionist theories associated with much of the research discussed in this chapter.

CONNECTIONS

Storing Information

To remember is to live.

Memory is a key psychological process. Without it we would not be able to learn, function effectively, or retain any knowledge of our life before the present moment. Over the centuries there have been many theories about how memory works. In recent times a great deal of research has been conducted on human memory. We now know that memory is not just a passive receiver of information but an active process that makes deductions about information and reconstructs events.

Memory allows us to recall birthdays, vacations, and other significant events that may have taken place hours, days, months, or even many years ago. As stated by the eminent cognitive neuroscientist Michael Gazzaniga of Dartmouth College: "Everything in life is memory, save for the thin edge of the present." Without memory we would not be able to hold a conversation, recognize our friends' faces, remember

KEY POINTS

- There are two main types of memory: short-term and long-term.
- The processes involved in memory are encoding, storage, and retrieval.
- There are three different aspects of short-term (working) memory, involving speech-based information, images, and attention, or strategy.
- According to the levels of processing theory, there are deep and superficial modes of processing information.
- Long-term memory is divided into explicit (consciously available) and implicit (for example, skills) memory.
- The hippocampus is the area of the brain responsible for sorting memories, and they are filed in the cerebral cortex.
- Long-term memory tends to deteriorate with age.

appointments, understand new ideas, succeed at studying and at work, or even learn to walk. The novelist Jane Austen (1775–1817) aptly summarized the mysterious qualities of memory: "There seems something more speakingly incomprehensible in the powers, the failures, the inequalities of memory, than in any other of our intelligences."

The ancient Greek philosopher Plato (about 428–348 B.C.) was one of the first thinkers to develop theories about memory. He thought that it was like a wax tablet on which impressions were made (encoded) and then stored so that we could return to, or retrieve, them at a later

Ancient philosophers drew comparisons between memories and birds in an aviary. The problem was to retrieve the right memory once it had been stored, just as it is difficult to catch a particular budgerigar from this aviary.

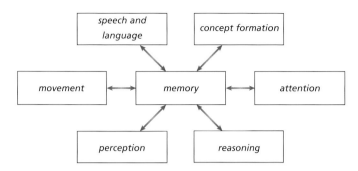

The different types of activity that memory is involved in.

time. Other ancient philosophers likened memories to birds in an aviary or to books in a library. They pointed out the difficulties of retrieving information after it had been stored—that is, catching the right bird or locating the right book. Contemporary theorists such as Ulric Neisser, Steve Ceci, Elizabeth Loftus, and

> *"Five senses; an incurably abstract intellect; a haphazardly selective memory; a set of preconceptions and assumptions so numerous that I can never examine more than a minority of them—never become conscious of them all. How much of total reality can such an apparatus let through?"*
>
> **C. S. Lewis, 1966**

Ira Hyman have come to appreciate that memory is a selective and interpretive process, rather than just the passive storage of information and is involved in numerous processes such as perception. These psychologists have all carried out experiments to show that memory reconstructs, integrating prior beliefs, expectations, or information (including misleading information) that was given at the time of encoding. Ceci, for example, repeatedly asked children who had never visited a hospital emergency room about events that had or had not occurred in their lives. At first they accurately reported

that they had never been to the emergency room, but after the third trial the children started to say that they had and to give detailed stories. This is known as the mousetrap experiment since one of the children described having his hand caught in a mousetrap and being rushed to hospital. The children were not given misinformation but were asked repeated questions, and this led to them using their imaginations to create memories.

The boxed quote from writer and philosopher C. S. Lewis indicates that our memory is far from perfect. That is because it is not possible to remember everything that we experience. We need to remember some things in order to function effectively in the world, but there are other things that we do not need to remember. Which bits we remember seems to depend on their functional significance. In our evolutionary past people may have survived by remembering information that signaled threat (such as the appearance of a potential predator) or reward (such as the discovery of a possible food source). Our memory works like a sieve or filtering mechanism ensuring that we do not remember absolutely everything (*see* box p. 90). We can also select, interpret, and integrate one thing with another to make use of what we learn and remember. These qualities have led many contemporary researchers to view memory as an active rather than a passive thing.

The logic of memory
Any effective memory system—whether it is a synthesizer, or sound mixer, a videocassette recorder, the hard disk of your computer, or even a simple filing cabinet—needs to do three things well. It has to be able to:
- encode (take in) information;
- store or retain that information faithfully and, in the case of long-term memory, over a significant period of time;
- retrieve (be able to access) stored information.

To continue with the example of a filing cabinet, you place a document in a certain file, where it should remain. When you need the document, you go back to the filing cabinet. But unless you have a good search system, you may not be able to find the file easily. Memory, therefore, involves the ability to retrieve information, as well as taking it in and storing it. All three components of encoding, storage, and retrieval have to work well together if our memory is to perform efficiently.

If we do not pay attention when we are presented with information, we may not encode it efficiently, or we may not encode it at all. If we do not store the information effectively, we say that we have forgotten it. With retrieval an important distinction is often made between availability and

> *"There's rosemary, that's for remembrance; pray, love, remember."*
> —**William Shakespeare, Hamlet, 1601–1602**

accessibility. For example, sometimes we cannot quite recall someone's name, but it feels as if it is right on the tip of our

---

THE MAN WITH A PERFECT MEMORY

People often wish for a perfect memory, but being unable to forget has distinct disadvantages, as this particular case study shows. It is reported in *The Mind of a Mnemonist* (1968) by the psychologist A. R. Luria. In the 1920s Shereshevskii (or S) was working as a journalist; his editor noticed that he was very good at remembering instructions. However complex the briefing he received, he never had to take notes and could repeat everything almost word for word. S took this for granted, but his editor persuaded

> *"The truth is, a person's memory has no more sense than his conscience, and no appreciation whatever of values and proportions."*
> —*Mark Twain, 1906*

him to see Luria for tests. Luria set a series of increasingly complex memory tasks, including lists of more than 100 digits, long strings of nonsense syllables, poetry in unknown languages, complex figures, and elaborate scientific formulas. S could repeat this material perfectly and could also repeat it in reverse order. He could even recall the information several years later.

His secret seemed to be twofold. He was able to create a wealth of visual images without much effort. He also had the power of synesthesia, which means that certain stimuli provoke unusual sensory experiences. A particular sound might evoke a specific smell, or a certain word might summon a particular color. Even information that appeared dry and dull to other people created a vivid sensory experience for S, not only in visual terms but also in terms of sound, touch, and smell. So S could encode and store any information in a rich and elaborate way.

Unfortunately, his abilities meant that S remembered virtually everything. New information (such as idle gossip) set off an uncontrollable train of distracting associations for him. Eventually S could not even hold a conversation, let alone function as a journalist. He was forced to become a professional mnemonist, giving demonstrations of his extraordinary skills on stage. He became increasingly unhappy, however, as his memory became more and more cluttered with useless information.

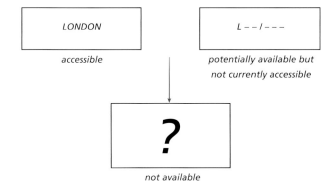

tongue. We may know what the first letter of the name is and the number of syllables it contains, but we just cannot produce the word itself. This is called the "tip of the tongue phenomenon," or TOTP. We know we have the information stored somewhere. We may also have partial knowledge of it, which means that the information is, in theory, potentially available, but it is not currently accessible—we fail to recall it.

Memory can fail to work due to a blockage in any one or more of these three components (encoding, storage, and retrieval). In the TOTP example it is the retrieval component that is failing (*see* diagram below). So all three components are necessary for effective memory, but no one component is sufficient.

The processes of memory

Plato and his contemporaries based their speculations about the mind on their own personal impressions. However, contemporary researchers conduct rigorous, highly controlled experimental studies to collect objective information about the workings of memory in people. The results often contradict the "common sense" approach favored in the past.

One of the major findings of the last hundred years is that there are different

Any effective memory system needs to be able to carry out these three functions: encoding or acquiring information, storing or retaining it, and finally be able to retrieve or have access to it.

The tip of the tongue phenomenon occurs when information has been stored away but cannot be retrieved. The question is "What is the capital of England?" The answer is either accessible, potentially available, or not available at all.

types of memory. We now know that there are different kinds of memory: the sensory store, short-term (working or primary), and long-term (secondary) memory. There are also different types of long-term memory such as explicit and implicit, episodic and semantic, and procedural.

The sensory store (*see* diagram p. 92) appears to operate below the threshold of consciousness. It receives information from the senses and holds it for about a second while we decide what to attend to. If you are at a cocktail party, for example, and hear your name being mentioned in a conversation elsewhere in the room, your attention is automatically diverted to that other conversation (*see* box p. 26). With sensory memory what we ignore is quickly lost and cannot be retrieved: It decays just as lights fade and sounds die away. You can sometimes catch an echo of what someone said when you are not paying attention, but a second later it has gone altogether.

Paying attention to something transfers it to working memory, which has a limited capacity of around seven items plus or minus two. This store is used when, for example, you dial a new phone number. As soon as your working memory is full, the old information is displaced by an input of new information. Less important items—such as a phone number you have to call only once—are held in the working memory, used, and then discarded. This process is used for everything that is processed consciously—it is what you are currently thinking about. Continuing to process information transfers it to long-term memory, which seems to have almost unlimited capacity. More important information, such as the new phone number you have to learn when you move, is placed in the long-term bank, which is the primary focus of this chapter.

Baddeley's working memory model supposes that working memory consists of three components: the articulatory loop that holds vocal information; the visuospatial scratchpad that is responsible for storing images; and the central executive that controls aspects of attention and strategy.

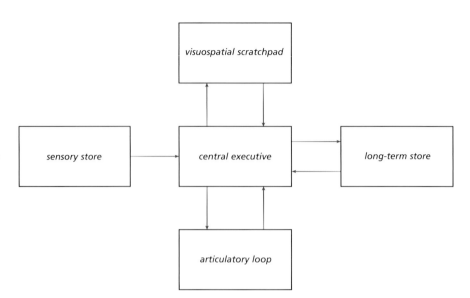

Previously people believed that working memory was a passive process, but we now know that it does more than just hold information. According to the modal model of working memory (*see* diagram p. 93), which is generally accepted by psychologists, people can do concurrent information processing or manipulation in working memory while holding information in four or five memory slots (*see* box p. 93). Working memory is also capable of other cognitive activities.

Working memory

There is now good evidence that short-term memory is also made up of at least three components. In 1986 the psychologist Alan Baddeley published a short-term memory model that consists of an articulatory loop, a visuospatial scratchpad, and a central executive.

The articulatory loop is made up of two parts: an inner voice and an inner ear. The inner voice repeats the information (covert speech) that is to be stored until you have worked on it, and the inner ear receives the auditory representation. After a while the loop starts to fade, and the central executive restarts it (like a traffic director). Brain imaging shows that two of the brain areas that usually process

speech or auditory signals are active when people store information in their working memories. If you either block your ear with external noise or block your speech system (by talking or chewing to occupy the muscles needed for pronunciation), it cannot be used for covert speech, and your memory performance drops because the auditory loop is blocked.

> *"A memory is what is left when something happens and does not completely unhappen."*
> —*Edward de Bono, 1969*

The visuospatial scratchpad provides a medium for the temporary storage and manipulation of images. Its existence has been deduced from studies showing that concurrent spatial tasks interfere with each other. If you try to perform two nonverbal tasks simultaneously (such as patting your head and rubbing your stomach), the visuospatial scratchpad may become overstretched and be unable to perform effectively. One function of the central executive is to link the visuospatial scratchpad with the auditory loop.

The central executive is also thought to control the attentional and strategic aspects of working memory. It may also be involved in coordinating the articulatory loop and the visuospatial scratchpad if both are active at the same time. After damage to the frontal lobe area of the brain, patients often have difficulty planning and making decisions. They are

"As the last taste of sweets, is sweetest last, writ in remembrance more than things long past."
—*William Shakespeare,*
Richard II, *1595–96*

able to carry out automatic and routine actions but are unable to interrupt or correct them. Baddeley called this dysexecutive syndrome because the damage was to the central executive.

Working memory could be likened to the random-access memory (RAM) capacity of your computer. The operations currently being carried out by your computer—in terms of its processing resources—are occupying RAM, the computer's "working memory." The hard disk is like long-term memory. Information you put there remains stored when the computer is switched off and

EXPERIMENT

MEMORY SPAN

In the 1950s, after a series of experiments, the psychologist George Miller found that healthy young people typically retained seven items, plus or minus two items, in their working memory. If you try to remember a list of words, for example, you tend to remember the last few words in the list best because they are still being held in your working memory.

It has been suggested that there is a link between the size of working memory and someone's intellectual performance—that is, that working memory span determines a person's ability to perform several tasks at the same time and not get confused between them. For example, participants in an experiment on working memory might be asked to work on equations and to also remember a list of words for later recall.

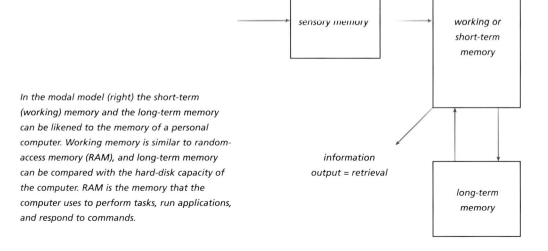

In the modal model (right) the short-term (working) memory and the long-term memory can be likened to the memory of a personal computer. Working memory is similar to random-access memory (RAM), and long-term memory can be compared with the hard-disk capacity of the computer. RAM is the memory that the computer uses to perform tasks, run applications, and respond to commands.

can be kept indefinitely. Switching off power is like falling asleep. When you wake up after a good night's sleep, you still have access to information stored in your long-term memory, such as who you are and what happened on an especially eventful day in your personal past. But typically, you cannot remember the last thoughts you held in your working memory before you went to sleep because that information is not usually transferred into your long-term memory.

The computer disk example also helps explain the distinction between encoding, storage, and retrieval in memory. The huge amount of information on the Internet can be thought of as a massive long-term memory system. Unless you have effective tools for searching and retrieving information from the Internet, however, that information is useless. It may theoretically be available, but it is not accessible when you need it.

> *"We soon forget what we have not deeply thought about."*
> —*Marcel Proust, 1913–1927*

Levels of processing

In 1972 experimental psychologists Fergus Craik and Robert Lockhart developed the "levels of processing" framework, which was to have a great influence on later theories about memory. Its key principle echoed Marcel Proust (*see* quote above). Subsequent formal experiments tested people's ability to remember things after a time lapse. They showed that "deeper" processing of information is superior to more "superficial" processing.

Craik and Lockhart also showed that elaboration of material can improve our ability to memorize items. What does this mean? Suppose you were asked to study a list of words and then tested on your memory of them. Typically you would remember more of them if you defined

each word on the list or else gave each one a personal association—this technique is known as elaboration of material. You would remember fewer of them if you provided a rhyming word for each word or gave each letter a number reflecting its position in the alphabet because that is a more superficial task in semantic terms. Semantics is the study of meaning in language.

According to the "levels of processing" theory, if a particular operation or procedure produces better memory performance, it arises from a deep mode of processing. Conversely, if another operation or procedure shows poor memory performance, it can be argued that this must have been due to more superficial processing.

To test the levels of processing theory adequately, psychologists need to devise a method of measuring the depth and shallowness of memory processing that works independently of the subsequent memory performance. This model is generally accepted by psychologists today, however, especially after Craik and Lockhart conducted further experiments showing that the intention to learn and remember information is totally insignificant—all that is necessary is for deep processing to take place.

The hippocampus is highlighted in magenta on this picture of the brain. The hippocampus is the area of the brain that sorts memories, deciding which ones are important enough to be stored in long-term memory.

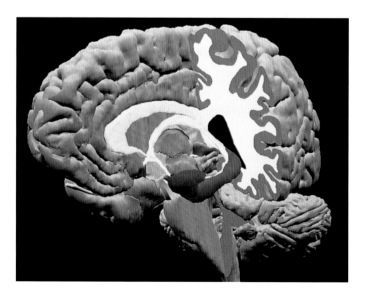

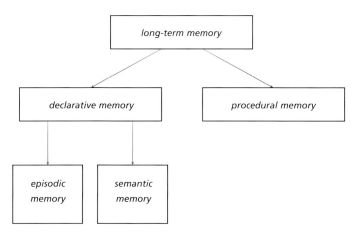

```
              long-term memory
             /                  \
declarative memory          procedural memory
    /         \
episodic    semantic
memory      memory
```

These are the proposed subdivisions of long-term memory. Endel Tulving divided declarative (explicit) or consciously accessible memory into two types: episodic memory for certain events and semantic memory, which is the general store of knowledge that we draw on.

Using the computer analogy, the "software" of memory is its functional components and the processes it is capable of. Memory also works at another level—the "hardware" of the central nervous system underlies the way that memory works. Deep within our brains memories are sorted in a part of the brain called the hippocampus (*see* Vol. 2, pp. 20–39). The hippocampus acts as a gatekeeper, determining whether information is significant enough to pass into long-term storage. The hippocampus can also be described as the "printing press" for new memories. Important memories are "printed" by the hippocampus and filed away indefinitely in the cerebral cortex. This outer, folded layer of the brain contains a thicket of billions of nerve cells. Electrical and chemical impulses cause it to retain information. The cerebral cortex can be seen as the "library" for important memories.

Long-term memory
Information stored in the long-term memory can be divided into two types: explicit memory that is consciously accessible and is also known as declarative memory, and implicit or nondeclarative memory. Explicit memory is usually divided into at least two types. The psychologist Endel Tulving labeled them episodic memory, which involves remembering particular events or specific episodes in your life, and semantic memory, which concerns the general knowledge that we acquire about the world (*see* box below).

It is still uncertain whether these two aspects of explicit memory (semantic and episodic memory) represent truly separate memory systems or are different parts of the same system. The distinction has, however, been useful in characterizing clinical memory disorders that seem to affect one system or area of memory more than the other. For example, researchers have found that certain disorders of the brain, such as semantic dementia, can affect semantic memory. In contrast, Tulving has argued, controversially, that the condition known as "amnesiac syndrome" is characterized by a selective impairment in episodic memory but not in semantic memory (*see* p. 111).

GENERAL VS. PERSONAL

FOCUS ON

We acquire a huge supply of general knowledge about the world throughout our lives. It is called semantic memory. Answering the questions posed below will require you to tap into your semantic memory.

• What is the capital of France?
• How many days are there in the week?
• Who is the current president of the United States?
• Are bats mammals?
• What is the chemical symbol for water?

• What is the longest word in the English language that you can think of?
• What direction would you travel in if you flew from London to New York?

In contrast, if you were asked what you had for breakfast yesterday, or what happened on your last birthday, your response would draw on your episodic memory, which relates to specific events, or episodes, that have occurred in your life.

Implicit or procedural memory involves skills that we know but could not always describe, such as riding a bicycle, playing basketball, or typing. There seems to be general agreement among psychologists that implicit memory is independent of explicit or consciously accessible memory.

RETRIEVAL

Having encoded, or received, and stored information that has been processed by the senses, we then have to be able to effectively retrieve it from our filing system. What we are able to retrieve depends largely on the context in which the information was encoded or classified in the first place and to what extent it matches the retrieval context. This is called the encoding specificity principle. For example, many of us have been embarrassed by our failure to recognize friends or acquaintances when we meet them in an unusual context. If we are used to seeing someone at school dressed in a particular way, in a uniform, for example, we may not recognize them when we see them dressed differently for a social occasion like a wedding (*see* box p. 97).

Recall

There are two types of retrieval: recall and recognition. When investigating recall in an experimental context, researchers might present people with information, such as a story, during what is called the learning episode. The researchers then ask them to recall certain aspects of the story.

Free recall is when people are asked to remember as much of the story as they can without any assistance. The "tip of the tongue phenomenon" mentioned earlier (*see* p. 91) illustrates the nature of one common problem in free recall—we often have only partial access to information that we are trying to retrieve.

Cued recall is when people are presented with a prompt (such as a category or the first letter of the word) to retrieve a certain piece of information. For example, they might be asked: "Tell me all the names of people beginning with 'J'

who were in the story that I read to you yesterday." Cued recall tends to be easier for people than free recall. This may be because the researchers are doing some of the memory work for them in providing the cues. Although cues can be useful in retrieving information, they can also introduce distortion and bias.

Recognition

Recognition is the easiest type of retrieval. Some of the actual memory material is presented, and you have to make a decision about it. "Forced choice recognition" is when you are presented with, say, two items, only one of which you have seen previously. You are then asked to point out which of the two items you saw before. It is a forced choice in that you have to choose one of the two items. It can be compared to "yes/no recognition," when you are shown a series of items one at a time and asked whether you have seen the item before. You simply have to answer yes or no in response.

Experiments have indicated that two independent processes can contribute to recognition: context retrieval and familiarity. Context retrieval depends on explicit recollection of time and place. For example, you may recognize someone as the person you saw on the bus when you were coming home from college last Friday. On a different day you may see someone who looks vaguely familiar. You know you have seen them before, but you cannot remember when or where. This type of recognition taps into a familiarity process, but there is no explicit recollection, so it is a less detailed form of recognition.

Physical and psychological influences
Recall performance is also influenced by your physical or psychological state. If you learn something when you are very calm and are tested when you are very excited, your ability to recall information is reduced. But if you learn while calm and then are tested while calm, or learn while you are excited and then are tested while excited, you tend to perform better. This is known as state-dependent learning, and it is important for students faced with exams. If you study for an exam while you are very calm, but then feel very nervous or excited in the actual examination, you might not recall information as well as someone whose mood is more even. That is because being in the same mood creates another additional retrieval cue as a pathway into the memory storage. Memory seems to be affected by our physical or psychological state in a variety of circumstances. In controlled conditions researchers have found that the effects are consistent only when tests use free recall.

When either cued recall or recognition is tested, differences in state or context have less predictable effects. That is mainly

THE EFFECT OF CONTEXT

EXPERIMENT

In 1975 and 1980 D. R. Godden and Alan Baddeley conducted two famous experiments to determine the effects of context on recall and recognition. A group of deep-sea divers was asked to learn information when they were on the beach. Later they were asked to learn information when they were underwater. The divers were then tested in both the same context and the different context.

The studies showed that the divers' recall memory was strongly influenced by whether they were in the same context when they encoded the information as they were for the memory test. The divers remembered far more information if they were asked to learn underwater and then were tested underwater, or if they learned on dry land and then were tested on dry land. But if the context in which they learned and were tested was different, then the divers' level of memory performance dropped markedly. However, this was only true for recall, not for recognition memory, so it seems that the cues provided by being in the same context at learning and test are important in effective recall but less important for recognition.

According to Godden and Baddeley, if this diver learns something underwater and then is tested underwater, her recall will be better than if she is tested on land.

because a certain amount of the information provided at learning and test is constant during recall and recognition tests. The potential for a mismatch between learning and remembering is substantially reduced. Also, the familiarity part of recognition does not depend on context, although the explicit recollection component may be state-dependent.

> *"The existence of forgetting has never been proved: We only know that some things don't come to mind when we want them to."*
> —*Friedrich Nietzsche, 1878*

Forgetting

Forgetting can be defined as the loss of information, interference, or other blockage of retrieval. Forgetting may well occur not because of storage limitations, but because similar memories become confused and interfere with each other when we try to retrieve them. In order to understand better how memory works, we need to understand some of the factors that can influence the forgetting of information.

There are two traditional views of forgetting. One view argues that memory fades or decays, just as objects might fade, erode, or tarnish over time. The second view sees forgetting as a more active process. It suggests that there is no strong evidence for the fading or eroding of information in memory. Forgetting occurs because memory traces are disrupted, obscured, or overlaid by other memories. In other words, forgetting happens because of interference.

The consensus view is that both of these processes occur, but it is difficult to separate the importance of time—which causes memories to fade away or decay—from interference by new events because they often occur together. Try to remember what happened in the Wimbledon men's tennis final in 2001. Your memory may be imperfect because of the passage of time, or because memories of later Wimbledon men's tennis finals interfere with your memory of the 2001 final, or for both reasons. However, there is some evidence that interference may be the more important reason for forgetting. If you have not seen another tennis match since this one, you might remember it better than someone who has seen other tennis matches.

Winner Goran Ivanisevic kissing the trophy after the 2001 Wimbledon men's final. Forgetting what happened in a notable event such as this might be due to a fading or eroding of the memory, or it could be that more recent tennis matches have obscured your memory of this final.

FLASHBULB MEMORIES AND THE REMINISCENCE BUMP

People seem to remember certain events—especially if they are particularly unusual and arousing—very vividly for a long time. Two different aspects of this phenomenon are flashbulb memories and the reminiscence bump.

A flashbulb memory is a vivid record of the circumstances in which people learn about a particularly significant or emotional event. People who were alive when John F. Kennedy was assassinated or when Princess Diana died are often able to remember where they were and who they were with when they heard the news of one or both of these deaths. There may be evolutionary reasons for such vivid and long-standing memories.

The reminiscence bump occurs when old people are asked to remember events from across their life span. They tend to remember many more events from the period between adolescence and early adulthood. It has been suggested that this is because of the particular significance of events that occurred during that period. Some involved strong emotions—meeting a partner and becoming a parent—while others—starting work or backpacking around the world—were significant in other ways. Theories about the processes underlying these phenomena are controversial, but they are subjects of great interest in memory literature.

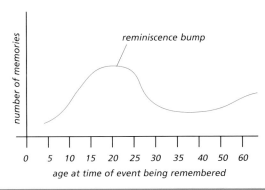

reminiscence bump

number of memories

0 5 10 15 20 25 30 35 40 50 60

age at time of event being remembered

The reminiscence bump is the tendency of old people to remember more events from adolescence and early adulthood than from later life.

Our experiences undoubtedly interact in our memories and tend to run into one another. As a result, our memory of one experience is often interrelated to our memory of another experience. The more similar two experiences, the greater the likelihood that they will interact in our memory. This can be helpful since new learning can build on old learning. But if it is important to separate two memories of different occasions, interference can mean that we remember less accurately than we would like. For example, memories from two different birthdays might become confused with one another.

The Ebbinghaus tradition
The German experimental psychologist Hermann Ebbinghaus (1850–1909) is famous for his research into forgetting. In one experiment Ebbinghaus taught himself 169 separate lists of 13 nonsense syllables. Each syllable was formed from a consonant, a vowel, and a consonant (for example, PEL or KEM). Ebbinghaus relearned each list after an interval ranging from 21 minutes to 31 days. To test how much he had forgotten, he used a measure called the savings score (how much time it took him to relearn the list).

Ebbinghaus noted that his rate of forgetting was roughly exponential. This means that forgetting is rapid at first. His observation has stood the test of time and has been shown to apply across a range of different materials and learning conditions. For instance, if you stop studying French when you leave school, your vocabulary will decline rapidly in the next 12 months. However, the rate at which you forget vocabulary will gradually slow down, and you will reach a plateau during which your knowledge stays the same. If you study French again five to ten years later, you might be surprised at how much vocabulary you have retained. Also, although you have forgotten some of your French vocabulary, you can relearn it much faster than someone who has never learned French. So although you have no conscious knowledge of this vocabulary, there must be some preservation of the memory record at an unconscious level.

A closely related point was made by the psychologist B. F. Skinner (1904–1990) when he wrote, "Education is what survives when what has been learned has been forgotten." We might adjust this to explicitly forgotten. Ebbinghaus described his nonsense syllables, chosen at random, as being "uniformly unassociated," which he regarded as a strength of his approach. And it is true that the great advantage of an experiment like Ebbinghaus's is that it excludes irrelevant factors. However, some argue that it oversimplifies memory, reducing its subtleties to a series of artificial, mathematical components. Although Ebbinghaus's methods are scientifically rigorous, they risk eliminating those aspects of memory in people that are most essential to the way it functions in real life. Researchers who make these criticisms suggest that using meaningful memory materials such as stories or shopping lists would be more relevant to the overall study of how memory works in people.

The Bartlett tradition

The work of psychologist Sir Frederick Bartlett (1886–1969) exemplifies the second great tradition in memory research. In his book *Remembering*, published in 1932, Bartlett attacked the Ebbinghaus tradition. He argued that the study of nonsense syllables does not tell us much about the way memory operates in the real world. Ebbinghaus used nonsense syllables and tried to eliminate meaning from his test materials, whereas Bartlett focused on meaningful materials —or materials onto which we try to impose meaning—remembered under relatively natural conditions.

In some of Bartlett's studies subjects were asked to read a story to themselves (*see* box below). Later the subjects were asked to recall the story. Bartlett found that people recalled the story in their own way, but also found some general trends:
- The stories tended to become shorter.
- The stories became more coherent as people made sense of unfamiliar material by changing it to fit their preexisting ideas and adapted it to their cultural expectations.

THE WAR OF THE GHOSTS

EXPERIMENT

When Bartlett followed Ebbinghaus's lead and tried to carry out further experiments using nonsense syllables, the result was, he said, "disappointment and a growing dissatisfaction." Instead, he chose to work with ordinary prose material that "would prove interesting in itself." This was precisely the kind of material that Ebbinghaus had rejected in his experiment.

Bartlett used two basic methods in his experiments: serial reproduction and repeated reproduction. Serial reproduction is similar to the game "Chinese Whispers." One person passes some information to a second person, who passes the same information to a third, and so on. The "story" that reaches the final person in the group is then compared with the original. Repeated reproduction is when someone is asked to repeat the same piece of information at certain intervals—from 15 minutes to a few years—after first learning it.

Bartlett's most famous experiment used a North American folktale called "The War of the Ghosts." He chose the story because it did not relate to the English culture of his subjects and would seem disjointed and rather incoherent to nonnative ears. From his experiments Bartlett concluded that people tend to rationalize material. In other words, they try to make the material easier to understand and also to turn it into something they feel more comfortable with. According to Bartlett, remembering is an imaginative reconstruction or construction. We built this construction out of a whole active mass of organized past reactions or experiences and outstanding details that usually appear as images or in language form. It is, therefore, hardly ever really exact, even in the most basic cases of rote recapitulation. Remembering is not the reactivating of a large number of "fixed, lifeless, and fragmentary traces."

• The changes people made matched the reactions and emotions that they had experienced when they first heard the story.

Bartlett argued that what people remember is to some extent driven by their emotional and personal commitment to—and investment in—the original event. The memory system retains "a little outstanding detail," and the remainder is an elaboration or a reconstruction based on the original event. Bartlett referred to this as the "reconstructive," as opposed to the "reproductive," nature of memory. In other words, instead of reproducing the original event or story, we make a reconstruction based on our existing "mental set." As an example, think of the way two people supporting two different countries (Canada and the United States, for example) will report the events in a sports game (ice hockey or tennis, for example) they have just watched between these two countries. The same objective events occurred on the field, but the Canadian supporter will most likely report the events in a radically different way than the American supporter.

The essence of Bartlett's argument—that people attempt to impose meaning on what they observe in the world and that this influences their memory of events—may not be important in a laboratory experiment using relatively abstract, meaningless materials. However, according to Bartlett, this "effort after meaning" is one of the most significant features of the way people remember and forget in the real world.

Organization and errors
In the 1960s and 1970s researchers carried out studies to discover how well chess players could remember the positions of chess pieces on a board. The studies showed that chess masters could remember 95 percent of the pieces on the chessboard after a single five-second glance. Weaker chess players, on the other hand, were able to position only 40 percent of the pieces correctly and needed

eight attempts to reach 95 percent accuracy. These findings suggest that the advantage enjoyed by the chess masters stemmed from their ability to perceive the chessboard as an organized whole, rather than as a collection of individual pieces.

Experiments in which expert bridge players were asked to recall bridge hands, and electronics experts were asked to remember electronic circuits produced similar results. In each case it appears that the experts are able to organize the material into a coherent and meaningful pattern that results in significant enhancement to their memory. We have already seen that organizing information at the time of retrieval (in the form of cuing) can aid recall, but these studies reveal the benefits of organization at the time of learning as well. In the laboratory researchers have compared memory for the learning of relatively unstructured material to the recall of material that had some structure imposed at the time of learning. If, for example, you try to memorize a random list of words, you will find it easier if the list you are learning is organized into categories, say,

> "One must have a good memory to . . . keep the promises one makes."
> —Friedrich Nietzsche, 1878

of vegetables or furniture. When people are later asked to remember the list that was organized during encoding, their performance is substantially better than their memory of the random list.

Meaningful organization of information during learning can lead to enhanced memory performance in testing, but it can also result in distortions. We know that memory is anything but infallible. Most people have a poor memory for many aspects of their daily life and everyday environment. If a piece of information is not useful in everyday life, then it is unlikely that we will successfully remember it. For instance, can you remember whether the head on a coin in your pocket faces to the left or the right? Generally speaking, people are very bad at answering this question correctly despite using the coins almost every day. Some might argue that we have no need to remember which way the head faces in order to use coins effectively in daily life, but that we would correctly observe and remember an unusual event, such as a crime.

Errors can be caused by a number of factors, including inattention, which leads to incomplete encoding, and initial misunderstanding, which can lead to intrusion errors. They are aspects that conform to your original understanding but were not part of what you are trying to remember. These errors are often not detectable since the reconstructions are as detailed, vivid, and confidently recalled as accurate memories. Hypnosis or memory-producing drugs do not produce more accurate memories either.

Memory and crime

Considerable weight is still placed on eyewitness testimony by the legal profession, the police, and the press. Eyewitnesses may be expected to produce a level of detail and evidence regarding an event that is quite unrealistic in the context of what we know—from carefully conducted scientific experiments—about the way our memories work. Eyewitnesses' reports of crimes may also depend on their emotional investment and their personal perspective. They may, for example, be more sympathetic toward the perpetrator of the crime or the victim.

In a crime many factors can combine and work together to make eyewitness reports unreliable and to obscure or distort the memory of an eyewitness, causing them to give an inaccurate report:

- When people experience extreme stress, their attention can be narrowed in focus, which means that their perception is often biased.
- People tend to remember less accurately when they are confronted by or are in a violent situation.
- A weapon at the scene of a crime can distract attention from the perpetrator of the crime.
- Although people are much better at recognizing faces than recalling other information from the crime scene, clothing is a particularly powerful source of bias in recognition. Someone wearing clothing similar

---

 ## THE SEVEN SINS OF MEMORY

In 2001 Daniel L. Schacter in his book *The Seven Sins of Memory* proposed that memory's malfunctions are caused by seven fundamental transgressions, or "sins."

- **Transience**: Weakening or loss of memory over time means that although we can remember what we did earlier today, in a few months' time we will most likely have forgotten most, if not all, of these details.
- **Absent-mindedness**: A breakdown between attention and memory means either that we did not register the information in the first place, or that we do not look for it because our attention is focused elsewhere.
- **Blocking**: We may try desperately to retrieve information but are thwarted. The "tip of the tongue phenomenon" (*see* p. 91) is an example of this malfunction.

- **Misattribution**: We assign memory to the wrong source. For instance, we might read about something in the newspaper but later wrongly remember the information as having been passed on by a friend.
- **Suggestibility**: False memories are implanted as a result of leading questions, comments, or suggestions.
- **Bias**: Our current knowledge and beliefs have a powerful influence on how we remember our pasts. As a result, we unconsciously distort past events or learned material in the light of our current perspective.
- **Persistence**: Repeated recall of disturbing information or events that we would prefer to banish from our minds. This could range from an embarrassing blunder at work to a seriously traumatic experience, such as rape.

to that of the criminal could be incorrectly identified as the criminal.

• People tend to be poorer at recognizing the faces of individuals from racial and ethnic groups other than their own even when they have extensive experience in interacting with people from other groups. This phenomenon does not seem to be related to racial prejudice.

Another powerful influence in the distortion of memory is the use of leading questions—making assumptions or implying what happened. "Did you see the man who raped the woman?" is an example of a leading question since it assumes that a rape has taken place. It can result in far more confirmations of an alleged crime than a question such as "Did you see a man rape the woman?"

If you witness a traffic accident at an intersection on the highway, and you are later asked whether the car stopped before or after the tree, you are subsequently likely to "insert"or add a tree into your memory of the scene even if there was no tree there in the first place. Once the tree has been inserted, it behaves as if it were part of the original memory, making it difficult to tell the difference between the real memory and what has been subsequently introduced. A bias has been introduced by the question.

A central message of these studies is that memory is not a passive process: It is a "top-down" as well as a "bottom-up" process. People do not just receive information and store it in their memory; they impose meaning on that information, molding memories to make them consistent with their world view. This indicates memory is an active process.

Influencing memory

In laboratory experiments in the mid-1970s Elizabeth Loftus found that people respond just as rapidly and confidently to leading or misleading questions as they do to questions phrased without bias. Even if participants notice that new information has been introduced, it can still become part of their memory of the

Memories of what happened at the scene of a traffic accident can be biased by the questions eyewitnesses are asked. For example, if witnesses are asked whether the car hit the signpost, they will insert a signpost into the original memory.

incident. Memory bias, therefore, can be introduced retrospectively. In one experiment in 1974 Loftus and her colleague John Palmer asked groups of students to watch a series of films, each showing a traffic accident. Afterward they had to answer questions about what had happened. One of the questions was, "How fast were the cars going when they ------ each other?" The gap was filled with a different word for each group of students and could be any one of the following: "smashed," "collided," "bumped," "hit," and "contacted."

The researchers found that the students' estimates of the cars' speed were influenced by the choice of verb in the question. Loftus and Palmer concluded that the students' memory of the accident had been altered by the implied information given in the question.

Loftus and Palmer then asked students to watch a film of an accident involving several cars that lasted for about four seconds. Again, the students were asked about the speed of the cars, with the word "smashed" being used for one group and "hit" for another. A third group was not asked this particular question. A week later the students were asked to answer more questions, one of which was "Did you see any broken glass?"

Loftus and Palmer found that not only did the verb in the speed question influence the students' estimates of speed,

> "The palest ink is better than the best memory."
> —Chinese Proverb

it also influenced their answer to the broken glass question. Those who had estimated a higher speed were more likely to remember seeing broken glass, although there had not been any in the film. Those who had not been asked the speed question were least likely to remember seeing broken glass. A year later

MISTAKEN IDENTITY

CASE STUDY

The Australian psychologist Donald Thompson had been very active in arguing for the unreliability of eyewitness evidence. On one occasion he took part in a television debate on the subject of eyewitness testimony, giving hints on remembering faces. Some time later the police arrested him but refused to explain why. When a woman picked him out of a lineup at the police station, he discovered he was to be charged with rape.

When he asked for further details, it became clear that the rape had been committed while he was taking part in the television discussion. Obviously, he then had a very good alibi because a large number of witnesses, including a police officer, had taken part in the same discussion.

It turned out that the woman had been raped in a room with the television on and that the program had been broadcast while the offense was committed. This was an instance of what is known as transference of memory, source amnesia, or (according to Dan Schacter) misattribution. The woman's memory of the rapist had been contaminated by the face she saw on the television at the same time. The face was correctly recognized, but its source was misattributed.

There have been other recent studies reported in which people have been unable to recognize when two people have changed places. This phenomenon is called "change blindness." It indicates that people are not very good at judging whether a change has taken place in their immediate environment.

Loftus carried out yet another experiment. Again she showed participants a film of a traffic accident. This time she asked some of them, "How fast was the white sports car going when it passed the barn while traveling along the country road?" There was no barn in the film. A week later those who had been asked this question were more likely to say they remembered seeing a barn. Even if participants were asked simply, "Did you see a barn?" they were more likely a week later to "remember" seeing it.

Loftus concluded that the actual memory can be changed by the introduction of misleading information. Critics of this experiment argued that just as children will give the answer they think is expected of them rather than say they do not know, participants in the tests were simply conforming to what they thought was expected of them. Loftus was convinced that this was not the case and proceeded to find more convincing evidence to support her conclusion about memory and misleading information. In 1978 Loftus, Miller, and Burns again presented participants with a traffic accident, but this time it was on a series of slides. The accident showed a red Datsun turning at an intersection and hitting a pedestrian. One group saw the car stopping first at a stop sign, while another group saw it stopping at a yield sign. The critical question this time was "Did another car pass the red Datsun while it was stopped at the stop {yield} sign?" For half the participants from each group the word "stop" was used, and for the other half from each group the word "yield" was used. This meant that half of each group was asked a question consistent with what they had seen, while the other half of the group was asked a misleading question.

Twenty minutes later all the participants were shown pairs of slides. One slide from each pair showed what the group had seen, and the other was slightly different. One of the pairs showed the car stopped at a stop sign, and the other showed it stopped at a yield sign. The participants had to choose the most accurate slide for each pair. The researchers found that those who had been asked the question that was consistent with what they had seen were more likely to choose the correct slide, while those who had been asked the misleading question were more likely to choose the wrong slide.

This suggests that some people were in fact remembering information that had been introduced after the event rather than the event itself. The researchers had successfully misled them into misreporting the events of the accident. These findings have great significance for police interviewing techniques, as well as very controversial implications for events associated with

possible child abuse. Are people in therapy recovering genuine memories of what happened during their childhood, or are they being induced or misled by the therapist's suggestions to remember things that did not really happen?

IMPROVING MEMORY

It is easy to damage the neural systems underlying memory, through alcohol and drug abuse or head injury, and the like, and comparatively difficult to enhance them. It might be possible to improve our "neural hardware" in the future, perhaps through genetic manipulation techniques or the interfacing of carbon-based

> *"Memory depends very much on the perspicuity, regularity, and order of our thoughts. Many complain of the want of memory, when the defect is in the judgment; and others, by grasping at all, retain nothing."*
> **Thomas Fuller, 1662**

hardware (that is, our brain) and silicon-based hardware (or computers). There have been claims that certain "smart drugs" and neurochemical agents can improve the functioning of the neural components underlying memory, but these substances are only consistently helpful for some people with impaired memory due to brain damage or illnesses, such as dementia. The only way to improve memory is to make sure that the "software" running on these neural systems is working at its best.

When Ebbinghaus was learning his nonsense syllables, he found that there was a direct relationship between the number of learning trials and the amount he retained. Ebbinghaus concluded that the amount learned depended simply on the time spent learning. If you doubled the amount of time spent learning, you would double the amount of information stored. This became known as the "total time hypothesis" and is the basic relationship underlying all literature on human learning. However, we now recognize that Ebbinghaus's techniques were, in some ways, artificial. This means that despite the general relationship between the amount of practice and the amount remembered, there are other ways in which you can get a better return for the time spent learning.

Ebbinghaus also noted the "distribution of practice effect." It demonstrates that it is better to distribute learning trials across

> *"Do not trust your memory; it is a net full of holes; the most beautiful prizes slip through it."*
> —*Georges Duhamel, 1919*

an extended period of time rather than to mass them together in a single block. Little and often is the key principle here. Cramming for an examination, therefore, cannot replace solid, sustained study.

"Errorless learning" is a flexible strategy in which a new item is initially tested after a short delay. As the item becomes better learned, the practice interval is gradually increased. The aim is to test each item at the longest interval at which it can be reliably reproduced. This seems to work quite effectively as a learning technique. A beneficial by-product of errorless learning is that the motivation of the learner is sustained because the rate of memory failure is kept at a low level.

Motivation to learn information is another important factor, although its effect may well be indirect. It influences the amount of time spent attending to the material to be learned, and that affects the amount of learning taking place.

The way in which we process information is crucial. People seek meaning in information they are trying to remember. If there is an absence of meaning, they try to impose their own. A

general rule is that it often helps to relate new material to yourself and to your circumstances as richly and elaborately as possible in the available time.

Victorian educators placed a lot of emphasis on repetition and rote learning, but repetition of information does not ensure that attention is being paid to it. Nothing is likely to get into long-term memory unless you pay attention to it. If you remember something for yourself, it tends to strengthen the memory more effectively. There is a complex, mutually reinforcing relationship between attention, interest, expertise, and memory. The more expert you become in a particular field, the more interest you will have in it, and those two aspects will reinforce each other in improving your memory for material in that field.

Artificial memory aids help remind us of things. In times gone by people used to tie a knot in their handkerchief. This did not tell them what to remember, just that they had to remember something. Nowadays many of us have access to a number of artificial external memory aids, such as computers, personal digital assistants (PDAs), timers, tape recorders, diaries, minutes, company reports, lecture

Today people have access to numerous electronic gadgets that act as memory aids. They include computers, personal organizers, and tape recorders. Other artificial external memory aids include diaries, minutes, reports, and notes.

STUDYING FOR TESTS

Here are some practical ideas to improve your memory that are based on psychological research and theories.

• Select a working environment that does not have many distractions so you can focus on the target information rather than on your surroundings.

• Try to encode the information as actively as possible. For example, imagine yourself questioning the author of the piece so you have to think about the work; try to relate what is being said to what you already know.

• Organize the information. This provides a structure, so if you can recall a fragment of information, you may well recall all of it. Relating newly learned material to existing knowledge makes it easier to understand new material.

• Relate new material to yourself and your own interests as richly and elaborately as possible in the available time.

• Practice is important. Whether you are learning facts, a dance sequence, or a foreign language, nothing can substitute for practice. Massing all your practice together into a marathon learning session is not an efficient way of learning—little and often is a much better strategy.

• Use unoccupied moments. Keep notes on cards, or use a PDA or tape recorder to refresh your memory.

• Think about the interrelationships between different concepts, facts, and principles in the field that you are studying. That will help you when you are learning material for a test and will often also help you in answering questions during the test itself.

• The best way to learn a subject is to teach it, because to convey the information to someone else, you must not only be able to reproduce it, but also to understand it. Only move on in your study when you can reproduce the material spontaneously without being prompted and explain it comprehensibly to someone else.

• If you can imagine applying the topics you are studying to situations or problems in your everyday life, you are more likely to do a better job of reproducing that information during a test. It makes the information more practical and relevant to situations you find yourself in.

notes, and so on. People with so-called "exceptional memories" often use mnemonics. A mnemonic is a visual or verbal method of organizing information

> *"In any well-made machine one is ignorant of the working of most of the parts—the better they work the less we are conscious of them . . . it is only a fault which draws our attention to the existence of a mechanism at all."*
>
> *Kenneth Craik, 1943*

to make it easier to remember. The two most popular visual mnemonics are the "method of loci" and "peg words."

Mnemonics
The method of loci (*loci* is Latin for "places") is based on an event that took place in about 500 B.C. The Greek poet

Simonides attended a celebration to deliver a praise speech, or eulogy. Shortly after he finished his speech, he was called away. Almost immediately after he left, the floor of the banqueting hall collapsed, and a number of guests were injured or killed. Many were unrecognizable, making it impossible for relatives to identify them. According to the orator Cicero, Simonides found that he could easily remember where most of the guests had been located at the time he left, which made it much easier to identify the relevant bodies.

Based on this experience, Simonides was said to have devised a technique of visualizing a room or building in great detail and then imagining various to-be-remembered objects or pieces of information in particular locations. Whenever Simonides needed to remember what these items were, he would imagine himself walking through the room or building and "picking up" those pieces of information. The technique seems to work particularly well with concrete words, such as names of objects. But it can also work

These children taking an examination have developed memory skills and also have an awareness of how good their memory is in different situations. Knowledge and language ability are important in their memory development, as is the physical development of the neuronal network in the brain.

with abstract words, such as truth, hope, and so on, provided you can come up with a representative image of the abstract concept and locate it appropriately.

Peg words help you remember lists of items. Each number is assigned a word: 1 is a bun, 2 is a shoe, 3 is a tree, 4 is a door, 5 is a hive, 6 is sticks, 7 is heaven, 8 is a gate, 9 is wine, 10 is a hen. If the first word on your list is cat, you link this image with the number 1, bun. So you might create a visual image of a cat eating a bun. If the second word is dog, you might think of a dog chewing a shoe, or even a dog wearing a shoe—generally speaking, the more bizarre the image, the better this technique seems to work.

Although classical mnemonics relied mainly on visual imagery, in later times verbal mnemonics were developed. Mnemonics using verbal materials tend to fall into one of two categories: either a reduction code or an elaboration code. A reduction code reduces the amount of information. For example, to remember certain rules of trigonometry, schoolchildren were once taught to use the nonsense word SOHCAHTOA, whereas an elaboration code increases it. Another way to learn the same trigonometric relationships, is to use

the expression Some Old Horses Chew Apples Heartily Throughout Old Age. In each case the coding technique produces information that is easier to remember because it is more meaningful to the user than the original source information.

People who are fascinated by numbers sometimes find that strings of numbers have rich personal associations. They become stored in long-term memory, making it easier to remember long strings of digits in a series of chunks rather than as individual digits. For example, someone interested in numbers or mathematics may have committed to memory that the first four digits of pi are 3.142. They then use this information to help them code other numbers for subsequent remembering. More musical people may find that by setting particular words to a very memorable tune, memory for those words can be enhanced.

MEMORY DEVELOPMENT
Studying the way memory changes between birth and death reveals a great deal not only about how memory changes with age, but also about the structure and processes underlying normal adult memory. Studying memory disorders also reveals more about normal memory.

Studies of explicit memory show that even the youngest children seem capable of recognition memory. By about five months children also seem to have a rudimentary recall ability. Memory development can be seen as the gradual emergence of more complex strategies for encoding and retrieving memories. As children begin to use language, they start to use linguistic labels to encode materials more richly and as cues when retrieving items. Children also develop a better awareness of how good or poor their memory is in particular situations, and how likely they are to be able to remember certain pieces of information. Studies of implicit memory indicate that it may be present in its full form in children as young as three years. Some people believe that implicit memory develops very little beyond the age of three or four years old.

What underlies memory development is not yet known. A child's knowledge and language ability are undoubtedly important, but biological factors are likely to be central, too. For example, the network of nerve cells in the frontal lobes of the brain seem to mature relatively slowly. This may provide part of the

> *"Every man's memory is his private literature."*
> —Aldous Huxley, 1932

explanation for another little-understood phenomenon called infantile amnesia (*see* box). Hardly anyone can reliably remember information from before the age of about four years, although it is a time when experience is at its richest. Another explanation for this is that memories of experiences before the age of four may well exist, but in a form that no longer allows the individual to access them. This may be due to differences in the way in which young children and adults encode their memories. Once a child develops an adult's form of encoding, the early experiences are lost.

Aging and memory

Everyone experiences memory lapses, failure, and errors, but in old people they tend to be automatically attributed to the effects of aging rather than just to normal variations between individuals, with aging being but an incidental factor. This important point was captured several centuries ago by the famous scholar and wit Samuel Johnson (1709–1784) when he wrote: "There is a wicked inclination in most people to suppose an old man decayed in his intellects. If a young or middle-aged man, when leaving a company, does not recollect where he laid his hat, it is nothing; but if the same inattention is discovered in an old man, people will shrug up their shoulders, and say, 'His memory is going.'"

INFANTILE AMNESIA

CASE STUDY

Very few people can remember anything before the age of about four—a phenomenon known as infantile amnesia. When people claim to remember earlier memories, it is often difficult to prove that they are genuine rather than implanted, as shown by this story from from the eminent Swiss developmental psychologist Jean Piaget (1896–1980).

"One of my first memories would date, if it were true, from my second year. I can still see, most clearly, the following scene, in which I believed until I was about fifteen. I was sitting in my pram, which my nurse was pushing in the Champs Elysées, when a man tried to kidnap me. I was held in by the strap fastened round me while my nurse bravely tried to stand between me and the thief. She received various scratches, and I can still vaguely see those on her face. Then a crowd gathered, a policeman with a short cloak and a white baton came up and the man took to his heels. I can still see the whole scene, and can even place it near the underground station. One day my parents received a letter from my former nurse saying that she had been converted to the Salvation Army. She wanted to confess her past faults, and in particular to return the watch she had been given on this occasion. She had made up the whole story, faking the scratches. I, therefore, must have heard, as a child, the account of this story, which my parents believed, and projected it into the past in the form of a visual memory."

Given the progressive increase in the average age of the population in the majority of western countries, it is important to identify which memory changes can truly be attributed to aging. However, there are some significant points to take into consideration. If we compare the memory of 20-year-olds today with 70-year-olds today, there is a whole range of different factors that could explain differences in memory performance apart from a 50-year age gap. For instance, education and health care over the life span of the 70-year-olds is likely to have been far inferior to that for the 20-year-olds. Factors like these can easily distort the outcome of studies into the effect of aging on memory.

Comparing the memory of a group of current 20-year-olds with the memory of a group of current 70-year-olds is an example of a cross-sectional experimental design. In a longitudinal study psychologists might follow the same people from the age of 20 through to 70 to see what changes in memory occur as people age. There are some advantages to this longitudinal method in that researchers are comparing memory changes occurring within the same individuals. However, it has been noted that there is a tendency for more high-functioning people to remain in a longitudinal study. In other words, the people who are getting positive feedback from participation in a longitudinal study may continue to participate, resulting in an artificially positive impression of the effects of aging. The other problem, of course, is finding a researcher who will be around long enough to conduct this kind of research and analyze the data over a 50-year time period.

Studies of aging and memory have produced some consistent findings, however. Working memory seems to remain quite efficient over the years, but tasks requiring working memory become more difficult. If people are shown a sequence of digits and asked to repeat them in reverse order, for example, older participants are less apt to do well than younger ones. But both old and young perform well when asked to repeat a sequence of digits in the same order in which they were shown.

Long-term memory performance declines significantly with age, especially in situations requiring free recall. Recognition holds up well, but it becomes more familiarity based. When recognition demands contextual memory—which is the more recollective component of recognition memory—deficits do emerge with age. This may mean that old people are more susceptible to suggestion and bias in their memory.

Implicit memory is usually tested by evaluating behavior rather than recollection of the memory experience. Results show it not only matures early in children, but also holds up well in old age.

Aging has little effect on semantic memory, which seems to improve throughout life; for example, people's vocabulary usually increases as they age.

Studies have shown that working memory does not deteriorate, but long-term memory becomes less efficient with age. This decline is usually gradual. Sometimes elderly people find it hard to remember events that happened more recently, but earlier events are very clearly remembered.

The frontal lobes seem to mature relatively late, which, as we have seen, can be linked to children's awareness of their memory abilities. Evidence also suggests that age-related memory loss arises partly because the frontal lobes deteriorate relatively early. Prospective memory (remembering to do something in the future) has been linked to the frontal brain functions.

Brain damage

One area of considerable interest to researchers is whether the changes in memory due to "normal" aging are actually signs of brain damage. For example, "mild cognitive impairment" has been defined as a category lying between normal aging and full-blown dementia (see Vol. 6, pp. 20–67). A lot of people diagnosed with mild cognitive impairment slip into full-blown dementia within five years.

Memory dysfunction is typically an early hallmark of dementia. This is particularly the case in the most common form of dementia—senile dementia of the Alzheimer type. In the early stages of the illness only memory is affected, but later on many other capacities can be impaired, such as perception, language, and executive or frontal lobe functions. Unlike people suffering from more selective forms of amnesia, Alzheimer patients appear to be deficient on tests of implicit as well as explicit memory.

The "amnesiac syndrome" is the purest example of memory impairment and involves some form of specific brain injury. Such damage usually involves two key areas of the forebrain—the hippocampus (see Vol. 2, pp. 86–109) and the diencephalon (see Vol. 2, pp. 20–39). Such patients exhibit severe anterograde amnesia and a degree of retrograde amnesia. Anterograde amnesia refers to a loss of memory for information that occurred after the brain injury, whereas retrograde amnesia refers to the loss of information occurring before the injury.

Generally, patients with amnesia have normal intelligence, language ability, and immediate memory span. It is their long-term memory that is impaired. The nature of this impairment is a matter for debate, with some theorists arguing that there is a selective loss of episodic memory, and others arguing for a wider-ranging deficit encompassing declarative memory. Explicit (or declarative) memory refers to memory for facts, events, or propositions that can be brought to mind and consciously expressed. In contrast, it is well known that amnesia has little effect on existing implicit or procedural memory. Sufferers can also form new procedural memories (that is, skills or habits that had not previously been learned), such as juggling or riding a unicycle. In other words, amnesiac patients perform normally—or very close to normally—on a wide range of implicit or procedural memory tasks whether these tasks tap into new or old skills.

To summarize, amnesiacs may be unable to learn new information over a substantial time span, although they can

> *"The advantage of a bad memory is that one enjoys several times the same good things for the first time."*
> *—Friedrich Nietzsche, 1881*

typically recite back information within their attention span; they may well retain childhood memories but find it almost impossible to acquire new ones; they may remember how to tell the time, but not know what year it is; they may readily learn new skills like typing, but then deny ever having used a keyboard. Different subtypes of amnesia have different characteristics depending on the precise location of the brain damage. It seems then that it is the "printing press" of long-term memory (located in the brain by the hippocampus or diencephalon) rather than the "library" (located in the cerebral cortex) that has been damaged in amnesiac individuals because old

THE FAMOUS CASE OF N.A.

N. A. was a much studied patient who was made amnesiac after sustaining a very specific and quite unusual brain injury: "I was working at my desk. . . . My roommate had come in [and] he had taken one of my small fencing foils off the wall and I guess he was making like Cerano de Bergerac behind me. . . . I just felt a tap on the back. . . . I swung around . . . at the same time he was making the lunge. I took it right in the left nostril, went up, and punctured the cribriform area of my brain."

Here is an excerpt from a conversation between N. A. and psychologist Wayne Wickelgren, who was introduced to N. A. in a room at the Massachusetts Institute of Technology (MIT). N. A. heard Wickelgren's name, and he said:

"Wickelgren, that's a German name isn't it?"

Wickelgren said, "No."

"Irish?"

"No."

"Scandinavian?"

"Yes, it's Scandinavian."

After another five minutes of further conversation Wickelgren left the room. Five minutes later he returned. N. A. looked at Wickelgren as if he had never seen him, and the two were introduced. Their conversation continued exactly as it had before.

N. A. retained his knowledge of language. He could understand what was said to him and respond sensibly. His short-term memory enabled him to keep track of what was being said in the conversation, but he seemed to lack the ability to retain new information over any significant period of time. That is, he lacked the ability to put new information into long-term memory. This is one of the central characteristics of amnesia.

Memory impairments rarely occur in isolation. Therefore, it is important in both clinical practice and research to carry out a range of systematic assessments of patients with memory disorders. For example, one of the most common memory impairments occurs in "Korsakoff's syndrome," which usually affects other psychological capacities in addition to memory. Therefore, it is advisable to assess other mental abilities such as perception, attention, and intelligence, as well as language and frontal lobe (or executive) functions in someone with memory loss.

Psychological damage

It is possible that not all memory disorders result from illness or injury. Some psychologists believe that some memory disorders are caused by psychological or emotional factors rather than neurological brain injury. For example, there are instances of individuals entering a dissociative state in which they seem to become partly or totally separated from their memories. An example of a dissociative state is the fugue state, when someone completely loses track of their personal identity and the memories that went with it. They are usually unaware that anything is wrong and will often adopt a new identity. The fugue only becomes apparent when the patient "comes to" days, months, or even years after the precipitating event.

Another form of dissociative state defined by some psychologists is multiple personality disorder, in which a number of personalities apparently emerge to handle different aspects of an individual's past life. This serves to protect an individual from potentially harmful memories and can be connected with crime.

An example is the 1977 Los Angeles case of the Hillside strangler. Kenneth Bianchi was charged with the rape and murder of several women; but despite strong evidence against him, he denied his guilt and claimed that he could remember nothing about the murders. Under

memories (books) are preserved in the library. Different types of amnesia have different characteristics depending on the location of the brain damage.

Loss of memory is extremely debilitating given the range of everyday activities in which it is important, and it can place great strain on caregivers. For example, it can be extremely frustrating when someone asks the same question over and over and over again because they cannot remember having asked the question or doing the task before. External aids, such as personal organizers can help, but memory is not like a muscle that can be improved using exercise machines.

ASSESSMENT TOOLS

FOCUS ON

Psychologists use a number of standard tools, called psychometric tests, to assess patients with memory impairments. The Wechsler Memory Scale (WMS) and the Wechsler Adult Intelligence Scale (WAIS) are both useful for assessing amnesiac patients. There is usually a substantial difference between the two scores, indicating that the amnesiac person has a particular impairment in memory but not in intelligence.

Current intelligence is measured using WAIS and then compared with an indicator of IQ from before the illness to see if there has been any significant decline in intelligence as a consequence of the clinical disorder.

Both the WAIS and WMS scales are periodically updated and are standardized with respect to the normal healthy population. This means that the WMS or the WAIS can be administered and the results compared against the general population (see Vol. 5, pp. 118–141). The scales have been devised so that the mean of the general population is 100, with a standard deviation of 15. Anyone scoring 85 on the WAIS is scoring one standard deviation below the mean of the general population.

However, the assessment of memory provided by the WMS is not comprehensive, and other tests, such as assessment of remote memory and recognition, should also be used. Questionnaires about memory can also yield valuable information that clinical psychometric measures do not provide. Insights into the patient's everyday difficulties may be given by the caregiver or the patient.

hypnosis another personality called Steve emerged who claimed responsibility for the rapes and murders. When removed from the hypnotic trance, Bianchi claimed to remember nothing of the conversation between Steve and the hypnotist. If two or more personalities can exist within a person, there is a legal problem of which one should be charged with the crime. In this case the ruling went against Bianchi since the court did not accept that he possessed two personalities.

At his trial psychologists pointed out that Bianchi's other personality emerged during sessions in which the hypnotist suggested to Bianchi that he would reveal another part of himself. The hypnotic effects could have been due to compliance with instructions given by the examiners allowing the suggestion that another personality could exist, and Bianchi may have seized the opportunity to confess. Furthermore, the prosecution argued that Bianchi's general knowledge of psychiatric illness and, in particular, cases of multiple personality may have provided him with a basis for convincing responses.

Because of its dramatic nature so-called multiple personality disorder has been the subject of media interest, and a number of books describing individual cases have been written. *The Three Faces of Eve* and *Primal Fear* are two examples of films based on the disorder. In *Primal Fear* a man accused of murder successfully fakes multiple personality disorder to avoid conviction for the crime.

In real life it seems that memory loss can be faked, and detection of it remains a challenge. Faking means that someone is performing at a lower level than they are capable of. This may be done consciously for financial reward or to generate increased attention from caregivers, or the motivation might be at a deeper unconscious level.

CONNECTIONS

- The Human Computer, pp. 6–23
- Attention and Information Processing, pp. 24–43
- Ancient Greek Thought: Volume 1, pp. 10–15

- Biology of the Brain: Volume 2, pp. 20–39
- Consciousness: Volume 2, pp. 110–139
- Infant Cognition: Volume 4, pp. 24–39
- Memory Development: Volume 4, pp. 78–93
- Mental Disorders: Volume 6, pp. 20–67

Language Processing

"Language is the autobiography of the human mind."

Max Muller

Language clearly distinguishes us from other animals. Because infants learn language so quickly, some psycholinguists have suggested that people are born with a predisposition to acquire language. This ability develops spontaneously along a predictable time course but requires exposure to a rich linguistic environment to reach full maturation. Over time the main focus of the study of language has moved from its philosophical meaning, through cognitive and perceptual models of language processing, to investigations of the relationship between language and the brain.

We know that recognizing speech or reading printed words is more complex than recognizing the sound of footsteps or distinguishing a picture of an apple from one of an orange. What makes language different is that it is the most powerful communication tool people possess. Through language we communicate not only ideas and feelings but also culture, ways of life, and world views. The faculty of language is common to all people, and at the same time, it makes us different from each other. For example, we have different languages, dialects, or accents. Language is the function that most clearly distinguishes us

KEY POINTS

• People are the only life-form able to produce language. Other species communicate in less complex ways. Some scientists believe chimpanzees can learn and use language in a humanlike way.
• An important feature of language is syntax, the rules governing how we combine words to generate meaning.
• Language has a building-block structure. It consists of linguistic units (morphemes), visual units (graphemes), and acoustic units (phonemes), which combine to produce words.
• There are critical stages in childhood for language exposure and production.

• Chomsky claimed that people are born with an innate ability to learn and use language: a Language Acquisition Device.
• Speech perception and reading involve a series of complex processes to translate symbols into meaning.
• Neuroimaging studies on brain-damaged patients have enabled scientists to relate areas of the left hemisphere of the brain to language processing.
• Linguistic determinism, the belief that language shapes and limits the way we think, is the central point of the Sapir–Whorf hypothesis. A diluted version of this theory is accepted today.

A group of Moroccan men talking to each other. Although people speak different languages throughout the world, the ability to communicate in this way distinguishes people from all other animals. Babies acquire language very quickly. This has led some psychologists to believe we are born with the ability to acquire language.

WHAT IS LANGUAGE?

There is not one single definition of language. Definitions vary across fields such as psychology, cognitive science, linguistics, and philosophy. They also change over time. Here are a few examples:

"Language is a purely human and noninstinctive method of communicating ideas, emotions, and desires by means of voluntarily produced symbols"
—Edward Sapir, 1921

"A language is a set of (finite or infinite) sentences. Each is finite in length and constructed out of a finite set of elements"
—Noam Chomsky, 1957

"Language is a means of communicating, generally through spoken sounds, that express specific meanings, and are arranged according to rules"
—Papalia and Wendkos Olds, 1985

"Language is an organized system of symbols with meanings that are shared, and are used to communicate"
—Lyle E. Bourne and Nancy Felipe Russo, 1998

Despite their disparity, these definitions agree that language involves a system of symbols organized according to rules to create a message that has a common meaning for the users and the recipients.

---

from animals. Although animals do have communication systems, they are far less complex than human language.

Language in nonhuman species
Many nonhuman species possess powerful ways of communicating information within their group. Insects, for example, release chemicals called pheromones that allow them to communicate with other members of the same species. Honeybees also use body language to communicate.

They perform complex dances when returning to the hive to let other bees know where they found a new source of food and how much of it there is. Researchers have shown that bee dances are made of distinct patterns and that they can be combined in various ways to convey a wide variety of messages.

One of the most intriguing animal languages is that used by chimpanzees. Although attempts to teach chimps vocal communication have failed because they

Communication systems used by other animals are far less complex than human language. These ants release chemicals, leaving trails that act as messages for other members of the same species. They communicate on a basic level and could not convey ideas, such as how they feel about the world or philosophical concepts, as people can.

lack the necessary voice organs, teaching sign language has proved rather successful. Washoe, the first chimpanzee to be involved in language-acquisition experiments in the 1960s, learned 132 manual signs in four years. She was capable of putting several signs together to express a few meaning relations similar to young children's sentence fragments (for example, "more fruit," "Washoe sorry").

Another famous chimpanzee, Sarah, learned to associate symbols made of plastic with nouns, verbs, or relationships (for example, "is the color of"). She could arrange symbols on a magnetic board to form short sentences like "Sarah insert apple in dish." She was also able to produce new meanings by substituting one word for another in a given sentence—thus she could turn "Randy give apple Sarah" into "Randy give banana Sarah." Sometimes she used conditional connectors such as "if… then…"

Such studies prove that animals can communicate successfully. Some of them even seem to be able to learn and use language in similar, though less complex ways, than people. Does this mean that chimpanzees possess the ability to acquire

> *"Is it just an historical accident that animals have not evolved a language, or are they in principle incapable of learning one?"*
> —*Trevor Harley, 2001*

language? If so, would Ivan Pavlov's assertion that "It is nothing other than words which has made us human" imply that chimpanzees are just like us?

Many scientists do not think that the evidence of chimpanzee communication demonstrates that animals can be compared to people in terms of their linguistic ability. They point out the following limitations: First, the chimps' language behavior might be the product of sophisticated imitation rather than true

Washoe was the first chimp to take part in language-acquisition experiments in the 1960s. She learned 132 manual signs in four years and was capable of constructing simple sentences. It is debatable whether or not these experiments provide evidence that chimpanzees are capable of learning language in the same way as people. They could combine words correctly by chance.

linguistic processing. Second, chimps do not develop language spontaneously, and when taught, they do not show a great creativity in their productions. Third, they learn slowly, need careful training, and are inflexible with respect to the way in which they give responses.

The debate on chimpanzee language is far from over. Many people still believe that chimpanzees can learn a humanlike language and that the difference between people and chimpanzees is simply a matter of degree. In this view chimpanzees can learn language, but not as well as people—they are able to achieve the comprehension skills of two-and-a-half-year-old children. The key argument is that chimpanzees sometimes show evidence of combining signs according to specific rules of ordering, for example, "banana is behind orange" as opposed to "orange is behind banana." Whether chimpanzees can combine words adequately in a systematic way, or whether they do so only once in a while by chance is not clear. However, this introduces a critical concept in defining language—the way in which we combine words.

Syntax

Research on animal language suggests that the most important feature of language is the way that words work together. For example, in English we can combine the words "Mary," "Paul," and "pushes" in two different ways with different meanings: "Mary pushes Paul" and "Paul pushes

> *"Any language is necessarily a finite system applied with different degrees of creativity to an infinite variety of situations, and most of the words and phrases we use are 'prefabricated' in the sense that we don't coin new ones every time we speak."*
> —David Lodge, 1980

Mary." They contain the same words, but what makes them different is the word order. The associations between a specific word order and a meaning are governed by rules. There are a limited number of rules for each language. The rules that govern how words are assembled into well-formed structures are termed syntax.

With each rule we can create an infinite number of sentences by simply replacing the words in a sentence with other words (for example, "John pushes Bill," "Bill watches Mary"). Being able to generate infinite different meanings from a limited number of rules applied to a limited number of words makes language unique.

So, what do we know when we know language? Just as a communication system is termed a language if it is structured around syntactical rules, in order to "know language," or possess the language faculty, we learn and use these syntactical rules. As an illustration, if we are justifiably to claim that we know a language, we must be able to comprehend: (1) the difference between "Cats like birds" and "Birds like cats"; (2) the equivalence between "The cat catches the fish" and "The fish is caught by the cat"; and (3) the meaning of "The woman who saw the officer arrest the robber who stole the bag that belonged to the student pulled her curtains."

The structure of language

Sentences have a critical role in language because they allow us to express whole ideas and thoughts. They convey meaningful data, otherwise known as

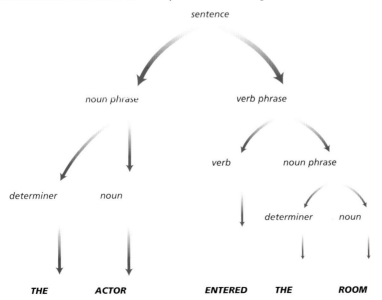

A syntactic structure tree applied to the sentence "The actor entered the room." The whole unit is a sentence. Within that the noun phrases are "The actor" and the "the room," and the verb phrase is "entered the room." The sentence can be further broken down into individual words that are either determiners such as "a," "an," or "the," nouns such as "actor," and verbs used to describe actions.

NOAM CHOMSKY: PREDISPOSED TO LEARN LANGUAGE

FOCUS ON

One of the most most influential advocates of the importance of syntax in language is Noam Chomsky. Chomsky claimed that verbal communication is so complex, and yet learned so easily by children, that there must be something special about it. In his view the unique feature that people possess is an innate ability to learn and use syntax. People are born with the predisposition to understand and use rule-based communication. One of the reasons why we should believe this theory is that the linguistic environment to which children are exposed in their early years is simply not rich enough for them to learn the complexities of language. The sentences they hear are often incomplete and sometimes incorrect; most importantly, children hear too few examples of each syntactical structure to be able to generalize on their own. Chomsky says that we are born with some sort of Language Acquisition Device, or an inbuilt Universal Grammar, which gives us a headstart when learning a language. Chimpanzees and other nonhuman animals probably do not possess such inbuilt capacity.

semantic information. Sentences are made of words organized in a way that is defined by syntactic rules. Words themselves are composed of morphemes. A morpheme is the smallest linguistic unit that conveys meaning. For example, the word "blueish" is made of two morphemes: "blue" and "ish." Many words are made of only one morpheme (for example, "tree," "person"). We also follow rules to combine morphemes into words. For example, if you attach the morpheme "un-" to the beginning of a verb, it means that you are undoing or reverting the action specified by the verb (for example, "untie," "unleash").

Phonemes are the speech sounds that words are made of. Each phoneme is represented by a conventional symbol. For example, the word "bat" is made of three phonemes: /b/, /æ/, and /t/. The only difference between the words "bat" and "pat" is the initial phoneme (/b/ versus /p/). Each language has a different set of phonemes. Some phonemes are common to many languages (such as, /b/, /p/, /t/), while others are specific to only a few (such as the click sounds of the Khoisan languages spoken in southern Africa). Phoneme inventories can contain as few as 11 phonemes (for example, in Rotokas, an Indo-Pacific language) or as many as 141 (in !Xu, a Khoisan language).

English contains about 40 phonemes. Although we can represent a word by

a string of phonemes (such as, /kritik/ for the word "critic"), it is customary to group phonemes into syllables (such as, /kri·tik/). A syllable is a speech element bigger than a phoneme consisting of vowels, consonants, or a combination of both. Each syllable corresponds to a specific articulatory gesture in which an increase in air pressure is released from the lungs as a chest pulse. The vowel is the nucleus of the syllable. Syllables can contain up to three consonants before the nucleus (as in "string") and five after the nucleus (as in "strengths"). Syllables are important in language processing because they probably play a central role in speech production and perception.

There are rules about how phonemes should follow each other within words. They are known as phonotactic rules. For instance, English words can end but not begin with the "ng" sound found in "sing." Similarly, /b/ cannot follow /p/ at the beginning of a word, for example, "pbant" is illegal. These rules about phonemes differ from one language to another.

A visual representation of the speaking voice or a speech waveform that is produced by computer. The vibrations of the voice cause changes in air pressure that are recorded. Each phoneme, or linguistic unit, is represented by a different pattern.

A radio announcer talking into a microphone. The words he speaks consist of phonemes, or speech sounds. The rules governing how phonemes are used are called phonotactic rules. Sentences and words can be broken down into morphemes—a morpheme is the smallest meaningful linguistic unit.

Language is more than just phonemes, syllables, words, and sentences. Rhythm, intonation, and speed matter, too. Such features, termed suprasegmentals, carry a lot of meaning. The sentence "I like jello" means something different if we put the emphasis on "I" (I like jello more than my neighbor does) or "like" (I like jello as opposed to disliking it). Placing emphasis on the end of the sentence by raising its pitch can create yet another meaning, since it can signal the interrogative mode—that is, a question. An important type of information is prosody, which in this context means the melody and stress structure of speech. Modifying a word by stressing its first or the second syllable can change its meaning (for example, the noun REfill and the verb reFILL). Misstressing words, as when learning a foreign language, has a generally amusing effect and can cause misunderstanding.

Breaking down language into sentences, words, syllables, and phonemes and analyzing features such as stress and pitch are useful because they help us organize our knowledge. More importantly, this typology reflects crucial distinctions in the language-processing system. Indeed, accessing each level might require distinct perceptual and processing mechanisms (for example, perceiving phonemes and segmenting syllables) and might tap into different memory banks (such as phonemic representations, mental lexicon, syntactical knowledge). These language levels may be controlled by separate areas of the brain.

KEY TERMS

- **Morphemes**—the smallest units of speech that carry meaning, usually a whole word but can be part of a word.
- **Mental lexicon**—the total stock of words in a language that an individual knows.
- **Phonemes**—speech units that are combined to produce words, shown as a conventional symbol, for example /b/.
- **Syllable**—an element of speech larger than a phoneme consisting of a vowel, or nucleus, and one or more consonants, or a combination of vowels and consonants.
- **Prosody**—the rhythm and stress or intonation of spoken language.
- **Syntax**—the rules governing how we combine words enabling us to generate well-formed meanings.
- **Grammar**—the system of rules defining the structure of language, for example, inflection and syntax.
- **Phonology**—the science or description of speech sounds.
- **Linguistic faculty**—the ability to produce speech and understand language.

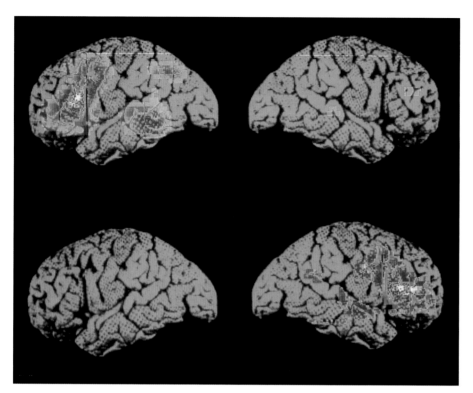

A scan of the areas of the brain active in word recognition with a right-handed person at the top and a left-handed person at the bottom. The people are thinking of verbs related to nouns that they have heard. Brain activity, measured as blood flow, is colored red and yellow.

Language and the brain

Every human perceptual, mental, and motor (physical) function is processed by the brain. But is language processing distributed throughout the brain, or is it localized in a specific area? Will damage to one part of the brain affect the whole language function, or is it possible to sustain serious head injuries and remain linguistically capable as long as the damage is not to a specific area?

Scientific knowledge of the relationship between language and the brain comes from two sources: neuropsychological studies of people with brain injury who show language impairments, and brain-imaging studies, in which brain activity in healthy individuals is monitored while they are engaged in language processing. Franz Gall was the first scientist to associate areas of the brain with specific functions. His assumption was proved correct, but he attributed the wrong areas of the brain to different cognitive functions (*see* Vol. 1, pp. 30–39).

Aphasia is the most common language disorder caused by brain damage. The first cases of aphasia were observed by pathologist Paul Broca. Nonfluent aphasia is a type of aphasia characterized by slow, laborious speech that is not fluent (effortless). It is typically caused by brain damage (from, for example, a cerebrovascular accident, tumor, hemorrhage, or penetrating head injuries) in a specific region of the brain. This region in the motor association cortex in the left frontal lobe is now known as Broca's area (*see* Vol. 1, pp. 90–95). About a quarter of all penetrating head injuries lead to aphasia. The incidence of this language disorder is about 1 in 200, with males particularly at risk. About a quarter of all patients recover within three months, while another quarter remain severely affected years later.

Lesions farther back from Broca's area have a different effect on speech. Damage to association areas in the left temporal (front) and parietal (middle) lobes generally causes receptive aphasia or Wernicke's aphasia, a condition named after German neurologist Carl Wernicke (1848–1904). This condition is characterized by serious difficulty understanding speech, while speech production remains fairly fluent. Thus, contrary to nonfluent aphasics, receptive aphasics do not understand when they are spoken to, but they answer anyway— in a voluble and often irrelevant manner.

Scientists have now found many other language impairments associated with certain brain areas (*see* Vol. 2, pp. 20–39). For example, a condition called conduction aphasia is characterized by a poor ability to repeat words (for example, saying "pubble" for "bubble") despite relatively good comprehension. This impediment is generally caused by a lesion (injury) in the arcuate fasciculus, which connects Broca's area with Wernicke's area (*see* Vol. 1, pp. 118–125).

Some aphasics suffer from a condition known as agrammatism. These patients are poor at sentence construction, leaving out function words (for example, "Peter come…night") and say words in the wrong order. Similarly, some patients are affected by neologistic jargon aphasia. Subsequent to a lesion in Wernicke's area, these patients have difficulty retrieving the words they intend to say and replace them with made-up words (for example, "stringt" for "stream" or "orstrum" for "saucepan," "stroe" for "stool"). The syntactical structure of their sentences is, however, generally correct.

Not all lesions in the so-called language areas lead to a language impairment. Conversely, language impairments can sometimes originate from "nonlanguage" areas. On the whole, however, neuropsychological studies strongly support the view that the language faculty is localized in particular parts of the brain rather than distributed throughout it. Furthermore, the existence of selective linguistic deficits, such as agrammatism or neologistic jargon aphasia, which result from localized brain damages, suggests

that some specific linguistic functions may have their own brain location. This is generally accepted by scientists today.

Neuroimaging studies
Neuroimaging (brain imaging) enables us to see pictures of the living brain. Like neuropsychological studies, neuroimaging indicates that the left hemisphere participates in linguistic tasks more actively than the right hemisphere. Moreover, neuroimaging indicates that distinct brain regions are activated during phonological, prosodic, syntactical, and semantic processing. However, a problem is that the region apparently activated by a specific type of language processing can vary from one study to another. This could be because not all studies use the same stimuli or pose the same task. Scientists tend to say that each study highlights a different aspect of processing in a specific condition. Therefore the "big picture" has to emerge from a large number of investigations considered as a whole, which has yet to happen.

In sum, it would appear that if there is such a thing as a language device in the brain, it is probably located in the left hemisphere, and only people possess it. Nevertheless, it is unlikely that specific language abilities are controlled by brain areas entirely independently of each other and dedicated to one task alone. There is a considerable overlap in brain activity across linguistic tasks, and this overlap varies from one person to another and from one type of stimulus to another.

LANGUAGE COMPREHENSION
Understanding spoken language is fast and automatic. Every day we hear thousands of words and sentences, and usually make sense of them immediately. However, as simple and effortless as it may seem, recognizing speech involves a great deal of knowledge about sounds, words, and grammatical rules, together with fine-tuned hearing and processing skills. Language processing may be described at four levels: perceptual, lexical, sentential,

and discourse. Sentential processing involves the syntax or construction of language and the semantics or imposing meaning on phonemes. Even though these levels feed back to each other extremely quickly, creating interactive processing, they are best described separately.

Speech perception

The entire act of comprehending speech begins with the perception of air pressure changes (the acoustic signal) and ends with the total integration of the message. At the start of language processing our perceptual system has to interpret the acoustic signal as a string of phonemes. But mapping the acoustic signal onto the 40 or so English phonemes is more complicated than it seems. The listener must deal with the fact that phonemes do not have their own "acoustic signature." For example, the phoneme /s/ is acoustically different in "sue" and "see" because, due to the following vowel, our lips are rounded in the case of "sue" and stretched in the case of "see." This effect is one of coarticulation, or the joining together of sounds. This difference is reflected in the acoustic signal. Thus the /s/ phoneme does not have one but many acoustic signatures.

This contrast between the acoustic signal and the phonemes forces our perceptual system to evaluate every bit of the single phoneme compared with the surrounding phonemes. That is, we need to take account of how phonemes are coarticulated or combined before we can decide which phoneme we are hearing. The fact that we can nevertheless deal with such acoustic differences in the signal has led some scientists to claim that there must be something special about the way we perceive speech as opposed to other sounds (such as music). People must be equipped with a special device that solves speech perception problems by quickly computing how sounds are coarticulated. We can perceive speech because we know how to produce it. This bold hypothesis was expressed in the motor theory of

GARDEN-PATH SENTENCES

CASE STUDY

Garden-path sentences are ones that look as if they are grammatically incorrect and can be misinterpreted by the reader, but are, in fact, correct, if poorly phrased. That is because the syntax is ambiguous and misleading to readers, or as the saying goes, "leads them up the garden path." Garden-path sentences enable psychologists to formulate theories about how we comprehend and process sentences (see p.123). Here are some examples:

The man who hunts ducks out on weekends.
The cotton clothing is usually made of grows in Mississippi.
I kissed Joan and Mary laughed.
Fat people eat accumulates.
She told me a little white lie will come back to haunt me.
That Jill is never here hurts.
The man who whistles tunes pianos.
We painted the wall with cracks.
I convinced her children are noisy.

speech perception devised by Alvin Liberman and colleagues at the Haskins Laboratory in New York and New Haven during fifty years of research that started in the 1950s.

Lexical access

Once the acoustic signal has been interpreted as a string of phonemes, lexical access can begin. Lexical access is the process of matching a string of phonemes to various possible words. Unfortunately, in actual speech there are few clear pauses between words. The speech acoustic signal is said to be continuous. So in theory we can (mis)perceive the word "lettuce" in "let us" and "decay" in "bloody cable." That is why lexical access must operate along with a process known as word segmentation. Research shows that listeners use different types of information to locate word boundaries in the signal. They include sense, pronunciation, stress, and pauses.

In truth, it is unlikely that on hearing "bloody cable" we will consider the word "decay" for very long because this interpretation generates two nonsense words, "bloo" and "ble." Generally, we prefer segmentation solutions that yield real words and meaningful sentences. It is because we know the words "bloody" and "cable" that we are able to correctly segment them from the input.

Some phonemes are pronounced slightly differently when they begin or end a word (listen to the difference between "gray chip" and "great ship"). Our perceptual system is sensitive to these differences and interprets them as cues for the boundaries between words.

> *"The structure of every sentence is a lesson in logic."*
> —*John Stuart Mill, 1843*

In English far fewer words begin with /z/ (as in "zero") than with /k/ or /s/. Similarly, most English words begin with a stressed syllable (such as, "painter," "table"). These types of regularity—there are many others—influence how we segment the acoustic signal. For instance, we tend to perceive strong syllables as the beginning of new words (sometimes even making segmentation mistakes, like perceiving "a tension" instead of "attention"). If all goes well at the segmentation stage, the words making up the acoustic signal will be recognized.

Next, the listener needs to make sense of the words' individual meanings in the context of the sentence. A crucial step in sentence comprehension is parsing. Parsing involves taking account of word order and other information to decide which word is the subject of the sentence, which is the object, and so on. It also involves assigning each word its appropriate grammatical category (that is, noun, verb, adjective, adverb). This is the stage at which we become aware of the difference between "The dog chases the cat" and "The cat chases the dog." Using our knowledge of syntactical rules will usually do the job. But some sentences

remain ambiguous even after the word order has been properly figured out. For instance, in "Proud parents and children joined in for a song" it is not clear whether only parents or both parents and children are proud. Prosodic cues, such as intonation, stress, and timing, might help. If only parents are proud, there will probably be a short pause after "parents," with "parents" said *ritardando* (slowing down), and the stressed, initial syllable in "children" receiving higher pitch.

When we hear the beginning of a sentence, we usually do not know what word is coming next. Similarly, at the end of a sentence we cannot go back in time and hear the initial words again. The sequential nature of speech has important consequences for the time course of how we process (understand) sentences. Imagine hearing the sentence: "The horse raced past the barn fell." When we hear "fell," we realize that the initial syntactical structure we built was incorrect (that is interpreting "raced" as part of the verb phrase instead of the subject noun phrase). We then have to reinterpret the sentence, parsing "raced" as a passive participle, as in "The horse, which was raced past the barn, fell." Reparsing garden-path sentences, as they are called, can sometimes take an extra half second.

Discourse processing

When sentences are assembled into discourse (or a logical sequence of events), they create rich messages that contain several major ideas. However, our memory capacity does not allow us to remember all the words of the discourse. Instead, we can extract only key words and ideas. How we do this is the research topic of discourse-processing specialists.

One outdated idea is that the flow of information processing is entirely bottom-up. In this view all of the words are extracted, and the meaning of each is given equal weight. The problem with this hypothesis is that it does not explain why we can sometimes anticipate words in sentences. For example, when we hear

SPEECH RECOGNITION BY MACHINES

FOCUS ON

For decades science-fiction writers have envisioned a world in which people use speech to communicate with machines. Today this is becoming a reality with speech-based interfaces beginning to emerge. We can now buy speech-recognition software from computer stores and install it on our personal computers. The most common languages implemented on speech-recognition software are American English, Spanish, and Mandarin Chinese. Speech-recognition software should have at least two of the following capabilities:

Talker-generality: To be useful to more than one user, the software should not be restricted to a single voice. Instead, it should be able to recognize speech spoken by anyone regardless of features of the person's speech such as accent, delivery speed, age, and sex.

Domain-generality: Current software is often limited to a specific domain of expertise, for example, weather forecasts, flight schedules, or medical diagnosis. Versatility requires that larger vocabularies be recognized as well.

Speech segmentation: Speech-recognition machines should be able to recognize natural speech, which includes very few clear markers of word boundaries (for example, pauses). One easy way to overcome this problem is to ask speakers to pause after every word. A better way is to improve software so that it can segment the continuous speech input into words as part of its recognition routine.

"Traffic is not bad in England, but what confuses the American visitor is driving on the . . . " we probably anticipate the word "left" rather than "right" or "sidewalk." There is a strong top-down element of discourse processing in which our knowledge of the language, of the world, and of the topic helps fill in gaps.

In the 1990s the psychologist Walter Kintsch proposed a discourse-processing theory that first involves condensing the story to a few propositions such as "It's six o'clock," "The lady needs bread," "She goes to the bakery," "The bakery is on a popular street," "The lady has an argument with the baker," and so on. The propositions are stored in short-term memory and then completed by top-down information retrieved from long-term memory. For example, we know that stores on popular streets stay open late, and that the lady is short-tempered, so we are not surprised that she had an argument with the baker, and so on. In the end, the integration of

A business meeting. There are different psychological theories about how people process speech, and what the impact of modern technology is on comprehension. An important part of understanding language is our prior knowledge of how it works and of the topic being talked about.

symbols as letters, group them into words, look them up in their mental lexicon, and access their meaning. Further processes involve using syntactical rules to make sense of sentences and draw inferences from long-term memory to comprehend the text as a whole. Many of the higher-level processes (such as syntactical processing) are common to both spoken and written language recognition. However, the two activities also differ in important ways.

The major difference is how the information reaches our senses. While the auditory signal is transitory (sounds come and go, a feature known as rapid fading) and consequently beyond a listener's control, written words remain visible on paper as long as necessary. This difference has consequences for the type of perceptual mechanisms used in reading. For example, our eyes can jump back to earlier words if needed (*see* box below).

Another fundamental difference is that speech has been with us for at least 30,000 years. In contrast, the oldest written artifacts are only 6,000 years old. Similarly, speech comprehension and production

This child learning to read is not aware of the complex processes involved, even at a very basic level of reading ability.

propositions (bottom-up) and inferences drawn from long-term memory (top-down) results in a streamlined representation of the discourse in which most of the details have been lost.

Reading
Like speech comprehension, reading involves a series of well-orchestrated processes. Readers must recognize written

---

HOW OUR EYES SCAN THE TEXT

FOCUS ON

As we read, it seems to us that our eyes are moving smoothly across sentences from left to right, identifying one word at a time. However, eye-movement research reveals a totally different picture. Our eyes move in saccades, which are rapid jumps from one location of the text to another a couple of syllables away. Each saccade lasts for about 15 milliseconds (ms, or thousandths of a second). No reading takes place during saccades. After each saccade there is a period of relative stability, known as fixation, during which the text is taken in. The duration of a fixation ranges from 100 to 400 ms in skilled readers, but can be well beyond 500 ms in poorer readers.

Fixations are not random. They tend to fall on content words (nouns, verbs, adjectives) rather than on function words (articles, conjunctions, prepositions) and on long words rather than short ones. This selectivity is guided by efficiency since long content words generally contain more

information. The fact that our fixations do not fall on every part of a sentence does not mean that we "skip" some information. Indeed, each fixation has a perceptual span (that is, the total field of view) of 3 or 4 letters on the left of the fixation point and about 15 letters on the right. So, the whole of a sentence ends up being covered.

Written sentence processing is mostly sequential, with our gaze sweeping across a sentence from left to right. However, such a strategy fails in cases of garden-path sentences (*see* pp. 122–123). In these cases our eyes need to move backward through the text, making a right-to-left saccade, which is known as a regression. Regressions constitute about 15 percent of all saccades. They are an indication that the reader has misperceived or misunderstood some portion of the text and needs to reanalyze it. The percentage of regressions is greater in poor readers than in skilled readers.

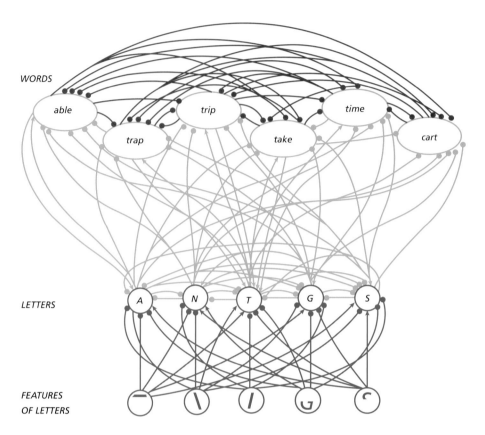

James McClelland and David Rumelhart's interactive activation network of word recognition shows the three levels of word recognition: features, letters, and words. These three levels are a two-way process, so as the person recognizes the word, that influences their recognition of features and letters.

WORDS

able trip time
trap take cart

LETTERS

A N T G S

FEATURES OF LETTERS

come naturally to the young learner, while reading and writing are the result of long, formal, and effortful training. Finally, unlike speech, written sentences have clear boundaries between words. Written words are separated by blank spaces, while, as we saw before, boundaries between spoken words are blurred by coarticulation. So the problem of word segmentation, which is so critical in speech processing, is virtually absent in reading.

Written word recognition
A great deal of research on reading is carried out using single words presented in isolation. There are three levels involved in word recognition: The feature level is the simple physical attributes of letters, for example, "k" is made of one vertical bar and two diagonal bars; the letter level; and the word level. Although it might be thought that feature identification should precede letter identification, and letter

identification should precede word recognition, this is not always the case. If readers are presented with a string of letters briefly flashed on a computer monitor and later asked which of two letters (for example, "d" or "k") ended the string, they are more accurate when the string is a word (such as, "work") than a nonword (such as, "owrk"). This result is known as the word superiority effect: Word knowledge makes letter identification easier. Therefore the connections between the three levels go both ways, bottom-up and top-down, which is known as interactive activation.

Interactive activation among the three representation levels (features, letters, and words) is found in many models of written word recognition. James McClelland and David Rumelhart's 1981 model has bottom-up connections (from features to letters to words) as well as top-down connections (from words to letters to features). Top-down connections are crucial in explaining the word superiority effect. Indeed, with brief presentation of the word "work" the unit corresponding to "work" at the word level becomes activated. In turn, this unit activates the letter units "w," "o," "r," and "k" at the letter level via bottom-up connections from the word level. The perception of the letter "k" is therefore reinforced. The same top-down facilitation applies to every-day situations as well, such as deciphering unfamiliar handwriting or reading a street sign as we quickly drive past it.

Reading by eye or by ear

As we gaze over a text, we cannot help "sounding" out the words we read. Often we even recognize the inner voice as being our own. The merging of the auditory and the visual language systems is not surprising given that written words are roughly a transcription of speech.

Max Coltheart's dual-route model of reading shows another theory of word recognition. The direct route is visual, and the phonological route involves reading aloud or by ear.

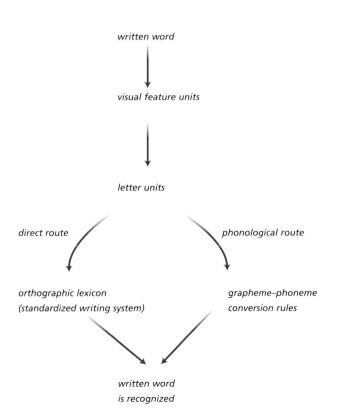

written word

visual feature units

letter units

direct route phonological route

orthographic lexicon
(standardized writing system)

grapheme–phoneme
conversion rules

written word
is recognized

Moreover, because reading is a late appearance in both human evolution and child development, some of its mechanisms could have "piggy-backed" those of speech recognition.

However, one theory argues that reading is exclusively visual: We read by eye. Here a process of visual analysis identifies letters and assigns them to a graphic code. These letters are called graphemes and are the smallest basic unit of a writing system. A grapheme is a unit of one or more letters that represents one phoneme. The whole visual pattern is then recognized as a word in the mental lexicon. Because the reading-by-eye theory does not involve any phonology, it is better at explaining why we do not confuse single-syllable words such as "two" and "too" when we read. Each word is treated as a different token (almost like an object) regardless of its phonological similarity to other words. This theory makes it easier to understand how some people can read at very rapid speeds. If we had to sound out every word, we could never speed-read. In contrast, visual processing allows larger chunks of letters and words to be taken in at once.

However, there is also evidence for an automatic grapheme-to-phoneme conversion during reading—in other words, reading by ear. Children learn speech before they learn to read. Therefore the obvious way to learn how to read is to link graphemes to phonemes we already know (for example, the letter "l" is pronounced /l/, "ph" is pronounced /f/). When people read difficult materials, they often move their lips as if accessing phonology helps them recognize words. Such phonological conversion is crucial when we encounter new words or pseudowords (false words) and have to read them out loud. Finally, reading by ear might be more efficient. That is, the phonological approach to reading is more economical in terms of the number of processes required and memory banks involved. For example, if we convert our graphemes into phonemes, we do not

127

INTRAUTERO SPEECH PERCEPTION

The auditory system begins functioning during the last trimester of gestation, and language development can begin before an infant is even born. However, not every sound frequency reaches the ear of the fetus. Low-frequency sounds (bass sounds) are best transmitted through the mother's uterine wall. The sound quality is similar to what you would hear if you put your ear against a wall and listen to the neighbors talking. Although this impoverished input is not sufficient to learn phonemes and words, it familiarizes infants with the intonation of their mother's voice and with the overall prosody (rhythm) of the language. Recent studies even show that infants exposed to a specific piece of music repeatedly during the mother's pregnancy exhibit a preference for that piece of music for up to a full year after birth (*see* Vol. 4, pp. 40–57).

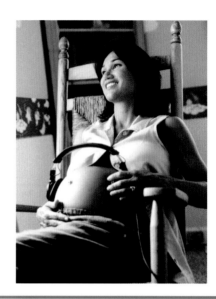

A fetus can hear some sounds in the womb.

need a separate way of writing them. The phonological representations generated by the conversion route would connect directly into the phonological lexicon used for spoken-word recognition. Both approaches seem plausible, even necessary. Without direct visual mapping we could never learn that the letters "au" are pronounced differently in "cause" and "gauge." Without phonemic conversion we could never learn new words. To overcome the problem, psychologists assume that we read and pronounce written words by eye and by ear. In such dual-route models (*see* diagram p. 127) we decode the written input using two mechanisms together: the direct route, which maps the input to lexical representations by simple visual association, and the phonological route, which involves grapheme-to-phoneme conversion. Which route dominates depends on many factors, such as the type of words we are reading.

LANGUAGE ACQUISITION

Whatever their talent, motivation, or personality, children in every part of the world acquire language. Children raised by English-speaking parents learn English as fast and as naturally as Spanish children learn Spanish. In a mere four or five years after they are born, children manage to learn the speech sounds, vocabulary, syntactical rules, and communicative skills of their environment.

One of the most intriguing questions is how children learn language so easily. Given the speed and regularity with which children do so, people often contend that humans must be born equipped to learn language. But at the same time, exposure to language through parents or siblings seems necessary as well. Indeed, children who are deprived of language exposure during their early years are rarely able to master language as fully as infants raised in a normal linguistic environment. Psychologists try to understand how much is innate (that is, language as a gift from nature) and how much is learned (that is, language as the result of nurture from the environment). Language acquisition occurs in various stages, and these stages generally follow a typical timetable that starts from the moment of birth, or possibly even before then in the womb.

The first twelve months

Despite the fact that infants rarely talk before at least eight months, familiarization with speech sounds is well on its way before that age. For example, soon after birth, if presented with a choice of English or French, American infants will tend to listen longer to English, and French infants to French. This indicates that exposure to the mother's voice during the last months of pregnancy has familiarized infants with their native language. However, they fail to distinguish between languages with similar accents and rhythms, such as English and Dutch. This more subtle type of distinction appears a few months later.

At the phonemic level young infants show impressive perceptual capacities as well. For example, they can discriminate critical phonetic contrasts, such as that between /ba/ and /pa/. Although this does not seem complicated to adult language users, it is quite an accomplishment given how similar these two syllables sound. Infants can also distinguish some nonnative sounds, that is, sounds that are not encountered in their own language.

For instance, in Japanese the difference between /l/ and /r/ does not exist. As a consequence, adult Japanese speakers have difficulty in distinguishing between these two sounds (for example, they do not clearly distinguish "late" from "rate"). However, very young Japanese infants do not have this problem. The converse is true as well: English-learning infants are capable of discriminating some foreign phonetic contrasts that their own parents cannot detect.

Yet no matter how good they are at perceiving fine speech contrasts and remembering them, infants younger than six months do not generally understand words. Except for a few very frequent words such as their own first name and "mommy" and "daddy," the semantic level of their linguistic system is still relatively undeveloped.

The hypersensitivity to phonetic contrasts that characterizes the first six months disappears between six months and a year, during which period infants' perceptual capacities narrow down to only those phonetic contrasts that are relevant to their own language. This is a time of

This Japanese infant was born with the ability to recognize the difference between /l/ and /r/. In later life she will be unable to do so as easily because she will not encounter this difference in her native language.

MEASURING INFANT SPEECH RECOGNITION

Infants cannot use language to answer questions such as "Did you hear /ra/ or /la/?" and they cannot push buttons labeled "yes" and "no." So, investigators have developed indirect methods of answering their research questions. Among the most informative methods used with preverbal infants are the high-amplitude sucking procedure and the head-turn preference procedure.

The high-amplitude sucking procedure is used with young infants (birth to about four months). The objective is to determine if infants change their sucking behavior in response to a change in speech stimuli. Sucking behavior is estimated by infants' sucking rate on a pacifier connected to a recording device. If infants can perceive the difference between, say, /ra/ and /la/, their sucking rate should increase abruptly when repetitions of /ra/ syllables have become boring and are suddenly replaced by repetitions of /la/ syllables because of interest in the "new" stimulus. If they cannot perceive the difference between the two stimuli, there should be no noticeable difference in sucking rate when the stimulus shifts.

The head-turn preference procedure is appropriate with infants between 4 and 12 months (and sometimes up to 18 months). The experimenter measures the amount of time an infant listens to speech stimuli (for example, words containing the same vowel) presented over a loudspeaker. Listening time is estimated by how long infants fixate on (turns their heads toward) the source of the speech. The fixation time is taken as an indication of the infant's interest in the stimulus, but the word is not repeated often enough to become boring. Infants tend to listen longer to familiar words, such as "daddy," than to unfamiliar ones, such as "caddy." They also listen for longer to stories containing words they were already familiar with than ones with new words.

perceptual attuning. Put another way, infants of that age start developing what is commonly referred to as a "mother tongue"—that is when Japanese infants cease to be able to perceive the difference between /r/ and /l/.

Infants also begin to use complex strategies to segment words from fluent speech. Among them statistical regularities in the speech input prove a powerful tool. Statistical regularities come from the fact that some sounds tend to occur next to each other more often than others. For example, because "dog" is a word, the sounds /d/, /o/, and /g/ are heard next to each other more often than, say, the sounds /p/, /o/, and /g/, because "pog" is not a word. Therefore, after months of exposure to speech infants might tend to infer that /d/ /o/ /g/ go together and decide to store the sequence as a new word in their mental lexicon.

Of course, statistical regularities also apply to the association between a sound pattern (for example, /dog/) and the presence of a certain thing (for example, a fluffy animal running around the cradle), event, or mood. Most of the words that

children understand at that age are simple nouns, such as "duck," "spoon," or "dog," but infants also respond to some verbs such as "give" and "push," and even to short expressions, such as "peekaboo."

Although actual talking emerges mostly during the second year of life, babbling is often present before one year—the first vowel is /a/, the first consonants /p/ and /b/. Infants may even produce a few words as early as eight months. These words are rarely understandable by anyone but the parents and are invariably one syllable long. In addition to "no" the early vocabulary tends to refer to concrete things that can move around ("ball" and "car") rather than immobile objects ("ceiling") or internal mental states (such as words related to pain, fear, or joy).

Age one and beyond
During the second year of life the infant's language system grows rapidly in complexity and efficiency. Speech perception capacities are now better attuned to segmenting speech and discovering new words in the input. Syntax is falling in place as well, as infants

start grasping important notions, such as the past tense of verbs and the composite nature of sentences.

Most noticeable is the child's growing verbal activity. However, most of the sentences they produce are only one word long. This one-word stage is ambiguous because children might use a single word to mean different things. For example, they may use the word "ball" to mean anything that is round, anything that rolls, or any toy. Likewise, they may assign a word to a specific instance of that word (for example, "ball" refers only to a ball in the neighbor's backyard). This problem of appropriate syntax disappears quickly as the child is exposed to multiple examples of a word in various contexts.

An infants' second birthday usually corresponds to a dramatic acceleration in language acquisition. The child's vocabulary begins to spurt from a few dozen words at around 18 months to several thousand words by age five. This fast growth, known as lexical explosion, is fueled by the discovery of 10 words per day on average. At the same time, the one-word stage gives way to the two-word stage, a telegraphic (fragmented) style that precedes the emergence of real sentences. Children produce their first real sentences, which contain verbs and function words, as early as two and a half years. This stage is central to language acquisition because it implies that children start to have a

handle on syntactical rules. In fact, they master some of them so well that they sometimes use them inappropriately, adding, for example, the –ed suffix to all verbs in the past tense (such as "holded" for "held"). Thus from overgeneralizing word meanings the child moves on to overgeneralizing syntactical rules.

While the problem of syntactical overgeneralization is remarkably similar for children raised in different language environments, it gradually disappears as children come to realize that, alongside rules, there are exceptions to them. Their growing memory capacity allows them to store, for example, irregular verbs as individual cases, which are learned by rote. By age four or five children's language knowledge is often described as comparable to adults' in quality.

Language is so complex, but learned so quickly, that innate (inborn) factors must play a role in its acquisition. Children from any part of the world go through the same sequence of language development regardless of the amount of exposure to language (as long as there is at least some); so do children deprived of hearing or sight. This suggests there is an innate machinery for language that works despite wide variations in the environment.

However, this machinery has constraints, too. For example, there seems to be a critical period for learning a language. A critical period is one in early

---

THE AVERAGE TIME COURSE OF LANGUAGE PRODUCTION

KEY POINTS

3 months: Random vocalization, cooing, pitch modulation of vowel-like sounds

6 months: Babbling (/ba/, /pa/, and /mu/ are among the most frequently used syllables)

10–12 months: Repeat some sound sequences, occasionally produce short words

18 months: Able to say up to a few dozens words; can produce one-word sentences

24 months: Lexical explosion begins; learns about 10

words per day and can produce two-word sentences

30 months: Lexical growth continues at a rate of about one word per day; longer sentences with simple grammatical structures; many errors in speech but understands everything said by others

3 years: Able to understand simple questions

By age 6: Knows and can say between 1,000 and 10,000 words; grammatical complexity and sentence length increase; fewer speech errors occur

life when language acquisition is easy. After this period language acquisition becomes much more difficult or even impossible. According to American psycholinguist Eric Lenneberg (1921–1975), after a certain point in time some characteristics of the brain change so that nerve cell connections can no longer be modified. One of the known critical periods concerns the ability to learn the sounds of a language. This period ends at around one year of age, which means that it is more difficult to master the subtle phonetic differences between phonemes if one has not been exposed to these phonemes by age one (such as the distinction between French nasal sounds for English learners or the /r/-/l/ distinction for Japanese learners).

> *"If you cannot be the master of your language, you must be its slave. If you cannot examine your thoughts, you have no choice but to think them, however silly they may be."*
> —*Richard Mitchell, 1979*

A separate critical period extends to puberty at around 12 to 14 years of age. During this phase of development language skills can be reallocated as necessary to different parts of the brain. This property is known as neural plasticity. Learning foreign languages before puberty is also much less effortful—those who start them after this age may have accented speech or reduced fluency. Brain injuries affecting language areas can be overcome during this period but not as easily afterward.

The idea that people are born with a predisposition to learn language is supported by the observation that the linguistic input received by infants is quite poor or incomplete—termed the poverty of the input hypothesis. For instance, the speech that infants hear contains hesitations, false starts, unfinished sentences, mumbled words, and even ungrammatical forms. Moreover, children are not normally exposed to enough examples of grammatical constructions to extrapolate the correct grammar. Similarly, parents tend to correct the meaning of their child's early productions (such as "drink" rather than "eat" water) more often than they applaud their grammatical correctness (for example, "she goes" instead of "she go"). Yet, despite the poverty of the input, people still learn the subtleties of language, especially syntax, within a few years. Therefore, according to the poverty of input hypothesis, we must be born with a language-acquisition device.

Yet not everything is preprogrammed in language acquisition. The language we speak clearly depends on the environment in which we are raised. So, if there is such a thing as a language-acquisition device, it must be flexible enough to suit all languages, rather than language-specific.

Regarding syntax acquisition, some people have argued that what infants and children learn is not so much a set of rules as simple connections or associations between meanings and sounds. The difference between rules and connections is that rules are learned consciously and applied to all cases inflexibly, while connections are learned passively (unconsciously) and applied mainly to those cases that are similar to a prototype. Because learning by connections or associations has been shown to be a powerful strategy in many nonlinguistic activities, according to this theory syntax could likewise be "learned" rather than born out of an "innate" language device.

Wild children

The importance of social factors in language acquisition is illustrated most dramatically in cases of total deprivation of social interaction during the first years of life. Wild children, abandoned in forests and found alive years later, provide a demonstration of how critical exposure to

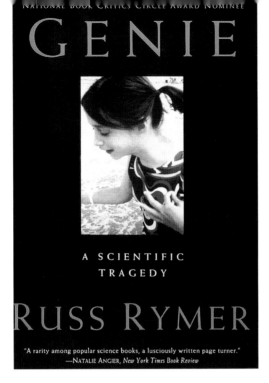

A SCIENTIFIC TRAGEDY

RUSS RYMER

"A rarity among popular science books, a lusciously written page turner."
—NATALIE ANGIER, *New York Times Book Review*

The front cover of a book documenting the life of Genie. Genie was not spoken to for the first 14 years of her life and, despite efforts to teach her to speak, never managed to use language normally. This shows that the ability to acquire language is not totally innate, and that there are critical periods for learning.

normal socialization is. Ramu, a young boy discovered in India in 1976, was apparently raised by wolves. He was found deformed, probably from lying in cramped positions in a den. He could not walk, and his favorite food was raw meat. Ramu died in February 1985 at the age of about 10. He had learned to bathe and dress himself, but he never learned to speak. Among the other 30 or so reported wild children the patterns of behavior were all very similar and animal-like. Although some of them eventually managed to speak a few words, none ever learned language to a normal level, and most had no comprehension of speech.

Unlike wild children, isolated children are individuals who were raised by people, but under extreme social and physical conditions. Genie was discovered in 1970 at the age of 14. From about 20 months she had been tied to a chair and denied normal socialization. When she was found, she had no language. In the course of her rehabilitation great efforts were made to teach her to speak. She was able to acquire some language (for example, "no more take wax," "another house have dog"), but could not use many function words (prepositions like "if" and

conjunctions like "and") and could not form elaborate sentences.

Wild children and isolated children clearly demonstrate the importance of normal social interaction during early life. If language acquisition were completely innate, language would emerge without exposure to socialization, or it could be rehabilitated easily. Moreover, the 20 months preceding Genie's isolation should have been sufficient to "trigger" her innate language-acquisition device. Yet Genie never became a normal language user.

It could also be argued that Genie did not reach linguistic maturity because, for the most part, she became exposed to language after she had reached puberty, that is, past the end of the second critical period. The importance of when we are exposed to language, as opposed to if we are exposed to it, is illustrated by another isolated child, Isabelle, who was hidden away during infancy and found when she was six. Within a year the girl had learned to speak. Her speech was virtually indistinguishable from that of the other children of her class, who had all been exposed to language for seven years. Rehabilitation was almost perfect because Isabelle was exposed to language before she reached puberty, as if she had beaten the innate language-maturation deadline. Both nature and nurture seem to influence the course of language acquisition, but neither operates in an all-or-nothing fashion. Therefore it is best to describe language acquisition as the result of an interaction between these two forces in which language is "preprogrammed" in our brains, but loosely so.

LANGUAGE AND THOUGHT

Much of our thinking—solving a problem, planning a sequence of events, analyzing the pros and cons of a decision—is accompanied by a silent inner voice that turns our thoughts into words. What if we did not have an inner voice? That is, what would happen to our thoughts if we did not have a language?

Would we be possibly be unable to think? Or would we think differently? Or would it not matter because thinking can exist without language?

The primacy of language hypothesis puts strong emphasis on the influence of language on cognition. In its extreme version it can be expressed as "I speak, therefore I think" and is best illustrated by the Sapir–Whorf hypothesis. Working in the early 1900s, Edward Sapir and his student Benjamin Lee Whorf claimed that language determines the way we think. It is because we have a word for love that we know what love feels like. This is linguistic determinism: Language determines the structure of our thoughts.

An immediate consequence of linguistic determinism is linguistic relativity. Because language shapes thinking, the language people speak makes them think differently. Taken to an extreme, if a language does not have a word for love, the speakers could not experience the feeling. More reasonably, societies with different languages develop distinct cultures because they attach different labels to objects, concepts, and feelings.

> *"We see and hear and otherwise experience very largely as we do because the language habits of our community predispose certain choices of interpretation."*
> —*Sapir and Whorf, 1929*

In *Language, Thought, and Reality*, published in 1956, Whorf illustrated this theory with examples from several languages and in particular from Hopi, a Native American language. Whorf alleged that in Hopi there are no words or grammatical constructions for the concept of time, so speakers must have a different understanding of time. This example has since been proven incorrect, but Whorf's theory remains an important illustration of the relationship between language and cultural differences. Several hypotheses on how language might impose its own "world view" on users received a great deal of attention in the past, and many researchers found the evidence compelling.

Nevertheless, the methods used by these early psychologists and anthropologists to assess language structure and thinking processes have proved unreliable. Scholars criticized the subjectivity of the investigators. The original Sapir–Whorf hypothesis no longer has many adherents today. People from different language backgrounds manage to communicate efficiently even when they do not share a common vocabulary. A language may not have a word to describe an object, but combining several other words can generally make the point (such as "baby bird" for "fledgling"). Similarly, even though Australian aboriginal languages have few words for numerals, speakers of these languages can count and calculate just as well as speakers of other languages.

Today people tend to accept a milder version of the Sapir–Whorf hypothesis in which language affects only some perception and memory (*see* box p. 135). For example, the speakers of a language with few color names may be less accurate in determining whether two colors are the same or different. Experiments have also shown that a person recalls things more easily if they correspond to readily available words. Words influence the way our perceptual and memory systems treat the outside world, but not how we think about it.

The Sapir–Whorf hypothesis, which came at a time of great popular interest in cultural differences and linguistic theories, is probably not an accurate description of how language and thought interact. Research into infant thinking shows that thought exists without language. Language and thought probably coexist with little interaction early in life and later merge into a more complex capacity, feeding into each other in an ever-changing cultural, social, and linguistic environment.

ALTERNATIVES TO THE SAPIR–WHORF HYPOTHESIS

Language might not "mold" our thinking. Here are two alternatives to the Sapir–Whorf hypothesis:

According to the independence hypothesis, language and cognition could be independent faculties, and we should be able to think just as well whether we possess the language faculty or not because language has its own module, separate from the cognitive functions. Not having an inner voice (a vocabulary and syntax) should not prevent us from planning complex events and understanding, for example, the difference between a scene in which Mary pushes John and one in which John pushes Mary. A milder version of this position, defended by Lev Semyonovich Vygotsky (1896–1934), contends that language and cognition are independent at birth but become interdependent as children grow older, with thinking progressively becoming more verbal.

The cognition hypothesis proposes that it is the development of intellectual functions that allows the emergence of language. According to Jean Piaget (1896–1980), children's intellectual development follows a sequence of well-defined stages that build on each other. Some cognitive skills are required for language to emerge. For example, Piaget claimed that a child has to attain the intellectual stage of object permanence (around nine months) to be able to represent concepts and objects with symbols and so to have access to language. Attaining the object permanence stage means that children realize that objects continue to exist even when they are removed from view. According to the cognition hypothesis, language does not fully develop in nonhuman species because they lack the intellectual capacity for its emergence.

Summary

Language is not just a series of meaningful sounds or pictures. It is organized around a finite number of syntactical rules and a finite vocabulary but has the capacity to generate an infinite number of sentences and meanings. Although some nonhuman species use elaborate communication systems, they do not possess such a powerful generative mechanism. Even when artificially taught to manipulate symbols according to combinatory rules, chimpanzees' productions remain poorer and less flexible than human language.

Language, whether spoken or written, has a building-block structure. Features (acoustic or visual) combine into phonemes or graphemes. Phonemes and graphemes themselves combine into morphemes, and morphemes into words. Syntax defines the acceptable ways in which words can be organized.

Evidence from brain-injured patients and neuroimaging studies gives an insight into the relationship between language processing and the brain. Linguistic functions are mostly localized in the temporal-frontal regions of the left hemisphere. Specific language impairments such as aphasia are usually associated with injuries or damage in distinct subareas of the brain.

Contrary to reading and writing, speech comprehension and production are learned instinctively. The development of language-specific speech perception strategies during the first year of life prepares the ground for the child's first words during the second year. Although people seem predisposed to learn language, they must be exposed to a great deal of linguistic stimulation—especially at critical stages of development before puberty—to achieve full mastery.

In the first half of the 20th century researchers supported the idea of linguistic determinism, which posits that language shapes the way that we think. However, the evidence proved unconvincing. Today, we accept a diluted version of the theory in which language sometimes biases perception and memory but does not determine the way we think.

CONNECTIONS

- Nature and Nurture: Volume 1, pp. 22–29
- Neuropsychology: Volume 1, pp. 90–95
- Psycholinguistics: Volume 1, pp. 118–125
- Infant Cognition: Volume 4, pp. 24–39
- Stages of Development: Volume 4, pp. 58–77
- Communication: Volume 5, pp. 72–93

Problem Solving

The search for correct answers

The psychology of problem solving is not just the study of our approach to questions such as might be encountered on a math test or a quiz. The subject also encompasses the more generalized reasoning processes that lead us to all kinds of everyday decision making and the way we estimate probability. How can I fix the door handle without the proper tools? How likely is this airplane to crash? Is it going to rain today? Problem solving is in this sense distinct from reasoning, which involves discernment and judgment. The study of problem solving also examines the nature of creativity.

Modern psychologists regard problem solving as a search process in which solvers use their mental faculties to find a path that leads to a goal. The route may be preplanned or found by chance; the ultimate objective may be identified from the start or stumbled on along the way.

KEY POINTS

- In humans problem solving is often a combination of trial and error and insight.
- Creativity is problem solving when there is no clear path to a solution.
- Problem-solving ability is not directly proportional to intelligence.
- Many external factors, such as functional fixity and the presentation of the data, may hinder problem solving.
- One important part of problem solving is means-end analysis (working back to the question from the required answer); another is the use of analogy.
- Logic may be helpful for solving some problems, but it is not a universal solution.
- Rational thought that stops when a "good enough" solution is reached is known as "satisficing."
- Human understanding of probability is notoriously poor.

How do people solve problems? What makes some problems harder than others? Can we improve our problem-solving ability? Can creative problem solving be examined scientifically? There are no straightforward answers to these questions, but the methods used to explore them are of great interest in themselves and cast fascinating light on the functioning of the human mind.

Trial and error

One of the simplest and most widely used methods of problem solving is trial and error. It is the process by which lots of possible solutions are tested, usually in a rather random fashion, until the right

U.S. psychologist Edward Lee Thorndike compared and contrasted the problem-solving strategies of his cats with those of humans in similar situations.

answer is found. U.S. psychologist Edward Lee Thorndike (1874–1949) studied this type of problem solving in cats. He observed that when his cats were trying to find their way out of a closed box to reach some food, they at first moved around the confined area unsystematically until finally by accident they moved the mechanism that opened the door. During subsequent attempts to escape from the same box the cats triggered the escape mechanism in a shorter time on each occasion. However, it did not seem that the cats had truly understood the solution to the problem of escaping from the box. Instead, they had simply used a trial-and-error strategy, getting a bit closer to the answer each time. The behavior of cats in such situations casts interesting light on that of humans, who are most likely to use trial and error when the way to solve a problem directly is not easily available or cannot be seen.

Insight

Trial-and-error learning differs from insight, which requires a leap of intuition for the solution to be identified. German Gestalt psychologist Wolfgang Köhler

> *"The insight learning of man operates with the aid of ideas which are free from narrow confinements."*
> —*Edward Lee Thorndike, 1930*

(1887–1967) (see Vol. 1, pp. 46–51) studied problem solving through insight by examining the ability of apes to reach bananas placed just beyond their grasp above or outside their cage. To get hold of the fruit, the apes had to stick two sticks together or move a box so that they could stand on it. It seemed that solutions to the problem would come suddenly to the apes after a period of inactivity and reflection.

Insight is sometimes regarded as a higher form of problem solving than trial

Cats can solve problems, but only through trial and error; what we call "insight" is beyond their mental capacity.

and error. In humans, however, the two methods are often complementary—in other words, the solution of most problems seems to involve a mixture of trial and error and insight. Psychologists have generally been more interested in the latter process, in which the solution seems to pop up out of nowhere. Insight seems to be particularly important in creative problem solving, in which there is no obvious route to a solution.

But insight remains easier to describe than to codify. Before looking more closely at the processes of problem solving, we will look in greater detail at the various types of problems.

Wolfgang Köhler's apes brought a form of insight to solving the problem of how to get hold of objects that were placed just beyond their reach.

FUNCTIONAL FIXITY

Problems can be divided into several categories. First are "problems of arrangement" in which various objects need to be shuffled into some other form. One example is jigsaw puzzles; another is finding solutions to anagrams, such as: "What fruit is made up of the letters ENRAOG?" Psychologist N. R. F. Maier conducted one of the classic studies of arrangement problems in 1931. He placed a person in a room containing various objects, including a pair of pliers. There were also two strings hanging from the ceiling. The problem was to find a way of tying the two pieces of string together. However, the strings were placed so far apart that it was not possible to grab one piece, hold it, and walk over to the other piece of string. The hoped for solution was to tie the pliers to the end of one string and hold the first string. The additional weight of the pliers made the string behave as a pendulum. Thus it became possible to grab hold of the two bits of string simultaneously and then tie them together. Most of the people who took part in this experiment were unable to find the correct solution.

Thumbtacks and candle

In another similar experiment carried out in 1945 the American psychologist K. Duncker gave participants a box of thumbtacks and a candle, and asked them to attach the candle to a wall in such a way that it would stay upright and burn properly. They came up with a range of contrived solutions, some of which were bizarrely excessive in their complexity. What most of them failed to figure out was that they should empty the box, pin it to the wall, and place the candle in it.

> *"When the problem-solving task is complex and requires a spectrum of perspectives, diversity increases the chances of a quality solution."*
> —*Roger N. Blakeney, 2000*

When another group of participants in the same basic experiment was first shown an empty box with the thumbtacks scattered over a table, the right idea was sown in their minds, and they found the solution to the problem more quickly.

Experiments such as these suggest that people find it hard to see how familiar objects can be used for unfamiliar purposes. The fact that pliers are used normally to pull nails out of wood can make it difficult to see what else they might be made to do; our notion of a box as a container is so firmly entrenched that we find it hard to think of any other use for it. This effect is known to psychologists as "functional fixity" or "functional fixedness."

Maier found that it was even harder for his subjects to find the correct solution to the first problem if they had recently used the pliers for their usual purpose. This suggests either that the information stored in the brain cannot reliably be accessed at the moment it is needed, or that the problem solvers have failed to make the mental connections that would have enabled them to think of the right answer.

Once we have noted how hard it can be to solve problems, we can applaud those who manage to do so. But the source of their inspiration and the manner in which they tapped it remain unknown.

At the start of a game of chess each player has 20 possible opening moves. From that point on the choices become even more numerous and complicated.

Problems of transformation

Another category is "problems of transformation," which involve changing one state into another through the application of a set of rules. For instance, some psychologists have studied various "river-crossing problems" (*see* box).

In attempting to solve problems of this type, subjects are faced with various choices. As the first step in solving the river-crossing problem, one can take the hen across the river, take the grain across the river, or take the cat across the river (three choices). Having done this, various other choices can be made. One problem-solving technique is termed the "state-space" for the problem. It is a mathematical representation of the possibilities or states for a problem. Solving the problem involves finding the shortest possible pathway through the space. Because several different choices can be made at every step, the number of possible routes to solving the problem quickly becomes very large. Indeed, for complex problems it is clear that people do not just randomly try out possibilities in the hope of hitting on the right solution. The classic example is chess. When deciding what move to make at a given point in a game, one strategy would be for a player to work out all the possible

EXPERIMENT

A RIVER-CROSSING PROBLEM

Suppose you are standing on one side of a river with a hen, a sack of corn, and a cat. You also have a boat. The task is to carry all the items over to the other side of the river. However, the boat is quite small and will carry only yourself and just one of the three items you have to transfer across the river. What makes the task difficult is that the hen cannot be left alone with the corn, or the hen will eat it. Also, the cat cannot be left alone with the hen, or the cat will chase away the hen. How can you move all the items over to the other side of the river in the shortest number of trips?

The solution is as follows. First, carry the hen to the other side of the river, then return. Next, take the corn to the other side of the river and return with the hen. Then, take the cat to the other side of the river, and leave it there with the sack of corn. Finally, return and take over the hen. Problems such as this can be made much more difficult (for example, by increasing the number of hens and cats). Another well-known similar problem is the Tower of Hanoi (*see* Vol. 1, pp. 104–117).

WATER JUG PROBLEMS

Problem 1

You have three water jugs. The largest jug, which is full of water, holds 24 pints. The second jug is empty but can hold 21 pints. The third jug is also empty but can hold three pints. Your task is to end up with 12 pints of water in the first jug, and 12 pints of water in the second jug. How can you do this, and how many moves will it take?

24 pints   21 pints   3 pints

Problem 2

You have three water jugs. The largest jug, which is full of water, holds eight pints. The second jug is empty but can hold five pints. The third jug is also empty but can hold three pints. Your task is to end up with four pints of water in the first jug, and four pints of water in the second jug. How can you do this, and how many moves will it take?

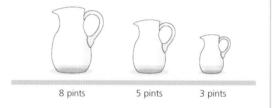

8 pints   5 pints   3 pints

consequences of each move. The thought process would be as follows: "If I make a certain move, what are all the possible moves my opponent can make next? For each of those possible moves that he or she might make, what are all the moves that I could then make?" This can carry on almost indefinitely. In chess there are so many possible moves that it would simply not be feasible to calculate all the consequences of any move that a player might make to a given point. Even if each calculation took only one second, it would take many years to examine all the

permutations and possibilities. If there were no shortcuts, the game of chess would never have been invented.

This all confirms the indispensability of insight—if humans had only trial and error at their disposal as a means of solving problems, their thought would have been unable to reach the heights it has in fact attained.

Means-end analysis

It is clear, therefore, that for complex problems we must have some strategy that prevents us from having to examine every possible path through the problem space. What might such a strategy be? One of the most widely used approaches is known as means-end analysis.

The classic example of the concept is nim, a popular game in which two players alternately remove objects from a table, the aim being to avoid having to remove the last one. There are many variant forms of nim, but it commonly involves 15 matchsticks; each player may remove between one and five matchsticks at every turn. By working backward, it is easy to see that if a player is faced with, for example, six or 12 matchsticks, it does not matter what his or her opponent does—in this situation, there can be only one winner.

In the 1950s American psychologists Allen Newell and Herbert Simon tried to formulate a generalized set of strategies that could be applied to many different problems of means-end analysis. For example, imagine the case of trying to figure out how to travel from your house in New York to a friend's house in London, England. You might have a set of rules to follow, such as these:

• If the distance to be traveled is less than one mile, walk.
• If the distance to be traveled is between one and five miles, catch a bus.
• If the distance to be traveled is between five and 100 miles, take a train.
• If the distance to be traveled is greater than 100 miles, take an airplane.

Because the distance to be traveled is

greater than 100 miles, the first rule that would be applied states "catch an airplane." However, there may be further conditions, termed enabling conditions, that need to be satisfied. In the case in point one of these conditions might be "be at the airport." You now have a new problem to solve, that of "getting to the airport." This is known as a subgoal because it is a small objective that will help you on the way to your ultimate goal of getting to London. Suppose the airport is three miles from your home. You can then apply the second rule (catch a bus) to help you get to the airport. Having gotten to the airport, you can then catch the plane to London.

If the airport in London is, say, 25 miles away from your friend's house, you can then activate the rule "catch a train for distances between 5 and 100 miles." As before, this will lead to new subgoals—in this case the subgoal of finding your way to the airport train station.

> "The computer [lets] the action taken reflect knowledge of the situation, to be sometimes this way, sometimes that, as appropriate."
> —Allen Newell, 1992

Newell and Simon showed that this kind of strategy can be successful in a wide range of applications. Yet it is not universally applicable. It is no good for the problem of the hen, the cat, and the corn, for example, because the solution requires returning the hen to the near side of the river after it has been transported to the farther bank. The point is that it is impossible to solve this problem by gradually increasing the number of items on the other side of the river. Instead, you have to go backward—away from the goal state—in order to achieve the desired result. That is what causes confusion.

Another illustration of the fact that problems can be particularly difficult if there is no smooth transition between where you start and where you need to end up is provided by the "water-jug problems" made famous by American psychologists A. S. and E. H. Luchins in 1942. Two examples are shown in the box on page 140. If you work through the problems, you will probably find the second harder than the first. That is not because it takes a greater number of moves to solve it. Rather, the second problem is harder because it requires several moves backward. It is not possible to solve the second problem simply by reducing the difference between the current state and the end state. People tend to find the second problem more difficult than the first because they are using difference-reduction strategy in an inappropriate context.

However, if the two problems are presented in reverse order, people are likely to find the "easier" problem harder than the one that is "objectively" more difficult. That is because the mind quickly becomes "set"—having once found a serviceable solution, it has to work hard to resist the temptation to apply the same formula to every new problem that reminds it of the earlier one.

Limitation of the General Problem Solver
Means-end analysis was seen originally as a problem-solving strategy that could be used in any situation. Indeed, the prototype model developed by Newell and Simon was known as the General Problem Solver (GPS). This machine was based on the assumption that human thought processes are comparable to the functioning of digital computers. However, this analogy, like so many others in the field of cognition, was good as far as it went, but did not go far enough. (For further details about the strengths and weaknesses of the GPS *see* Vol. 2, pp. 140–163.)

When psychologists examined the performance of people who are very skilled in one particular field (such as chess players), they usually found that expertise was restricted to a particular

THE BUDDHIST MONK PROBLEM

At six o'clock in the morning a Buddhist monk started climbing the path up a mountain to reach a temple at the top. He stopped many times on the path to rest. Sometimes he walked quickly; sometimes more slowly. Eventually, in the evening he reached the top of the mountain. The monk spent the night at the temple on the top of the mountain. At six o'clock the following morning he set off down the mountain using the same path as he had used to climb it. Again, he stopped several times, but it took him less time to go down the mountain than it had taken him to climb it.

The question is simply this: Is there a spot along the mountainside path that the monk will pass on both trips—up and down—at exactly the same time of day? Show why your answer is correct. (For the answer *see* the figure p. 143.)

area and not transferable or more widely applicable to other areas. These people's problem-solving skills appear to be strictly localized and are not the product of the particular application of some general-purpose strategy.

The way in which a problem is represented may also have a significant effect on the ease with which it can be solved. One famous illustration of the point is contained in the problem of the Buddhist monk described in the box above. Try and solve this problem before you read the rest of this chapter.

Most people find this question difficult to answer. However, it becomes quite easy when it is represented in the right way. We can draw a simple graph that shows the altitude of the monk up the mountain at various times of the day. It is shown in the figure (*see* p. 143). The red line shows the man's path up the mountain—his altitude along the path gradually increases throughout the day. The green line shows the monk's altitude along the path on the second day, when he starts at the top and gradually moves lower down the mountain as the day wears on. Once the

If the Buddhist monk problem is expressed in the form of a graph, it is clear that the climber must be at one point on the mountain at the same time on both days.

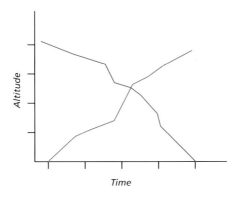

problem is set out in this way, it becomes clear that there has to be a point on the path, somewhere on the side of the mountain, that the monk passes at the same time of the day on his trip up and on his trip down.

Making analogies

Another way of solving problems is by comparing them with similar instances— this is known as using analogy. Some experiments have shown that solutions may be found more easily if suitable analogies are suggested. One famous example is the "radiation problem." Imagine you are a doctor who wants to destroy a cancerous tumor in the middle of the body of an otherwise healthy patient. You can use X-rays to kill the tumor. Yet if the X-rays are strong enough to kill the tumor, they will also harm healthy tissue and thus injure the patient.

> *"Understanding of spoken speech happens without 'thinking about it.' In contrast, we may sometimes 'think aloud' when solving puzzles."*
> *—Charles F. Schmidt, 2002*

So the problem is: How can the doctor kill the tumor without damaging the healthy and unaffected parts of the body? When the problem is presented in this form, few subjects are able to find a good solution quickly. However, in a study

by psychologists Mary Gick and Keith Holyoak in 1980 subjects were first told a different, analogous story about an army attacking a fortress. The roads leading to the fortress were littered with landmines and were therefore impassable by a large number of troops, but the commander of the forces managed to carry out an attack successfully by dividing his army into several smaller groups that traveled to the castle along different routes.

After hearing this story, many more people were able to find a good solution to the problem of using the X-rays to kill the tumor. If several different X-rays, pointing in different directions, are focused on the tumor, then the intensity of the beams at the tumor will be much greater than that of those passing through healthy tissue. That is because the intensity of the X-rays will be cumulative only at the place where they overlap. The fact that people were more likely to find this solution to the X-ray problem after they had heard the story about the army attacking the castle suggests that analogies can sometimes be useful in finding the answers to problems.

Yet it remains much easier to see the value of analogies than to find the right one at the perfect moment. People tend to choose analogies that resemble the problem superficially—if, for example, they are dealing with questions that involve water, they come up with the other facts they know about liquids. They may or may not be relevant to the matter at hand. In fact, of course, they need to find a comparison that is valid rather than one that merely looks similar.

Creativity

Creativity is a form of problem solving that needs to be applied in cases in which neither the form of the solution nor the path to it is clear in advance. Creativity requires neither judgment nor reason, the use of which depends on available, relevant information—the application of past experience to present and future difficulties. It is purely inspirational,

REMOTE ASSOCIATES TESTS

The following are some of the groups of three words used by S. A. and M. T. Mednick in their studies of creativity in 1962 and 1967 and by Kenneth S. Bowers and his colleagues in 1990 for use in their studies of intuition. The table is printed in ascending order of difficulty—easiest first, hardest last.

Three Clue Words	Answer
Falling Actor Dust	Star
Broken Clear Eye	Glass
Skunk Kings Boiled	Cabbage
Widow Bite Monkey	Spider
Bass Complex Sleep	Deep
Coin Quick Spoon	Silver
Gold Stool Tender	Bar
Time Hair Stretch	Long
Cracker Union Rabbit	Jack
Bald Screech Emblem	Eagle
Blood Music Cheese	Blue
Manners Round Tennis	Table
Off Trumpet Atomic	Blast
Playing Credit Report	Card
Rabbit Cloud House	White
Room Blood Salts	Bath
Salt Deep Foam	Sea
Square Cardboard Open	Box
Water Tobacco Stove	Pipe
Ache Hunter Cabbage	Head
Chamber Staff Box	Music
High Book Sour	Note
Lick Sprinkle Mines	Salt
Pure Blue Fall	Water
Snack Line Birthday	Party
Square Telephone Club	Book
Surprise Wrap Care	Gift
Ticket Shop Broker	Pawn
Barrel Root Belly	Beer
Blade Witted Weary	Dull
Cherry Time Smell	Blossom
Notch Flight Spin	Top
Strap Pocket Time	Watch
Walker Main Sweeper	Street
Wicked Bustle Slicker	City
Chocolate Fortune Tin	Cookie
Color Numbers Oil	Paint
Mouse Sharp Blue	Cheese
Sandwich Golf Foot	Club

coming "out of the blue." In everyday parlance we tend to describe a solution as creative only if it is unusual or unique and also useful in some sort of way.

In the 1960s many western psychologists took the view that creativity involved the ability to identify relationships between ideas that were superficially very different from each other—the capacity to detect likeness in unlike things. To support this hypothesis, they devised the Remote Associates Test, in which the subject is provided with three words and asked to think of another word that is related to all of them (*see* box). The tests certainly make an amusing parlor game, but do they reveal anything more than random verbal knowledge? And in what sense, if any, can they be said to measure creativity? In an effort to answer these questions, psychologists asked the working colleagues of people who had taken the Remote Associates Test to give their impressions of the subjects' creativity in their jobs. Although this experiment produced some evidence of a correlation between creativity and high test scores, the methodology was clearly impressionistic rather than rigorously scientific, and other, similar studies produced frustratingly conflicting results.

Thus far scientists have largely failed to identify the processes that lead to creative outcomes. Case studies of creativity depend too much on self-reports or after-the-event reconstructions to be reliable—thinking is significantly different from thinking about thinking.

Biographical extrapolations
Other studies have been made of creative people in an attempt to find out where their gift comes from and to identify characteristics of their family background and upbringing that might explain their success. American psychologist Anna Roe carried out a well-known study of this type in the 1950s. She looked at the biographies of 40 famous natural scientists and discovered that they were particularly likely to be male, first-born

PRACTICAL DAYDREAMS

Daydreaming is defined as the spontaneous recollection or imagination of experiences—one's own, or other people's—in the past or future while in the waking state. Although daydreaming is sometimes deprecated as a waste of time that would be better spent getting on with work, many scientists believe it performs an important role in human cognition and helps with problem solving.

Research has shown that daydreaming enables us—or at least gives us confidence—to plan for the future. The anticipation of possible future situations allows us to form responses to those situations in advance and may improve the efficiency with which we deal with them if and when they arise. By assessing the consequences of alternative courses of action in advance—weighing the pros and cons—daydreaming helps with decision making. It also provides a rehearsal function: "What will I say if he says that?" We can deal better with problems we have anticipated in this way than with those that come at us out of the blue—forewarned is forearmed.

Daydreaming also helps us learn from experience. If we look back at our previous actions, no matter whether they were successes or failures, and then think about what might have happened if we had acted differently, we can formulate strategies for the future. If events happen too quickly for us to take them in at the time, daydreaming may help us make better sense of them later.

Daydreaming is also thought to support creativity. Thinking about fanciful possibilities can lead or inspire us to find new and useful solutions to a problem. While daydreaming about one problem, it is possible to stumble on the solution to another. Each time we go over the past in our minds, we inevitably reappraise it in a slightly different light. It is partly for that reason that creativity has been described as decaying memory.

It is easy to read this description of daydreaming and feel that it strikes a chord with our own experience. But for scientists questions remain: How do we know when people are daydreaming; and even if we do, how do we know for sure what they are daydreaming about? Several methods have been used to find out. Those of Graham Wallas are described in the main text below. Before Wallas, Julian Varendonck (*see* p. 146) used a form of retrospective report in which he first recalled the final portion of a daydream and then worked his way back to its supposed beginning. In the 1970s psychologist Eric Klinger asked subjects to think aloud and describe their streams of thought as they occurred. In a variant method subjects would carry a beeper. When it sounded, they would fill out a questionnaire about their most recent thoughts. The possible limitation of such methods is that if the subjects have to think about thinking, it may alter or inhibit their flow—they may report what seems to have happened, rather than what really did occur.

children, middle-class, and to have professional fathers. Successful (and hence presumably creative) social scientists were also studied. Their profile turned out to be somewhat different from that of the first group—for example, they had notably higher divorce rates.

Such insights may be illuminating, but the evidence they provide is anecdotal and leads to no firm conclusions about either the psychological basis or the nature of creativity. Can creativity be studied scientifically? Some researchers have tried, with some success, to program computers to be "creative." In the 1990s one scientist, Pat Langley, developed a set of computer programs to discover simple scientific laws; another, Philip Johnson-Laird,

developed musical improvisation programs. To the extent that the outputs from these computer programs seem to us to be creative, it may appear that there is nothing mystical or magical about the creative process. But that conclusion is of limited usefulness because it brings us no closer to an understanding of the mental processes that underlie creativity.

The work of Graham Wallas
One of the best-known and, for a while, most influential accounts of the human creative process appeared in *The Art of Thought* (1936), a posthumously published work by the English political scientist and psychologist Graham Wallas (1858–1932). Wallas wanted to understand

how thinking worked so that it could be improved. He was particularly interested in a problem that had concerned the ancient Greek philosophers, namely, why it does not seem possible to improve our creativity in problem solving merely by "trying harder." In other words, why do we not seem to have conscious control over the process of creative thinking? Wallas speculated that if this was indeed the case, and we do not have any such control, it might not be possible to improve thinking. Clearly, such a conclusion, though limiting, would be an important advance in our understanding of the whole area. So is it true that some of the most important steps in problem solving are unconscious?

Four stages of thought

Wallas was influenced by *The Psychology of Daydreams* (1921), an important work by Julian Varendonck (1879–1924) that suggested that different kinds of links between ideas are formed while we are daydreaming or in the state of reduced consciousness experienced immediately before going to sleep (*see* box p. 145). Such links between previously unrelated ideas are usually known as "associations." This gave Wallas the idea that part of problem solving may take place in our unconscious

minds rather than just when we are actively thinking. Wallas reached the conclusion that there are four separate stages of creative problem solving.

The first stage is preparation. During the preparation stage the problem is

> *"To his disciples he [Graham Wallas] appears a brilliant man. It remains to be seen what else he will become."*
> —*Beatrice Webb, 1893*

investigated thoroughly. The mind attempts to solve the problem in many ways and becomes familiar with it. The second stage is known as incubation. In the incubation period no conscious thought is given to the problem. Meanwhile, however, the unconscious mind may be working away on the problem. The third stage, illumination, is the appearance of an apparently new solution to the problem. It may feel like a sudden insight. The final stage, according to Wallas, is verification. In verification the problem solver carefully and consciously tests to see if the new solution really does work.

Models of chemical compounds help us visualize the arrangement of their component atoms. Legend has it that one such model appeared to a scientist in a dream, thus enabling him to work out the structure of a highly complex chemical.

At first sight these categories may appear entirely plausible, and sound like an accurate account of common experience. Yet much of the scientific basis of Wallas's work has since been discredited. Later researchers have denied the existence of an incubation stage—they prefer the "fresh start" explanation, which states that people find the right answer after they have had time to forget the wrong paths they originally took or the misleading clues that steered them in the wrong direction.

Is it possible that our unconscious minds can be working to find a solution while we are consciously thinking about something else? If so, then perhaps we should always make sure that we allow time for incubation when we have a tricky problem to solve. Wallas certainly believed that this was important. He suggested that Charles Darwin's outstandingly creative problem solving may have been aided by the fact that the naturalist suffered from ill health and had to spend much of his time in physical and mental relaxation. Wallas worried that scientists in modern universities might not have enough time for incubation. "At Oxford and Cambridge, men on whose power of invention and stimulus the intellectual future of the country may largely depend are made personally responsible for innumerable worrying details of filling in forms and sending in applications." Wallas feared that this might be "destroying the possibility of incubation."

Despite the doubts about Wallas's methods, it is still important to know if he was right. Sometimes discoverers' explanations of how they came to make important breakthroughs seem to provide evidence for the importance of unconscious processes. One of the most famous examples is the flash of inspiration that came to the German chemist Friedrich August Kekule (1829–1896). His dream about snakes moving in circles and chasing their own tails is thought to have enabled him to identify the chemical structure of the benzene molecule as a ring of six carbon atoms. Of course, it is difficult to be sure that it was really the dream that provided the key to the problem—accounts such as this may be metaphors or post facto rationalizations. And, as previously stated, self-report (as this kind of evidence is known) is scientifically suspect.

Several psychologists have tried to find experimental evidence for incubation. Usually these studies give people the opportunity for incubation in an effort

> "Logically untrained individuals reason by using mental models. A conclusion is necessary if it holds in all the models of the premises."
> —Philip Johnson-Laird, 2002

to discover whether this makes it more likely that the solution will be found. Unfortunately, however, the results have again been inconclusive. All we can say is that incubation can sometimes help if it allows time for functional fixedness to be dislodged, and that enables solvers to see the problem clearly and objectively.

Improving creativity
Although it is not clear whether creativity can be increased, many people spend their time looking for ways to do so. In business one of the most commonly used techniques is brainstorming, or ideas meetings. Brainstorming involves first generating a large number of possible ideas and potential solutions to problems. All criticism and judgment are suspended during this period. Later, after many ideas have been generated, they are examined more carefully. The rationale behind brainstorming is that good ideas may be lost if a critical approach is adopted from the outset, or if people get "stuck" on the first few ideas they think of. You may have had the experience of having incompletely formed ideas criticized so harshly that you are reluctant to make more contributions

to the discussion until you have marshalled your thoughts more carefully. Several forms of brainstorming exist, and the technique can be used by groups or individuals. Brainstorming sessions should welcome all crazy ideas, encouraging people to come up with as many of them as possible and try to combine them with other ideas previously proposed. All this should take place in a relaxed, friendly, and noncritical environment. After this idea-generation phase is complete, it is time to return to the ideas and drop those that are not workable.

It is easy to describe brainstorming in such a way as to make it sound like the answer to nearly all corporate problems, and indeed it is widely practiced in many industries, often successfully. Yet scientific studies of the effectiveness of the technique have produced mixed results—the main problem with it is that it increases the quantity of ideas, but it might fail to improve—and may even diminish—their quality.

Other techniques may also be involved in finding creative solutions. Thinking visually often seems to be important. A well-known example is that of Albert Einstein (1879–1955), who is reputed to have imagined himself traveling along a beam of light. That is said to have helped him develop his theory of relativity. The use of metaphors and analogies may also be useful. It is said that Alexander Graham Bell (1847–1922) invented the telephone by thinking of possible mechanical equivalents to the organs in the human ear.

REASONING, LOGIC, RATIONALITY
Thus far in this chapter we have focused on what psychologists have learned about how we solve different types of problems, and why some problems are more difficult than others. However, problem solving is only one part of thinking and reasoning. We turn now to an examination of people's ability to reason logically.

There are many prescriptive theories about how people should reason—the rules they should follow in order to draw logical conclusions from various facts and premises. In practice, however, we do not always think in this way, and that has led some psychologists to question whether we are really rational at all. But others see no paradox in this, believing that it is perfectly reasonable to be logical when necessary and intuitive at other times.

In everyday situations the use of perfectly accurate reasoning may not always be the best method of problem solving. Sometimes we have to make decisions quickly and may not have time to analyze the problems in any detail. Even if we did have the time, analyzing problems in detail might prevent us from achieving our other goals. So perhaps rationality should be defined more broadly as the thought processes that are most likely to enable us to achieve our goals. This is known as "satisficing." The idea behind satisficing, which was introduced by the economist and psychologist Herbert A. Simon (1916–2001), who had previously worked with Newell on the GPS (*see* p. 141), is

> **"It is not of the essence of mathematics to be conversant with the ideas of number and quantity."**
> **—George Boole, 1854**

that sometimes it is best just to solve a problem well enough or to reach an accurate enough answer to a question or an estimate of quantity. It is not always desirable to calculate a perfect solution, especially when it would take a long time to do so. The rational course is to stop looking for a better solution to a problem when the cost of continuing to search for it becomes greater than the potential benefits of finding it. To put it another way, part of reasoning is the ability to decide when reasoning is inappropriate. If people do not "think things through" in a way that is pleasing to a logician or a philosopher, that may not always be because they are incapable of doing so, but may be simply because they have made the snap decision that prolonged deliberation is either a waste of time or inappropriate in the circumstances.

Boolean principles of thought

The Englishman George Boole (1815–1865) (*see* box) is widely regarded as one of the founders of modern mathematics. In 1854 he published a book in which he attempted to define the principles of reasoning. Although this work is commonly known as *An Investigation of the Laws of Thought*, its full title is *An Investigation of the Laws of Thought on Which Are Founded the Mathematical Theories of Logic and Probabilities*. This appendage is important because it shows that Boole was concerned not just with proofs in mathematics, but also with the kinds of thinking that could be used to draw correct conclusions from problems of any sort. One of the author's stated aims was "to investigate the fundamental laws of those operations of the mind by which reasoning is performed, [and] give expression to them in the symbolic language of a calculus." He assumed that the same rules of thinking could, and should, be applied in any area, not just in mathematics and logic.

Although Boole noted that people often failed to follow his "laws of right reasoning," he realized that such deviations could not be attributed only to their intellectual limitations. This is very different from the view of modern psychologists such as Daniel Kahneman and Amos Tversky, who argued that people's estimates of probabilities are so often at variance with mathematical facts and statistical theories that they do not reason according to logical rules.

Boole thought that the mind could be studied accurately only when it was working in a natural environment. He wrote: "What I mean by the constitution of a system is… its observed character, when operating, without interference, under those conditions to which the system is conceived to be adapted."

GEORGE BOOLE

BIOGRAPHY

Born in 1815, George Boole was largely self-taught, and he never gained a university degree, but he still became one of the world's leading mathematicians. His work has formed the foundation of modern digital computer technology and has been of great assistance to psychologists in their study of human problem solving.

Boole's earliest theories were founded on those of past masters, such as Isaac Newton (1642–1727). His first published paper—about possible new uses of algebra and calculus—appeared in a scholarly journal in 1844.

It brought him acclaim in the field of mathematics, but it was not long before he realized that his work had far broader applications. In an 1847 pamphlet Boole pointed out the analogy between algebraic symbols and symbols that can represent logical forms and syllogisms. He then made the revolutionary proposal that logic should be allied with mathematics, not with philosophy.

Boole's work helped establish the foundations of symbolic logic, and today's digital computer circuits use a form of notation known as Boolean algebra. Many years after his death in 1865 Boole's ideas led to numerous applications he could never have imagined. Among them are telephone switching and electronic computers, which use the binary digits that he first developed.

BIAS

You flip a coin many times, and it lands on heads four times in a row. You are then asked to bet on the next throw. It is highly likely that you will call tails on the entirely reasonable assumption that it has to come up sometime. But the truth is that there is no more or less likelihood of the coin coming up tails now than there was on any of the previous flips—the chances are always 50:50, the odds are always evens.

Someone asks you whether the letter "k" is more likely to appear as the first or third letter of any given word. You do not know for sure, but because more words starting with "k" spring immediately to mind than words in which it is the third letter, you answer "first." As it happens, you are wrong again.

Life is full of problems of this type in which we do not—cannot—know what is right, but have to make a decision nevertheless. Psychologists study the choices we make in the absence of full knowledge. For example, Daniel Kahneman and Amos Tversky (see pp. 156–157) told participants in one of their experiments about someone called Steve who is very shy and withdrawn, invariably helpful, but with little interest in people or in the world of reality. A meek and tidy soul, he has a need for order and structure, and a passion for detail.

The participants were then asked to guess what Steve does for a living—is he a librarian, a musician, a pilot, a physician, or a salesman? Most of them said "librarian."

The point is not whether they were right, but how they reached their conclusion. Here is another test problem—we do not give the right answer because there is none. Think about it, give your answer, and then think about the processes that brought you to your conclusion:

Linda is 31 years old, single, outspoken, and very bright. She majored in philosophy. As a student she was deeply concerned with the issues of discrimination and social justice, and also participated in antinuclear demonstrations.

Now rank the following statements in order of probability, using 1 for the most probable and 8 for the least probable:

(a) Linda is a teacher in elementary school.

(b) Linda works in a bookstore and takes yoga classes.

(c) Linda is active in the feminist movement.

(d) Linda is a psychiatric social worker.

(e) Linda is a member of the League of Women Voters.

(f) Linda is a bank teller.

(g) Linda is an insurance salesperson.

(h) Linda is a bank teller and is an active member of the feminist movement.

In other words, he thought it important to ensure that studies of the human mind were always carried out in normal, everyday circumstances.

Much of Boole's work can be seen as the forerunner of more recent, mainstream approaches to the study of the mind. Boole developed the relation between mathematics, logic, and human thinking in a detailed way and argued that Aristotle's rules of reasoning (see Vol. 1, pp. 10–15) were not the most basic principles involved in thinking.

The work of Gigerenzer

During the second half of the 20th century detailed research into people's reasoning capacity increased scientific understanding of their problem-solving ability. Many psychologists, such as the German Gerd Gigerenzer (born 1947),

have followed Boole and taken the view that attempts to show that humans are irrational are flawed. Gigerenzer argued that people may perform some tasks badly because information is presented to them in an unnatural way, or because they are interpreting the experimental task in a different way than the experimenter.

Another line of research has focused on various logical reasoning tasks. Again, much initial work appeared to show that

Every time you throw a die, you have a 1 in 6 chance of your chosen number coming up.

people behave irrationally on such problems, but in the 1990s psychologist John Anderson and others suggested that we should talk about "adaptive rationality" rather than "normative rationality"—in other words, that we should describe somebody's behavior as rational if it is optimally adapted to the environment and context, even though it does not obey the rules of formal logic.

Even if people behave irrationally or illogically, and thus perform poorly at certain tasks, that does not necessarily mean that they are themselves irrational or illogical. It may be rather that their errors are caused by processing limitations (for example, restricted memory capacity). Their mistakes may be purely random and fortuitous—there was no particular reason why they were made once, and nothing to suggest that they will be made again. Another possibility is that our brains are not large enough to perform perfectly on some tasks; it may also be that the experimenters use the

wrong set of logical rules to judge human performance. All of these possibilities have been put forward to explain why people may not be irrational after all.

PROBABILITY

One important area of reasoning concerns people's judgment of probability. How likely is it that some future event will take place? If a horse has won its last five races, how does that affect its chances of winning a sixth? How likely is it that the sun will shine tomorrow? How likely is it that Jane committed the murder? The development of probability theory, which can be used to answer such questions, started between about three and four hundred years ago.

Probabilities are expressed as numbers between zero and one in which higher numbers mean increased probability. Low probabilities refer to unlikely events. For example, if you roll a die, the chances of it coming up on any number are 1 in 6 (roughly 0.16). If you draw a card

A woman undergoing a mammogram. The test is not infallible, so even if her result is positive, she may not have breast cancer. Yet few people realize this because their problem-solving skills are weak when it comes to matters of probability.

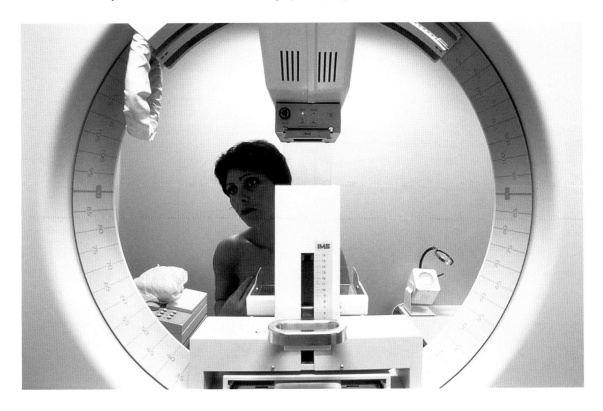

randomly from a pack of 52, the probability of that card being the ace of clubs is lower at 1 in 52 (roughly 0.02). Gigerenzer and others have suggested that our minds have not adapted well to dealing with information expressed in terms of probabilities. In particular, people have trouble making use of new information to change their estimates of how likely some event is.

The Eddy Test

A famous illustrations of this shortcoming appeared in an article published in 1982 in the *Journal of the American Medical Association*. The author, physician David M. Eddy, found that even doctors are bad at estimating medical probabilities (*see* box).

Suppose you are a doctor, and you are examining a patient who has come to you after having noticed a lump in her breast. The woman has been sent to have a test for breast cancer (a mammogram), and the test has come back positive. Your job is to tell your patient how likely it is that she has cancer, given the test result. Imagine that you know the following three things:
- The probability that any woman being screened is suffering from breast cancer is 1 percent (0.01).
- If the patient has cancer, there is an 80 percent (0.8) probability that she will test positive (this is known as the "hit rate").
- If the patient does not have breast cancer, the probability that she will test positive is 10 percent (0.1)—this is known as the "false positive rate."

Effectively, you now have to answer the following question: What is the probability that a patient with a positive

---

EXPLAINING THE EDDY RESULT

EXPERIMENT

Imagine a small town containing 1,000 women. All of them are tested for cancer. One percent of the women have cancer, while 99 percent do not. We can therefore divide the town's women into two groups: a small group of 10 who have cancer, and 990 who do not. Now consider what happens when we give the test to everybody. There is an 80 percent probability that a patient who has cancer will test positive (*see* main text). Or, of the 10 women who have cancer, eight (80 percent of them) test positive, while two test negative. This is illustrated in the top right-hand portion of the figure on the right. Now consider the test results of the rest of the women in the town—the 99 percent who do not have cancer. Remember what the statement said: If a patient does not have breast cancer, the probability that she will test positive is 10 percent. This means that on average, of the 990 cancer-free women, 99 (10 percent) will test positive, while the rest (891) will have a negative result.

The end result of all this testing is that of all the women in the town 107 have tested positive (99 plus 8). However, most of those 107 women who have tested positive do not have cancer—in fact, 99 of them do not. Only eight out of the total of 107 women who tested positive actually have cancer. Therefore, even a woman with a positive test has only a small probability (8 out of

107, or roughly 0.08) of actually having cancer. Therefore it is a mistake to think that a given woman is more likely than not to have cancer just because she comes back with a positive test result. Yet this is what most people conclude. The incorrect conclusion ignores the fact that many more women do not have cancer than do have cancer, so there is a strong probability that she will not have the disease. Because most people who have been tested do not have cancer, even if the test is quite accurate, there will still be many people who test positively and yet do not have the disease. That is because the test is not 100 percent accurate.

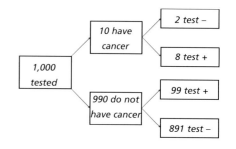

The likelihood of having cancer after an imperfect test

test result actually has cancer? Many psychology experiments have asked people questions such as this. With the figures above, most people would say that the chances are very high that the patient whose test is positive does have cancer. Most people estimate the chances at about 75 percent (0.75). In fact, the answer is only about 8 percent (that is, a probability of 0.08)—in other words, the chances are extremely small that the patient has cancer even though the test has come back positive. Why is the right answer so much smaller than most people think? It is because most patients (99 percent) do not have cancer, and so most of the positive tests results will come from women who do not have cancer and yet have tested positive for it (remember that 10 percent of patients who do not have breast cancer will get a positive result on the tests).

In view of the distress that the misinterpretation of these statistics can cause, many commentators believe it might be better to present these chances as real numbers ("one person in 10") rather than in terms of probability ("0.1").

Ignoring the base rates
These findings are clearly of great practical significance. Even doctors, when asked questions of this nature, typically make the error of assuming that a patient who comes back with a positive test result is very likely to have the disease. The basic error is usually called "ignoring prior probabilities" or "ignoring the base rates." Those are just two different ways of saying that in their calculations people do not seem to take account of how likely events are independently of the new evidence they are given. In the breast cancer example the prior probability (base rate) is 1 percent—in other words, just one woman in a hundred has breast cancer before they are all tested. It is this evidence that is not taken into account in people's probabilistic reasoning. Similar examples can be found in many other areas. For example, suppose that many—or even all—users of hard drugs started off using

soft drugs. Some people are tempted to conclude that "use of soft drugs leads to use of hard drugs." Yet this conclusion does not necessarily follow because there might be many more soft drug users who do not ever move on to hard drugs. Indeed, it could be the case that using soft drugs makes them less likely to move on to hard drugs. (Even if this is not true, the fact remains that we cannot conclude that use of soft drugs leads to use of hard drugs simply because some, many, most, or even all hard drug users started off using soft drugs.) Another example is the interpretation of the polygraph lie-detector tests sometimes used by police. A suspect may test positive on a polygraph, but there may still be a low probability that he or she is lying for as long as the test has even a small tendency to produce an incorrect false positive result.

Psychologist Egon Brunswik (*see* box p. 154) argued that people's reasoning can be assessed fairly only if they are tested in realistic, naturalistic situations—this is similar to the point made by George Boole. Meanwhile, Gigerenzer found that the failure to calculate probabilities accurately—the so-called base-rate neglect phenomenon—is caused not by people's fundamental incompetence or irrationality but by the fact that they are forced to process information in an unnatural way. Our reasoning capacities

A woman undergoes a polygraph test. This method has its uses, but it cannot reliably distinguish between truth and falsehood.

have evolved over tens of thousands of years, while probability theory has been developed only over the last few hundred. Gigerenzer further suggested that in more natural situations people would acquire information in the form of lots of concrete instances. For example, they would have encountered various people with or without some disease and showing or not showing specific symptoms. According to this account, if the information is presented as real frequencies rather than as abstract probabilities, people's estimates will be much more accurate. Gigerenzer and his colleagues have conducted numerous

The aftermath of an earthquake in San Francisco. This is not an unexpected event, given that the city lies on the San Andreas Fault, but people tend to overestimate the number of tremors that hit the city because every one makes headline news.

EGON BRUNSWIK

BIOGRAPHY

Egon Brunswik (1903–1955) was born in Budapest, Hungary, and studied psychology at the University of Vienna, Austria, obtaining a doctorate in 1927. From 1931 he spent a year as a visiting lecturer at the University of Ankara, where he established Turkey's first psychological laboratory. In 1935 he won a Rockefeller fellowship at the University of California. He settled in Berkeley, becoming a U.S. citizen in 1943 and professor of psychology in 1947. He formulated the concept of "probabilistic functionalism," the fundamental tenet of which is that in an uncertain environment organisms have to adapt to their surroundings by adopting the most likely means available to achieve goals. This, in his view, helped explain why people use apparently irrational methods of problem solving and reasoning. Egon Brunswik was a prolific writer, especially about the history of psychology. In January 2000 his 1952 book *The Conceptual Framework of Psychology* was included in a list of the 100 most influential works of the 20th century.

experiments to examine this issue, and the results have generally supported the view that probabilities are easier to calculate if information is presented in the form

> *"Proponents of unbounded rationality generally acknowledge that their models assume unrealistic mental abilities."*
> —*Gerd Gigerenzer, 2001*

of frequencies rather than in that of probabilities. Although this work is still controversial, it has important theoretical and practical applications.

In cases in which information is presented in terms of probabilities, it can be argued that probability is an ambiguous concept. Indeed, Gigerenzer suggested that people's reasoning about probabilities can be interpreted as rational if it is assumed that they are interpreting the idea of probability in a different way from the psychologists and researchers who have designed the experiments.

HIV counseling

People who may draw incorrect medical inferences when information is presented in the form of probabilities may produce

German schoolchildren reading about HIV and AIDS. Research has shown that some of the information given out by the country's medical authorities was disturbingly inaccurate and misleading.

more accurate responses when the same information is presented as frequencies. An example of this can be seen in testing for human immunodeficiency virus (HIV). In recent years it has been common to test low-risk populations for HIV. For example, this may be done before donation of blood or as a condition of applying for life insurance. It is clear that there are serious consequences if people are incorrectly advised about the implications of a positive test for HIV. The issue is essentially the same as that discussed above: How likely is a given individual to have HIV if he or she tests positive on the standard HIV test?

German errors

Gigerenzer and his colleagues examined a population in Germany in the 1990s. For this sample group overall, at that time, the probability of actually being HIV-positive even after having provided a positive test result was quite small—only around 50 percent (0.5). For people from a low-risk population (such as young, nondrug-using, heterosexual males) the chances of actually having HIV if they test positive is only about 1 in 2.

In order to examine what actual advice would be given to people who tested positive, one of the investigators went to 20 testing and counseling centers in Germany and took an HIV test in each. He also received counseling on the interpretation of a possible positive test. The investigator made it clear that he was from a low-risk population and asked counselors about the meaning of a positive test. The questions asked by the investigator were carefully designed to obtain the necessary detailed information. For example, one of the questions was "If one is not infected with HIV, is it possible to get a positive test result?" Most of the counselors answered this question incorrectly, saying that the chances were small or nonexistent. A second question was "What is the probability that a man in my risk group actually has HIV after getting a positive test?" Fifteen out of

twenty counselors replied "certain" or "almost certain," even though the actual probability was only about 50 percent. Clearly this is a very serious finding. It illustrates an error of reasoning that could be damaging to the individual receiving incorrect advice. It would be both more humane and more accurate to advise people who take the test that even if their results are positive, their chances of really having the condition that may lead to acquired immunity deficiency syndrome (AIDS) are no greater than one in two.

Two conclusions seem clear from this research. First, people have difficulty in dealing with information when it is presented in the form of probabilities. Second, it is possible to improve the accuracy of people's performance substantially by presenting the same information in a different format.

ESTIMATION OF FREQUENCIES

Another well-established finding is that people systematically overestimate the chances of unlikely events happening and underestimate the chances that likely things will happen. For example, in 1978 researchers Paul Slovic, Baruch Fischhoff, and Sarah Lichtenstein asked people to estimate the frequency of various causes of death. The frequencies of very unusual causes (such as death by floods or tornadoes) were systematically overestimated. People tend to think that the numbers killed in events such as tornadoes or floods are much greater than they in fact are. At the other end of the scale people typically underestimate the number of people who die through common causes, such as heart disease and various forms of cancer.

How do we account for such discrepancies between perception and reality? Several researchers, including the psychologists Daniel Kahneman (b. 1934) and Amos Tversky (1937–1996), have suggested that they occur because subjects rely on the availability of examples of the events in their memory. To answer questions about how often events happen, people think of examples of those events

The aftermath of a hurricane—what is the probability of a natural disaster in Kansas, and is it greater or less than the likelihood of one in Vermont? Not only do most people not know the answers to these questions, they do not know how to figure them out.

happening. The more examples that come to mind of death by a particular cause, the more frequent that cause will be judged to be. If that is how people estimate frequencies, it is possible to explain why they might make incorrect suppositions. When a death occurs due to an unusual cause—if, for example, a person is killed in a fairground accident—it is likely to be reported in the broadcast media, and as a result almost everybody will hear about it. When death occurs due to a more common cause, the event is less newsworthy. Thus when we are asked to

> *"Economic analysis presupposes the rationality of actors' decisions. Tversky and Kahneman challenged such presumptions."*
> —*Kenneth Arrow et al., 1996*

estimate the number of people killed each year at fairgrounds, we may overestimate the true frequency because we recall such incidents better than many more mundane, and thus unreported, causes of death. This type of thinking may lead us to the wrong answers, but it does not necessarily mean that we are incapable of rational thought, or that our problem-solving abilities are defective—we are merely making the best possible use, in the circumstances, of the inadequate data at our disposal.

HEURISTICS

"Availability" is an example of using something known as a heuristic. (The English word comes from the Greek meaning "to discover.") A heuristic is a shortcut that people might use in problem solving or reasoning. Often, as we have seen, it will not be possible to find the solution to a problem or to figure out the answers to a question in a completely systematic way. Even if such a solution were possible, it might take too long to compute. Kahneman and Tversky have

therefore suggested that people may use heuristics to solve problems. The advantage of using a heuristic is that it will usually allow one to reach approximately the right answer to a problem quickly and without too much mental effort. The disadvantage is that in some circumstances a heuristic may lead to the wrong answer. The availability heuristic about causes of death described above is a good example of the latter.

Another phenomenon is that of overconfidence. If people are asked a factual question (for example: "What is the capital of Nigeria?" or "How do you spell the word 'accommodation'?"), they will often not be sure whether they have provided the correct answer. However, subjects are often overconfident in their estimates of how likely they are to be right. For example, when they say they are 85 percent confident, in fact they might only be correct on about 60 percent of occasions. Sometimes, for questions on which they are very likely to be wrong, they may be underconfident. In general, therefore, people often seem to be more extreme in their judgments of confidence than they should be.

Is this similar to the estimation of the likelihood of having cancer if you test positive for the disease—another example of people making systematic errors? Not necessarily. It may be that as in the medical diagnoses described above, people are not interpreting probability as meaning "How often you will be right in the long run," but instead are assuming some other interpretation of what "probability" means in the question they are given. Gigerenzer examined this by changing the way that subjects were asked the question. Instead of asking subjects how certain they were about their answer, he asked them how often they thought they gave the right answer to a number of questions. Gigerenzer found that when the question was rephrased in this way, people were much more accurate. Thus it does seem that this is another case in which, rather than assuming that subjects are

and then adjusting their estimate away from that staring point. However, they may not adjust enough. Some studies have found strong evidence for anchoring in the decisions made by consumers. For example, imagine running a promotion in which you have to sell as many cans of soup as possible. You might put up a sign in your store saying "discounted cans of soup." You might put no limit on the number of cans of soup that can be purchased, or alternatively you could specify a maximum per customer. One study, by psychologist Brian Wansink in the 1990s, found that the average number of cans of soup purchased during such a promotion was twice as high when the poster read "maximum 12 per customer" as it was when there was no stated limit.

making systematic mistakes, we can instead imagine that they are interpreting the question in a different way from the one the experimenter intended. In addition, it is clear that people can become expert in judging how likely they are to be correct (this often happens with meteorologists, for example, whose weather forecasts are skillfully prepared and phrased in such a way as to minimize the possibility of error).

Decision making
Once people have—or believe they have—enough information about a problem, they make a decision. That decision may not be correct; sometimes it may even seem irrational. But it is likely to be the best they could have made in the circumstances, given that the information that went into making it was, almost inevitably, incomplete, and that their judgment was unlikely to have been perfect or entirely objective.

Such decisions are commonly informed by something known as the anchoring and adjustment heuristic. People who use it seem to estimate quantities or probabilities by starting with some number or estimate (which may have been provided for them by the experimenter)

What is the price difference between a $700 garment marked down to 50 percent of list price and another item reduced by 80 percent of $1,750? The answer is nothing, but shoppers may prefer larger discounts, perhaps regardless of what they end up buying.

Partitional pricing
Another form of anchoring in consumer decision making is termed partitional pricing. For example, suppose someone is choosing which of two Internet bookstores to purchase a novel from. One bookstore is advertising the novel at $12.95 plus $3.95 for shipping and handling. The other is selling the same item for $11.95 plus $4.95 for shipping and handling. The total cost is the same in both cases, but in the 1990s psychologist

> *"People [should be] given information in a format that meshes with the way they naturally think about probability."*
> —*Steven Pinker, 1997*

Vicki Morwitz and her colleagues found that people sometimes prefer the package that offers the lower price for the book itself. It has been suggested that this is because people anchor on the main price (that of the book itself) and fail to make sufficient adjustment for the additional cost of shipping and handling.

Furthermore, if people are asked to

The special deals offered by stores and businesses pose significant problem-solving difficulties for potential buyers who are anxious to figure out what represents the best value.

recall the price of the item some time later, the figure that they remember often seems to be determined mainly by the larger price component of the total amount. Of course, in real-world examples other factors may be important as well. It may be that people fail to take account of the cost of package and mailing because such costs are sometimes hidden in the small print. Besides, we generally remember how much the book cost, rather than the total price paid, including all the "added costs." However, in general there is considerable evidence that people do use anchoring heuristics under a range of realistic circumstances.

Loss aversion

Several other reasoning biases can be illustrated by reference to consumer choices and purchasing. One is loss aversion. Essentially it means that the loss of some quantity (say, $100) makes people more unhappy than a gain of $100 makes them happy.

For example, consider how storekeepers might represent the fact that they are charging different prices for some item in a store depending on whether the customer pays for it with cash or a credit card. This situation can be presented in two different ways. Either it can be advertised as a "cash discount," or it can be described as a "credit card surcharge." Even if the actual price change involved is the same in both cases, research has shown that people are more likely to use their credit card if the price difference is expressed as a cash discount. That is because the phrase "credit card surcharge" sounds like a loss and is therefore more unpleasant and worth avoiding.

Kahneman and Tversky developed a detailed mathematical model, called prospect theory, to describe a large number of systematic reasoning and choice preferences of this kind.

Mental accounting

A concept related to loss aversion is risk aversion. In general, people dislike risks but are more prepared to take them to prevent losses than to make gains. Consider why people might be risk averse. The figure on page 160 illustrates the increase in "utility" for a person as a

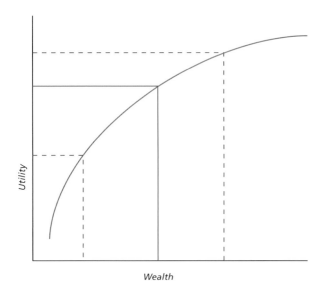

Utility

Wealth

function of the amount of money he or she gains. In simple terms utility is the amount by which we have moved toward what we want. It can be thought of as a bit like happiness, although that is not quite accurate because people might not want only happiness. It is usually assumed that utility increases more slowly as the amount of money gained increases. One way of thinking about this is that twice as much money makes you happier than you were before, but not twice as happy. So, for example, a win of $100 in a lottery might give you six extra units of utility. A

In economics pleasure (utility) increases as the amount of wealth acquired increases. But the graph does not rise at a 45-degree angle, as it would if wealth were directly proportional to pleasure. In fact, as we can see, it drops off: two Ferraris make us happier than one Ferrari but not twice as happy.

> **"If you are setting out to work in a new field you should thoroughly research that field. Right? Wrong! There is a flaw in this argument."**
> **—Edward de Bono, 1991**

larger win of $200 might give you 10 units of utility—more than the six that $100 gives you, but not twice as many. Consider therefore whether you would rather have a certain prize of $100 or a 50 percent chance of winning $200. Most people in this situation prefer the certainty of

$100—that is because they are what economists call risk averse, that is, they prefer the certainty of the smaller gain. We can explain this in terms of the shape of the utility curve, in which $100 will be worth six units of utility for you, while a 50 percent chance of winning $200 is worth only five units of utility (in other words, half of the utility that you would gain if you were to win the $200 prize).

One implication of this approach is that discounts on items in a store will seem more attractive if they are presented separately. For example, suppose a television set and a DVD player can be sold as a pair or together as a package. Suppose also that the price of these items has been reduced by a total of $200. It should be more effective for the seller to present this price change as a discount of $100 off the television set and a separate discount of $100 off the DVD player rather than a single discount of $200 off the combination. The reason for this is essentially the same as that outlined above. The utility of two separate gains of $100 might be worth 2 x 6 = 12 units of utility. A single gain of $200 might seem less attractive, being worth only 10 units of utility. Some studies have confirmed this theory and also shown that the opposite applies to price increases, which will be widely perceived as losses.

Scope for improvement?
Can people be taught to improve their reasoning and problem-solving abilities? According to one school of thought, a major purpose of education is to teach general thinking skills and critical thinking that can be applied to any situation. Another view is that education is primarily about teaching facts and inculcating understanding of specific subjects (such as English, geography, and mathematics). From time to time psychologists such as the Maltese-born British writer Edward de Bono (born 1933) have looked for ways to improve creativity and problem-solving skills. Might this be possible? One of the most

general problems in reasoning and problem solving seems to concern people's fixation on earlier solutions to problems. People often seem to find it hard to break free from what they already know or think they know. As a consequence, one useful general rule might be something like "always look for alternative possibilities." Clearly it is important to encourage people to believe that they can, through their own thinking, solve problems and arrive at correct conclusions. We have seen several examples in which people's intuitions can go badly wrong. Therefore it is important to show people that their preconceptions can often be misleading, and that it is always important to consider the evidence carefully.

Transferable skills

One potential problem in any effort to "teach thinking" is that it can be hard to ensure that the skills will transfer from the context in which they were originally taught into real-life situations, which are likely to be slightly different and more complex There are mixed findings in this area. Some studies appear to show that

training in statistics can lead to improved answers to questions that involve the use of statistics outside the classroom.

Other studies have tried to teach very general strategies to improve performance. In the 1980s psychologist Jonathan Baron and his colleagues had some success with a simple training program that emphasized three rules. Each of these rules was designed to overcome common problems. For example, one rule was "Take time to think." This was to counter the tendency to spend too little time on any given problem. Another slogan was "Always consider alternatives." This was to encourage problem solvers to consider other possibilities and delay decisions for as long as possible. A final slogan, "Keep at it," was designed to encourage persistence. In some experiments students have been encouraged to consider arguments from the opposite side of the case they are arguing. Again, there does seem to be some evidence that an open mind during thinking can be encouraged. However, at its worst, advising people to use such approaches is cracker-barrel wisdom, and its effect on pupils is seldom great.

Formal logic

In this final section we consider how people do and should perform on logical reasoning tasks. This has been investigated since the time of the ancient Greeks. Aristotle was concerned with a particular kind of reasoning known as deductive reasoning. For example, consider the following argument, the form of which is known as a syllogism:

All children are happy
                                (first statement),
    Andrew is a child
                                (second statement),
    Therefore Andrew is happy
                                (conclusion).

A syllogism draws a conclusion from two statements. The rules of logic that ancient philosophers examined were concerned simply with the rules that would guarantee that you would end up with a true conclusion if the first two

SYLLOGISMS

EXPERIMENT

All artists are beekeepers; all beekeepers are chemists. Most people find it fairly easy to conclude from these premises that "All artists are chemists." However, some syllogisms are much harder than this example. What, if anything, can be concluded from the premises: some artists are not beekeepers; all chemists are beekeepers?

Most people find this one much harder, partly because of the limitations of their problem-solving techniques, and partly because of the inherent shortcomings of the syllogistic method itself (see p. 163).

statements (the premises) were true. Therefore the correctness of the argument depends on two things: the truth of the premises and the structure of the argument being consistent with the rules of logic. In the example above, the argument structure is a good one. If it is true that all children are happy, and it is also true that Andrew is a child, then the rules of logic provide an absolute guarantee that the conclusion (Andrew is happy) is also true.

Of course, in reality it is unfortunately not true that all children are happy. Therefore the absolute truth of the conclusion in this case cannot be guaranteed. However, it is important to understand that this is not because of any problem with the logical rules that are being used to construct the argument. Instead, it is simply because one of the starting points (the premises) of the

argument happens to be false. If we follow the rules of logic, we can guarantee that we will draw only accurate conclusions from true premises. These rules are very general; that is, they apply whatever the premises and conclusions are about. Consider the following rule:

P → Q

This is the logical notation meaning "if P is true, then Q is true." P and Q can each stand for any simple statement. For example, P could stand for "It is snowing," and Q might stand for "It is cold outside." The statement as a whole would then be: "If it is snowing, it is cold outside."

But if we know that P → Q, this can help us draw other conclusions. For example, suppose we know that Q is not true. Then we can conclude that P is not true either. That is because the rule says that if P is true, then Q is true. If Q is not true, therefore, P must be untrue. This will

Portrait of a genius—the Spanish painter and sculptor Pablo Picasso (1881–1973). It is easier to describe his work than to know how it came into his mind and then found expression in his chosen media.

remain the case whatever P and Q stand for. In the case of the specific example, we could conclude from "It is NOT cold outside" that "It is NOT snowing." The rules of logic are powerful because they can be applied to any statement.

Logic in the real world

Rules of logic are about how people should deal with the available information if they are to be sure that they are reasoning correctly. Psychologists have investigated it extensively. However, the question of how people actually do reason is quite a different one. When you read the box on page 161, you probably found the first syllogism much easier to understand than the second one. Several theories have been developed to account for the kinds of errors that people make and to explain why some syllogisms are more difficult than others. It has been hard to account for this in terms of standard rules of logic, although many people have tried. One of the best-known alternative accounts was developed by Philip Johnson-Laird. He and his colleagues at Princeton University have argued that it is possible to reason without logical rules. Instead, he suggests that when people have to solve a syllogism, they construct a "mental model," a sort of image in their mind's eye of the premises and the objects involved in them. When they have constructed a mental model of the premises, they can examine it to see what other statements may be true of the same model. They can then use these other statements as their conclusion. Johnson-Laird takes the view that this kind of account can be used to explain the types of errors that people commonly make in syllogistic reasoning.

SUMMARY

This chapter has examined a number of different cases in which people seem to reason incorrectly and attempted to show how that can restrict their problem-solving abilities. Although it is not always clear why they are unable to perform these tasks, especially when they clearly know the rules to which they are expected to conform, their failures often cast light on the nature of problem solving.

It has often been concluded from such findings that "humans are irrational." In many cases, however, research has shown that people are performing the task

> *"The artist can do; the artist can't explain how. It does not follow, however, that nothing of interest can be learned about genius."*
> —Denis Dutton, 2001

correctly and logically but that they are treating it as a different type of problem than as intended by the experimenter: They have not failed to understand the problem but misunderstood the instructions, if they are given any, or if there are no instructions, they have chosen the wrong method of solving the problem.

This conclusion is supported by numerous cases in which people reason more correctly about probabilities when information is presented to them in what they regard as a natural way. As for creativity, while we may be able to describe some of its mechanics, its quintessence— for example, the inspiration that turns a painter from a journeyman into a genius —remains a mystery.

CONNECTIONS

- Representing Information: pp. 64–87
- Ancient Greek Thought: Volume 1, pp. 10–15
- Gestalt Psychology: Volume 1, pp. 46–51
- Cognitive Psychology: Volume 1, pp. 104–117
- The Mind: Volume 2, pp. 40–61
- Artificial Minds: Volume 2, pp. 140–163

Set Glossary

abnormality Within abnormal psychology abnormality is the deviation from normal or expected behavior, generally involving maladaptive responses and personal distress both to the individuals with abnormal behavior and to those around them.

abnormal psychology The study and treatment of mental disorders.

acquisition The process by which something, such as a skill, habit, or language, is learned.

adaptation A change in behavior or structure that increases the survival chances of a species. Adjective: adaptive

addiction A state of dependence on a drug or a particular pattern of behavior.

adjustment disorder A mental disorder in which a patient is unable to adjust properly to a stressful life change.

affect A mood, emotion, or feeling. An affect is generally a shorter-lived and less-pronounced emotion than mood.

affective disorder A group of mental disorders, such as depression and bipolar 1 disorder, that are characterized by pronounced and often prolonged changes of mood.

agnosia A group of brain disorders involving impaired ability to recognize or interpret sensory information.

Alzheimer's disease A progressive and irreversible dementia in which the gradual destruction of brain tissue results in memory loss, impaired cognitive function, and personality change.

amnesia A partial or complete loss of memory.

amygdala An almond-shaped structure located in the front of the brain's temporal lobe that is part of the limbic system. Sometimes called the amygdaloid complex or the amygdaloid nucleus, the amygdala plays an important role in emotional behavior and motivation.

anorexia nervosa An eating disorder in which patients (usually young females) become obsessed with the idea that they are overweight and experience dramatic weight loss by not eating enough.

antidepressants A type of medication used to treat depression.

antianxiety drugs A type of medication used to treat anxiety disorders.

antipsychotic drugs A type of medication used to treat psychotic disorders such as schizophrenia. Sometimes known as neuroleptics.

anxiety disorder A group of mental disorders involving worry or distress.

anxiolytics See antianxiety drugs

aphasia A group of brain disorders that involve a partial or complete loss of language ability.

arousal A heightened state of awareness, behavior, or physiological function.

artificial intelligence (AI) A field of study that combines elements of cognitive psychology and computer science in an attempt to develop intelligent machines.

attachment theory A theory that describes how infants form emotional bonds with the adults they are close to.

attention The process by which someone can focus on particular sensory information by excluding other, less immediately relevant information.

attention deficit disorder (ADD) A mental disorder in which the patient (usually a child) is hyperactive, impulsive, and unable to concentrate properly.

autism A mental disorder, first apparent in childhood, in which patients are self-absorbed, socially withdrawn, and engage in repetitive patterns of behavior.

automatization The process by which complex behavior eventually becomes automatic. Such a process may be described as having automaticity or being automatized.

autonomic nervous system A part of the nervous system that controls many of the body's self-regulating (involuntary or automatic) functions.

aversion therapy A method of treating patients, especially those suffering from drink or drug addiction, by subjecting them to painful or unpleasant experiences.

axon Extension of the cell body of a neuron that transmits impulses away from the body of the neuron.

behavioral therapy A method of treating mental disorders that concentrates on modifying abnormal behavior rather than on the underlying causes of that behavior.

behaviorism A school of psychology in which easily observable and measurable behavior is considered to be the only proper subject of scientific study. Noun: behaviorist

bipolar I disorder A mental (affective) disorder involving periods of depression (depressed mood) and periods of mania (elevated mood).

body image The way in which a person perceives their own body or imagines it is perceived by other people.

body language The signals people send out to other people (usually unconsciously) through their gestures, posture, and other types of nonverbal communication.

Broca's area A region of the brain (usually located in the left hemisphere) that is involved with processing language.

bulimia nervosa An eating disorder in which patients consume large amounts of food in binges, then use laxatives or self-induced vomiting to prevent themselves putting on weight.

CAT scan *See* CT

causality The study of the causes of events or the connection between causes and effects.

central nervous system The part of the body's nervous system comprising the brain and spinal cord.

cerebellum A cauliflower-shaped structure at the back of the brain underneath the cerebral hemispheres that coordinates body movements.

cerebral cortex The highly convoluted outer surface of the brain's cerebrum.

cerebrum The largest part of the brain, consisting of the two cerebral hemispheres and their associated structures.

classical conditioning A method of associating a stimulus and a response that do not normally accompany one another. In Pavlov's well-known classical conditioning experiment dogs were trained so that they salivated (the conditioned response or CR) when Pavlov rang a bell (the conditioned stimulus or CS). Normally, dogs salivate

(an unconditioned response or UR) only when food is presented to them (an unconditioned stimulus or US).

clinical psychology An area of psychology concerned with the study and treatment of abnormal behavior.

cognition A mental process that involves thinking, reasoning, or some other type of mental information processing. Adjective: cognitive

cognitive behavioral therapy (CBT) An extension of behavioral therapy that involves treating patients by modifying their abnormal thought patterns as well as their behavior.

cognitive psychology An area of psychology that seeks to understand how the brain processes information.

competency In psycholinguistics the representation of the abstract rules of a language, such as its grammar.

conditioned stimulus/response (CS/CR) *See* classical conditioning

conditioning *See* classical conditioning; instrumental conditioning

connectionism A computer model of cognitive processes such as learning and memory. Connectionist models are based on a large network of "nodes" and the connections between them. Adjective: connectionist

consciousness A high-level mental process responsible for the state of self-awareness that people feel. Consciousness is thought by some researchers to direct human behavior and by others simply to be a byproduct of that behavior.

cortex *See* cerebral cortex

cross-cultural psychology The comparison of behavior, such as language

acquisition or nonverbal communication, between different peoples or cultures.

cross-sectional study An experimental method in which a large number of subjects are studied at a particular moment or period in time. Compare longitudinal study

CT (computed tomography) A method of producing an image of the brain's tissue using X-ray scanning, which is commonly used to detect brain damage. Also called CAT (computerized axial tomography).

culture-specific A behavior found only in certain cultures and not observed universally in all humankind.

declarative knowledge A collection of facts about the world and other things that people have learned. Compare procedural knowledge

declarative memory *See* explicit memory

defense mechanism A type of thinking or behavior that a person employs unconsciously to protect themselves from anxiety or unwelcome feelings.

deficit A missing cognitive function whose loss is caused by a brain disorder.

delusion A false belief that a person holds about themselves or the world around them. Delusions are characteristic features of psychotic mental illnesses such as schizophrenia.

dementia A general loss of cognitive functions usually caused by brain damage. Dementia is often, but not always, progressive (it becomes worse with time).

Dementia of the Alzheimer's type (DAT) See Alzheimer's disease

dendrite A treelike projection of a neuron's cell body that conducts nerve impulses toward the cell body.

dependency An excessive reliance on an addictive substance, such as a drug, or on the support of another person.

depression An affective mental disorder characterized by sadness, low self-esteem, inadequacy, and related symptoms.

desensitization A gradual reduction in the response to a stimulus when it is presented repeatedly over a period of time.

developmental psychology An area of psychology concerned with how people develop throughout their lives, but usually concentrating on how behavior and cognition develop during childhood.

discrimination In perception the ability to distinguish between two or more stimuli. In social psychology and sociology unequal treatment of people based on prejudice.

dysgraphia A brain disorder involving an ability to write properly.

dyslexia Brain disorders that disrupt a person's ability to read.

eating disorders A group of mental disorders that involve disturbed eating patterns or appetite.

echoic memory See sensory memory

ego The central part of a person's self. In Freudian psychology the ego manages the balance between a person's primitive, instinctive needs and the often conflicting demands of the world around them.

egocentric A person who is excessively preoccupied with themselves at the expense of the people and the world around them.

eidetic An accurate and persistent form of visual memory that is generally uncommon in adults (often misnamed "photographic memory").

electroconvulsive therapy (ECT) A treatment for severe depression that involves passing a brief and usually relatively weak electric shock through the front of a patient's skull.

electroencephalogram (EEG) A graph that records the changing electrical activity in a person's brain from electrodes attached to the scalp.

emotion A strong mood or feeling. Also a reaction to a stimulus that prepares the body for action.

episodic memory A type of memory that records well-defined events or episodes in a person's life. Compare semantic memory

ethnocentricity The use of a particular ethnic group to draw conclusions about wider society or humankind as a whole.

event-related potential (ERP) A pattern of electrical activity (the potential) produced by a particular stimulus (the event). EVPs are often recorded from the skull using electrodes.

evoked potential See event-related potential (ERP)

evolution A theory suggesting that existing organisms have developed from earlier ones by processes that include natural selection (dubbed "survival of the fittest") and genetic mutation.

evolutionary psychology An approach to psychology that uses the theory of evolution to explain the mind and human behavior.

explicit memory A type of memory containing information that is available to conscious recognition and recall.

flashbulb memory A very clear and evocative memory of a particular moment or event.

fMRI (functional magnetic resonance imaging) An MRI-based scanning technique that can produce images of the brain while it is engaged in cognitive activities.

functionalism An approach to psychology that concentrates on the functions played by parts of the mind and human behavior.

generalized anxiety disorder (GAD) A type of nonspecific anxiety disorder with symptoms that include worry, irritability, and tension.

genes A functional unit of the chromosome that determines how traits are passed on and expressed from generation to generation. Adjective: genetic

Gestalt psychology A psychology school that emphasizes the importance of appreciating phenomena as structured wholes in areas such as perception and learning, as opposed to breaking them down into their components. Most influential in the mid-1900s.

gray matter The parts of the nervous system that contain mainly nerve cell bodies.

habituation See desensitization

hallucination A vivid but imaginary perceptual experience that occurs purely in the mind, not in reality.

heritability The proportion of observed variation for a trait in a specific population that can be attributed to genetic factors rather than environmental ones. Generally expressed as a ratio of genetically caused variation to total variation.

hippocampus A part of the limbic system in the temporal lobe that is thought to play an important role in the formation of memories.

Humanism A philosophy that stresses the importance of human interests and values.

hypothalamus A small structure at the base of the brain that controls the autonomic nervous system.

hysteria A type of mental disturbance that may include symptoms such as hallucinations and emotional outbursts.

implicit memory A type of memory not normally available to conscious awareness. Sometimes also known as procedural or nondeclarative memory. Compare explicit memory

imprinting A type of learning that occurs in a critical period shortly after birth, such as when chicks learn to accept a human in place of their real mother.

individual psychology An approach to psychology that focuses on the differences between individuals. Also a theory advanced by Alfred Adler based on the idea of overcoming inferiority.

information processing In cognitive psychology the theory that the mind operates something like a computer, with sensory information processed either in a series of discrete stages or in parallel by something like a connectionist network.

ingroup A group whose members feel a strong sense of collective identity and act to exclude other people (the outgroup).

innate A genetically determined trait that is present at birth, as opposed to something that is acquired by learning.

instinct An innate and automatic response to a particular stimulus that usually involves no rational thought.

instrumental conditioning A type of conditioning in which reinforcement occurs only when an organism makes a certain, desired response. Instrumental

conditioning occurs, for example, when a pigeon is trained to peck a lever to receive a pellet of food.

internalize To make internal, personal, or subjective; to take in and make an integral part of one's attitudes or beliefs:

introspection A behaviorist technique of studying the mind by observing one's own thought processes.

language acquisition device (LAD) According to linguist Noam Chomsky, a part of the brain that is preprogrammed with a universal set of grammatical rules that can construct the rules of a specific language according to the environment it is exposed to.

libido The sexual drive.

limbic system A set of structures in the brain stem, including the hippocampus and the amygdala, that lie below the corpus callosum. It is involved in emotion, motivation, behavior, and various functions of the autonomic nervous system.

long-term memory A type of memory in which information is retained for long periods after being deeply processed. Generally used to store events and information from the past. Compare short-term memory

longitudinal study An experimental method that follows a small group of subjects over a long period of time. Compare cross-sectional study

maladaptive Behavior is considered maladapative or dysfunctional if it has a negative effect on society or on a person's ability to function in society.

medical model A theory that mental disorders, like diseases, have specific underlying medical causes, which must be addressed if treatment is to be effective.

mental disorder A psychiatric illness such as schizophrenia, anxiety, or depression.

metacognition The study by an individual of their own thought processes. *See also* introspection

mnemonic A technique that can be used to remember information or improve memory.

modeling The technique by which a person observes some ideal form of behavior (a role model) and then attempts to copy it. In artificial intelligence (AI) people attempt to build computers that model human cognition.

modularity A theory that the brain is composed of a number of modules that occupy relatively specific areas and that carry out relatively specific tasks.

morpheme The smallest unit of a language that carries meaning.

motor neuron *See* neuron.

MRI (magnetic resonance imaging) A noninvasive scanning technique that uses magnetic fields to produce detailed images of body tissue.

nature–nurture A long-running debate over whether genetic factors (nature) or environmental factors (nurture) are most important in different aspects of behavior.

neuron A nerve cell, consisting of a cell body (soma), an axon, and one or more dendrites. Motor (efferent) neurons produce movement when they fire by carrying information *from* the central nervous system *to* the muscles and glands; sensory (afferent) neurons carry information *from* the senses *to* the central nervous system.

neuropsychology An area of psychology that studies the connections between parts of the brain and neural processes, on one hand, and different cognitive processes and types of behavior, on the other.

neurotransmitter A substance that carries chemical "messages" across the synaptic gaps between the neurons of the brain.

nonverbal communication The way in which animals communicate without language (verbal communication), using such things as posture, tone of voice, and facial expressions.

operant conditioning *See* instrumental conditioning

outgroup The people who do not belong to an ingroup.

parallel processing A type of cognition in which information is processed in several different ways at once. In serial processing information passes through one stage of processing at a time.

peripheral nervous system All the nerves and nerve processes that connect the central nervous system with receptors, muscles, and glands.

personality The collection of character traits that makes one person different from another.

personality disorder A group of mental disorders in which aspects of someone's personality make it difficult for them to function properly in society.

PET (positron emission tomography) A noninvasive scanning technique that makes images of the brain according to levels of metabolic activity inside it.

phenomenology A philosophy based on the study of immediate experiences.

phobia A strong fear of a particular object (such as snakes) or social situation.

phoneme A basic unit of spoken language.

phrenology An early approach to psychology that studied the relationship between areas of the brain (based on skull shape) and mental functions. Phrenology has since been discredited.

physiology A type of biology concerned with the workings of cells, organs, and tissues.

positive punishment A type of conditioning in which incorrect responses are punished.

positive reinforcement A type of conditioning in which correct responses are rewarded.

primary memory *See* short-term memory

probability The likelihood of something happening.

procedural knowledge The practical knowledge of how to do things ("know-how"). Compare declarative knowledge

prosody A type of nonverbal communication in which language is altered by such things as the pitch of someone's voice and their intonation.

psyche The soul or mind of a person or a driving force behind their personality.

psychiatry The study, classification, and treatment of mental disorders.

psychoanalysis A theory of behavior and an approach to treating mental disorders pioneered by Austrian neurologist Sigmund Freud. Adjective: psychoanalytic

psychogenic A mental disorder that is psychological (as opposed to physical) in origin.

psycholinguistics The study of language-related behavior, including how the brain acquires and processes language.

psychosurgery A type of brain surgery designed to treat mental disorders.

psychotherapy A broad range of treatments for mental disorders based on different kinds of interaction between a patient and a therapist.

psychosis A mental state characterized by disordered personality and loss of contact with reality that affects normal social functioning. Psychosis is a feature of psychotic disorders, such as schizophrenia. Adjective: psychotic

reaction time The time taken for the subject in an experiment to respond to a stimulus.

recall The process by which items are recovered from memory. Compare recognition

recognition The process by which a person realizes they have previously encountered a particular object or event. Compare recall

reductionism A philosophy based on breaking complex things into their individual components. Also, an attempt to explain high-level sciences (such as psychology) in terms of lower-level sciences (such as chemistry or physics).

reflex An automatic response to a stimulus (a "knee-jerk" reaction).

reflex arc The neural circuit thought to be responsible for the control of a reflex.

rehearsing The process by which a person repeats information to improve its chances of being stored in memory.

representation A mental model based on perceptions of the world.

repression In psychoanalysis an unconscious mental process that keeps thoughts out of conscious awareness.

response The reaction to a stimulus.

reuptake The reabsorption of a neurotransmitter from the place where it was produced.

risk aversion A tendency not to take risks even when they may have beneficial results.

schema An abstract mental plan that serves as a guide to action or a more general mental representation.

schizophrenia A mental disorder characterized by hallucinations and disordered thought patterns in which a patient becomes divorced from reality. It is a type of psychotic disorder.

secondary memory *See* long-term memory

selective attention *See* attention

self-concept The ideas and feelings that people hold about themselves.

semantic memory A type of long-term memory that stores information based on its content or meaning. Compare episodic memory

senses The means by which people perceive things. The five senses are vision, hearing, smell, touch, and taste.

sensory memory An information store that records sensory impressions for a short period of time before they are processed more thoroughly.

sensory neuron *See* neuron

serotonin A neurotransmitter in the central nervous system that plays a key role in affective (mood) disorders, sleep, and the perception of pain. Serotonin is also known as 5-hydroxytryptamine (5-HT).

shaping A type of conditioning in which behavior is gradually refined toward some ideal form by successive approximations.

short-term memory A memory of very limited capacity in which sensory inputs are held before being processed more deeply and passing into long-term memory. Compare long-term memory

social cognition An area of psychology that combines elements of social and cognitive psychology in an attempt to understand how people think about themselves in relation to the other people around them.

social Darwinism A theory that society behaves according to Darwinian principles, with the most successful members thriving at the expense of the least successful ones.

social psychology An area of psychology that explores how individuals behave in relation to other people and to society as a whole.

sociobiology A theory that seeks to explain social behavior through biological approaches, notably the theory of evolution. *See also* evolutionary psychology

somatic Something that relates to the body as opposed to the mind; something physical as opposed to something mental.

stereopsis The process by which the brain assembles one 3-D image by combining a pair of 2-D images from the eyes.

stimulus A type of sensory input that provokes a response.

subject The person studied in a psychological experiment.

synapse The region across which nerve impulses are transmitted from one neuron to another. It includes the synaptic cleft (a gap) and the sections of the cell membranes on either side of the cleft. They are called the presynaptic and postsynaptic membranes.

synesthesia A process by which the stimulation of one sense (such as hearing a sound) produces a different kind of sensory impression (such as seeing a color).

thalamus A structure in the forebrain that passes sensory information on to the cerebral cortex.

theory of mind The realization by an individual (such as a growing child, for example) that other people have thoughts and mental processes of their own. It is universally accepted that humans have a theory of mind, and research has shown that some other animals, such as chimpanzees and dolphins, might also have a theory of mind, but this is still debated. Theory of mind is of interest to developmental psychologists since it is not something people are born with, but something that develops in infancy.

tranquilizers A type of medication with sedative, muscle-relaxant, or similar properties. Minor tranquilizers are also known as antianxiety or anxiolytic drugs; major tranquilizers are also known as antipsychotic drugs.

unconditioned stimulus/response (US/UR) *See* classical conditioning

unconscious In psychoanalytic and related theories the area of the mind that is outside conscious awareness and recall but that informs the contents of such things as dreams. In general usage *unconscious* simply refers to automatic cognitive processes that we are not aware of or the lack of consciousness (that is, "awareness") at times such as during sleep.

working memory *See* short-term memory

Resources

Further Reading

Altmann, G. T. M. *The Ascent of Babel: An Exploration of Language, Mind, and Understanding.* Cambridge, MA: Oxford University Press, 1999.

American Psychiatric Association. *Diagnostic and Statistical Manual of Mental Disorders, 4th edition, Text Revision.* Washington, DC: American Psychiatric Press, 2000.

Argyle, M. *The Psychology of Interpersonal Behaviour (5th edition).* London, UK: Penguin, 1994.

Asher, S. R. and Coie, J. D. (eds.). *Peer Rejection in Childhood.* Cambridge, UK: Cambridge University Press, 1990.

Atkinson, R. L. *et al. Hilgard's Introduction to Psychology (13th edition).* London, UK: International Thomson Publishing, 1999.

Barnouw, V. *Culture and Personality.* Chicago, IL: Dorsey Press, 1985.

Baron, J. *Thinking and Deciding.* Cambridge, UK: Cambridge University Press, 1994.

Barry, M. A. S. *Visual Intelligence: Perception, Image, and Manipulation in Visual Communication.* Albany, NY: State University of New York Press, 1997.

Beck, J. *Cognitive Therapy: Basics and Beyond.* London, UK: The Guildford Press, 1995.

Bickerton, D. *Language and Species.* Chicago, IL: The University of Chicago Press, 1990.

Blackburn, I. M. and Davison, K. *Cognitive Therapy for Depression and Anxiety: A Practitioner's Guide.* Oxford, UK: Blackwell, 1995.

Boden, M. A. *Piaget (2nd edition).* London, UK: Fontana Press, 1994.

Brehm, S. S., Kassin, S. M., and Fein, S. *Social Psychology (4th edition).* Boston, MA: Houghton Mifflin, 1999.

Brody, N. *Intelligence (2nd edition).* San Diego, CA: Academic Press, 1997.

Brown, D. S. *Learning a Living: A Guide to Planning Your Career and Finding a Job for People with Learning Disabilities, Attention Deficit Disorder, and Dyslexia.* Bethesda, MD: Woodbine House, 2000.

Bruhn, A. R. *Earliest Childhood Memories.* New York: Praeger, 1990.

Buunk, B. P. "Affiliation, Attraction and Close Relationships." *In* M. Hewstone and W. Stroebe (eds.), *Introduction to Social Psychology: A European Perspective.* Oxford, UK: Blackwell, 2001.

Cacioppo, J. T., Tassinary, L. G., and Berntson, G. G. (eds.). *Handbook of Psychophysiology (2nd edition).* New York: Cambridge University Press, 2000.

Cardwell, M. *Dictionary of Psychology.* Chicago, IL: Fitzroy Dearborn Publishers, 1999

Carson, R. C. and Butcher, J. N. *Abnormal Psychology and Modern Life (9th edition).* New York: HarperCollins Publishers, 1992.

Carter, R. *Mapping the Mind.* Berkeley, CA: University of California Press, 1998.

Cavan, S. *Recovery from Drug Addiction.* New York: Rosen Publishing Group, 2000.

Clarke-Stewart, A. *Daycare.* Cambridge, MA: Harvard University Press, 1993.

Cohen, G. *The Psychology of Cognition (2nd edition).* San Diego, CA: Academic Press, 1983.

Cramer, D. *Close Relationships: The Study of Love and Friendship.* New York: Arnold, 1998.

Daly, M. and Wilson, M. *Homicide.* New York: Aldine de Gruyter, 1988.

Davis, R. D., Braun, E. M., and Smith, J. M. *The Gift of Dyslexia: Why Some of the Smartest People Can't Read and How They Can Learn.* New York: Perigee, 1997.

Davison, G. C. and Neal, J. M. *Abnormal Psychology.* New York: John Wiley and Sons, Inc., 1994.

Dawkins, R. *The Selfish Gene.* New York: Oxford Universty Press, 1976.

Dennett, D. C. *Darwin's Dangerous Idea: Evolution and the Meanings of Life.* Carmichael, CA: Touchstone Books, 1996.

Dobson, C. *et al. Understanding Psychology.* London, UK: Weidenfeld and Nicolson, 1982.

Duck, S. *Meaningful Relationships: Talking, Sense, and Relating.* Thousand Oaks, CA: Sage Publications, 1994.

Durie, M. H. "Maori Psychiatric Admissions: Patterns, Explanations and Policy Implications." *In* J. Spicer, A. Trlin, and J. A. Walton (eds.), *Social Dimensions of Health and Disease: New Zealand Perspectives.* Palmerston North, NZ: Dunmore Press, 1994.

Eliot, L. *What's Going on in There? How the Brain and Mind Develop in the First Five Years of Life.* New York: Bantam Books, 1999.

Eysenck, M. (ed.). *The Blackwell Dictionary of Cognitive Psychology.* Cambridge, MA: Blackwell, 1991.

Faherty, C. and Mesibov, G. B. *Asperger's: What Does It Mean to Me?* Arlington, TX: Future Horizons, 2000.

Fernando, S. *Mental Health in a Multi-Ethnic Society: A Multi-Disciplinary Handbook.* New York: Routledge, 1995.

Fiske, S. T. and Taylor, S. E. *Social Cognition (2nd Edition).* New York: Mcgraw-Hill, 1991.

Franken, R. E. *Human Motivation (5th edition).* Belmont, CA: Wadsworth Thomson Learning, 2002.

Freud, S. and Brill, A. A. *The Basic Writings of Sigmund Freud.* New York: Modern Library, 1995.

Gardner, H. *The Mind's New Science: A History of the Cognitive Revolution.* New York: Basic Books, 1985.

Garnham, A. and Oakhill, J. *Thinking and Reasoning.* Cambridge, MA: Blackwell, 1994.

Gaw, A. C. *Culture, Ethnicity, and Mental Illness.* Washington, DC: American Psychiatric Press, 1992.

Giacobello, J. *Everything You Need to Know about Anxiety and Panic Attacks.* New York: Rosen Publishing Group, 2000.

Gazzaniga, M. S. *The Mind's Past.* Berkeley, CA: University of California Press, 1998.

Gazzaniga, M. S. (ed.). *The New Cognitive Neurosciences (2nd edition).* Cambridge, MA: MIT Press, 2000.

Gazzaniga, M. S., Ivry, R. B., and Mangun, G. R. *Cognitive Neuroscience: The Biology of the Mind (2nd edition).* New York: Norton, 2002.

Gernsbacher, M. A. (ed.). *Handbook of Psycholinguistics.* San Diego, CA: Academic Press, 1994.

Gigerenzer, G. *Adaptive Thinking: Rationality in the Real World.* New York: Oxford University Press, 2000.

Goodglass, H. *Understanding Aphasia.* San Diego, CA: Academic Press, 1993.

Gordon, M. *Jumpin' Johnny Get Back to Work! A Child's Guide to ADHD/Hyperactivity.* DeWitt, NY: GSI Publications Inc., 1991.

Gordon, M. A *I Would if I Could: A Teenager's Guide to ADHD/Hyperactivity.* DeWitt, NY: GSI Publications Inc., 1992.

Goswami, U. *Cognition in Children.* London, UK: Psychology Press, 1998.

Graham, H. *The Human Face of Psychology: Humanistic Psychology in Its Historical, Social, and Cultural Context.* Milton Keynes, UK: Open University Press, 1986.

Grandin, T. *Thinking in Pictures: And Other Reports from my Life with Autism.* New York: Vintage Books, 1996.

Greenberger, D. and Padesky, C. *Mind over Mood.* New York: Guilford Publications, 1995.

Groeger, J. A. *Memory and Remembering: Everyday Memory in Context.* New York: Longman, 1997.

Gross, R. and Humphreys, P. *Psychology: The Science of Mind and Behaviour.* London, UK: Hodder Arnold, 1993.

Halford, G. S. *Children's Understanding: The Development of Mental Models.* Hillsdale, NJ: Lawrence Erlbaum Associates, 1993.

Harley, T. A. *The Psychology of Language: From Data to Theory (2nd edition).* Hove, UK: Psychology Press, 2001.

Harris, G. G. *Casting out Anger: Religion among the Taita of Kenya.* New York: Cambridge University Press, 1978.

Hayes, N. *Psychology in Perspective (2nd edition).* New York: Palgrave, 2002.

Hearst, E. *The First Century of Experimental Psychology.* Hillsdale, NJ: Lawrence Erlbaum Associates, 1979.

Hecht, T. *At Home in the Street: Street Children of Northeast Brazil.* New York: Cambridge University Press, 1998.

Hetherington, E. M. *Coping with Divorce, Single Parenting, and Remarriage: A Risk and Resiliency Perspective.* Mawah, NJ: Lawrence Erlbaum Associates, 1999.

Higbee, K. L. *Your Memory: How It Works and How to Improve It (2nd edition).* New York: Paragon 1993.

Hinde, R. A. *Individuals, Relationships and Culture: Links between Ethology and the Social Sciences.* Cambridge, UK: Cambridge University Press, 1987.

Hogdon, L. A. *Solving Behavior Problems in Autism.* Troy, MI: Quirkroberts Publishing, 1999.

Hogg, M. A. (ed.). *Social Psychology.* Thousand Oaks, CA: Sage Publications, 2002.

Holden, G. W. *Parents and the Dynamics of Child Rearing.* Boulder, CO: Westview Press, 1997.

Holmes, J. *John Bowlby and Attachment Theory.* New York: Routledge, 1993.

Hughes, H. C. *Sensory Exotica: A World Beyond Human Experience.* Cambridge, MA: MIT Press, 1999.

Hyde, M. O. and Setano, J. F. *When the Brain Dies First.* New York: Franlin Watts Inc., 2000.

Ingersoll, B. D. *Distant Drums, Different Drummers: A Guide for Young People with ADHD.* Plantation, FL: A.D.D. WareHouse, 1995.

Jencks, C. and Phillips, M. *The Black-White Test Score Gap.* Washington, DC: Brookings Institution Press, 1998.

Johnson, M. J. *Developmental Cognitive Neuroscience.* Cambridge, MA: Blackwell, 1997.

Johnson, M. H. and Morton, J. *Biology and Cognitive Development. The Case of Face Recognition.* Cambridge, MA: Blackwell, 1991.

Johnson-Laird, P. N. *The Computer and the Mind: An Introduction to Cognitive Science.* Cambridge, MA: Harvard University Press, 1988.

Jusczyk, P. W. *The Discovery of Spoken Language.* Cambridge, MA: MIT Press, 1997.

Kalat, J. W. *Biological Psychology (7th edition).* Belmont, CA: Wadsworth Thomson Learning, 2001.

Kaplan, H. I. and Sadock, B. J. *Synopsis of Psychiatry: Behavioral Sciences, Clinical Psychiatry.* Philadelphia, PA: Lippincott, Williams and Wilkins, 1994.

Karen, R. *Becoming Attached: First Relationships and How They Shape Our Capacity to Love.* New York: Oxford University Press, 1998.

Kirk, S. A. and Kutchins, H. *The Selling of DSM: The Rhetoric of Science in Psychiatry.* New York: Aldine de Gruyter, 1992.

Kinney, J. *Clinical Manual of Substance Abuse.* St. Louis, MO: Mosby, 1995.

Kleinman, A. *Rethinking Psychiatry: From Cultural Category to Personal Experience.* New York: Free Press, 1988.

Kosslyn, S. M. and Koenig, O. *Wet Mind: The New Cognitive Neuroscience.* New York: Free Press, 1992.

Kutchins, H. and Kirk, S. A. *Making Us Crazy: DSM: The Psychiatric Bible and the Creation of Mental Disorders.* New York: Free Press, 1997.

LaBruzza, A. L. *Using DSM-IV; A Clinician's Guide to Psychiatric Diagnosis.* St. Northvale, NJ: Jason Aronson Inc., 1994.

Leahey, T. A. *A History of Psychology: Main Currents in Psychological Thought (5th edition).* Upper Saddle River, NJ: Prentice Hall, 2000.

LeDoux, J. *The Emotional Brain.* New York: Simon and Schuster, 1996.

Levelt, W. J. M. *Speaking: From Intention to Articulation.* Cambridge, MA: MIT Press, 1989.

Lewis, M. and Haviland-Jones, J. M. (eds.). *Handbook of Emotions (2nd edition).* New York: Guilford Press, 2000.

Lowisohn, J. H. *et al. Substance Abuse: A Comprehensive Textbook (3rd edition).* Baltimore, MD: Williams & Wilkins, 1997.

McCabe, D. *To Teach a Dyslexic.* Clio, MI: AVKO Educational Research, 1997.

McCorduck, P. *Machines Who Think: A Personal Inquiry into the History and Prospects of Artificial Intelligence.* San Francisco: W. H. Freeman, 1979.

McIlveen, R. and Gross, R. *Biopsychology (5th edition).* Boston, MA: Allyn and Bacon, 2002.

McLachlan, J. *Medical Embryology.* Reading, MA: Addison-Wesley Publishing Co., 1994.

Manstead, A. S. R. and Hewstone M. (eds.). *The Blackwell Encyclopaedia of Social Psychology.* Oxford, UK: Blackwell, 1996.

Marsella, A. J., DeVos, G., and Hsu, F. L. K. (eds.). *Culture and Self: Asian and Western Perspectives.* New York: Routledge, 1988.

Matlin, M. W. *The Psychology of Women.* New York: Harcourt College Publishers, 2000.

Matsumoto, D. R. *People: Psychology from a Cultural Perspective.* Pacific Grove, CA: Brooks/Cole Publishing, 1994.

Matsumoto, D. R. *Culture and Modern Life.* Pacific

Grove, CA: Brooks/Cole Publishing, 1997.

Mazziotta, J .C., Toga, A. W., and Frackowiak, R. S. J. (eds.). *Brain Mapping: The Disorders.* San Diego, CA: Academic Press, 2000.

Nadeau, K. G., Littman, E., and Quinn, P. O. *Understanding Girls with ADHD.* Niagara Falls, NY: Advantage Books, 2000.

Nadel, J. and Camioni, L. (eds.). *New Perspectives in Early Communicative Development.* New York: Routledge, 1993.

Nobus, D. *Jacques Lacan and the Freudian Practice of Psychoanalysis.* Philadelphia, PA: Routledge, 2000.

Oakley, D. A. "The Plurality of Consciousness." *In* D. A. Oakley (ed.), *Brain and Mind*, New York: Methuen, 1985.

Obler, L. K. and Gjerlow, K. *Language and the Brain.* New York: Cambridge University Press, 1999.

Ogden, J. A. *Fractured Minds: A Case-study Approach to Clinical Neuropsychology.* New York: Oxford University Press, 1996.

Owusu-Bempah, K. and Howitt, D. *Psychology beyond Western Perspectives.* Leicester, UK: British Psychological Society Books, 2000.

Paranjpe, A. C. and Bhatt, G. S. "Emotion: A Perspective from the Indian Tradition." *In* H. S. R. Kao and D. Sinha (eds.), *Asian Perspectives on Psychology.* New Delhi, India: Sage Publications, 1997.

Peacock, J. *Depression.* New York: Lifematters Press, 2000.

Pfeiffer, W. M. "Culture-Bound Syndromes." *In* I. Al-Issa (ed.), *Culture and Psychopathology.* Baltimore, MD: University Park Press, 1982.

Pillemer, D. B. *Momentous Events, Vivid Memories.* Cambridge, MA: Harvard University Press, 1998.

Pinel, J. P. J. *Biopsychology (5th edition).* Boston, MA: Allyn and Bacon, 2002.

Pinker, S. *The Language Instinct.* New York: HarperPerennial, 1995.

Pinker, S. *How the Mind Works.* New York: Norton, 1997.

Porter, R. *Medicine: A History of Healing: Ancient Traditions to Modern Practices.* New York: Barnes and Noble, 1997.

Ramachandran, V. S. and Blakeslee, S. *Phantoms in the Brain: Probing the Mysteries of the Human Mind.* New York: William Morrow, 1998.

Ridley, M. *Genome: The Autobiography of a Species in 23 Chapters.* New York: HarperCollins, 1999.

Robins, L. N. and Regier, D. A. *Psychiatric Disorders in America.* New York: Free Press, 1991.

Robinson, D. N. *Toward a Science of Human Nature: Essays on the Psychologies of Mill, Hegel, Wundt, and James.* New York: Columbia University Press, 1982.

Rugg, M. D. and Coles, M. G. H. (eds.). *Electrophysiology of the Mind: Event-Related Brain Potentials and Cognition.* Oxford, UK: Oxford University Press, 1995.

Rutter, M. "The Interplay of Nature and Nurture: Redirecting the Inquiry." *In* R. Plomin and G. E. McClearn (eds.), *Nature, Nurture, and Psychology.* Washington, DC: American Psychological Association, 1993.

Sarason, I. G. and Sarason B. R. *Abnormal Psychology: The Problem of Maladaptive Behavior (9th edition).* Upper Saddle River, NJ: Prentice Hall, 1998.

Savage-Rumbaugh, S., Shanker, S. G., and Taylor, T. J. *Apes, Language, and the Human Mind.* New York: Oxford University Press, 1998.

Schab, F. R., & Crowder, R. G. (eds.). *Memory for Odors.* Mahwah, NJ: Lawrence Erlbaum Associates, 1995.

Segal, N. L. *Entwined Lives: Twins and What They Tell Us about Human Behavior.* New York: Plume, 2000.

Seeman, M. V. *Gender and Psychopathology.* Washington, DC: American Psychiatric Press, 1995.

Seligman, M. E. P. *Helplessness: On Depression, Development, and Death.* San Francisco, CA: W. H. Freeman and Co., 1992.

Shorter, E. *A History of Psychiatry: From the Era of Asylum to the Age of Prozac.* New York: John Wiley and Sons, Inc., 1997.

Siegler, R. S. *Children's Thinking (3rd edition).* Englewood Cliffs, NJ: Prentice Hall, 1998.

Simpson, E. M. *Reversals: A Personal Account of Victory over Dyslexia.* New York: Noonday Press, 1992.

Singer, D. G. and Singer, J. L. (eds.). *Handbook of Children and the Media.* Thousand Oaks, CA: Sage Publications, 2001.

Skinner, B. F. *Science and Human Behavior.* New York: Free Press, 1965.

Slavney, P. R. *Psychiatric Dimensions of Medical Practice: What Primary-Care Physicians Should Know about Delirium, Demoralization, Suicidal Thinking, and Competence to Refuse Medical Advice.* Baltimore, MD: The Johns Hopkins University Press, 1998.

Smith McLaughlin, M., Peyser Hazouri, S., and Peyser Hazouri, S. *Addiction: The "High" That Brings You Down.* Springfield, NJ: Enslow publishers, 1997.

Sommers, M. A. *Everything You Need to Know about Bipolar Disorder and Depressive Illness.* New York: Rosen Publishing Group, 2000.

Stanovich, K. E. *Who Is Rational? Studies of Individual Differences in Reasoning.* Mahwah, NJ: Lawrence Erlbaum Associates, 1999.

Symons, D. *The Evolution of Human Sexuality.* New York: Oxford University Press, 1979.

Symons, D. "Beauty is in the Adaptations of the Beholder: The Evolutionary Psychology of Human Female Sexual Attractiveness." *In* P. R. Abramson and S. D. Pinkerton (eds.), *Sexual Nature, Sexual Culture.* Chicago, IL: University of Chicago Press, 1995.

Tavris, C. *The Mismeasure of Women.* New York: Simon and Schuster, 1992.

Triandis, H. C. *Culture and Social Behavior.* New York: McGraw-Hill, 1994.

Tulving, E and Craik, F. I. M. *The Oxford Handbook of Memory.* Oxford, UK: Oxford University Press, 2000.

Vygotsky, L. S. *Mind in Society: The Development of Higher Psychological Processes.* Cambridge, MA: Harvard University Press, 1978.

Weiten, W. *Psychology: Themes and Variations.* Monterey, CA: Brooks/Cole Publishing, 1998.

Werner, E. E. and Smith, R. S. *Overcoming the Odds: High-Risk Children from Birth to Adulthood.* Ithaca, NY: Cornell University Press, 1992.

White, R. W. and Watt, N. F. *The Abnormal Personality (5th edition).* Chichester, UK: John Wiley and Sons, Inc., 1981.

Wickens, A. *Foundations of Biopsychology.* Harlow, UK: Prentice Hall, 2000.

Wilson, E. O. *Sociobiology: A New Synthesis.* Cambridge, MA: Harvard University Press, 1975.

Winkler, K. *Teens, Depression, and the Blues: A Hot Issue.* Springfield, NJ: Enslow publishers, 2000.

Wolman, B. (ed.). *Historical Roots of Contemporary Psychology.* New York: Harper and Row, 1968.

Wrightsman, L. S. and Sanford, F. H. *Psychology: A Scientific Study of Human Behavior.* Monterey, CA: Brooks/Cole Publishing, 1975.

Yap, P. M. *Comparative Psychiatry: A Theoretical Framework.* Toronto, Canada: University of Toronto Press, 1974.

Zarit, S. H. and Knight, B. G. *A Guide to Psychotherapy and Aging.* Washington, DC: American Psychological Association, 1997.

Useful Websites

Amazing Optical Illusions
http://www.optillusions.com
See your favorite optical illusions at this fun site.

American Psychological Association
http://www.apa.org
Here you can read a peer-reviewed e-journal published by the APA, follow the development of new ethical guidelines for pscychologists, and find a wealth of other information.

Association for Advancement of Behavior Therapy
http://www.aabt.org
An interdisciplinary organization concerned with the application of behavioral and cognitive sciences to the understanding of human behavior.

Association for Cross-Cultural Psychology
http://www.fit.edu/CampusLife/clubs-org/iaccp
Including a full-text downloadable version of their journal.

Bedlam
http://www.museum-london.org.uk/MOLsite/exhibits/bedlam/f_bed.htm
The Museum of London's online exhibition about Bedlam, the notorious mental institution.

Bipolar Disorders Information Center
http://www.mhsource.com/bipolar
Articles and information about bipolar 1 disorder.

Brain and Mind
http://www.epub.org.br/cm/home_i.htm
An online magazine with articles devoted to neuroscience, linguisitics, imprinting, and many other related topics.

Exploratorium
http://www.exploratorium.edu/exhibits/nf_exhibits.html
Click on "seeing" or "hearing" to check out visual and auditory illusions and other secrets of the mind.

Freud and Culture
http://www.loc.gov/exhibits/freud
An online Library of Congress exhibition that examines Sigmund Freud's life and key ideas and his effect on 20th-century thinking.

Jigsaw Classroom
http://www.jigsaw.org
The official web site of the Jigsaw Classroom, a cooperative learning technique that reduces racial conflict between schoolchildren. Learn about its history and how to implement the techniques.

Kidspsych
http://www.kidspsych.org/index1.html
American Psychological Association's childrens' site, with games and exercises for kids. Also useful for students of developmental psychology. Follow the "about this activity" links to find out the theories behind the fun and games.

Kismet
http://www.ai.mit.edu/projects/humanoid-robotics-group/kismet/kismet.html
Kismet is the MIT's expressive robot, which has perceptual and motor functions tailored to natural human communication channels.

Museum of Psychological Instrumentation
http://chss.montclair.edu/psychology/museum/museum.html
Look at images of early psychological laboratory research apparatus, such as Wilhelm Wundt's eye motion demonstrator.

National Academy of Neuropsychology
http://nanonline.org/content/pages/research/acn.shtm
A site where you can download the archives of Clinical Neuropsychology, *a journal that focuses on disorders of the central nervous system.*

Neuroscience for Kids
http://faculty.washington.edu/chudler/neurok.html
A useful website for students and teachers who want to learn about the nervous system. Enjoy activities and experiments on your way to learning all about the brain and spinal cord.

National Eating Disorders Society
http://www.nationaleatingdisorders.org
Information on eating disorders, their precursors, how to help a friend, and the importance of treatment.

Neuroscience Tutorial
http://thalamus.wustl.edu/course
The Washington University School of Medicine's online tutorial offers an illustrated guide to the basics of clinical neuroscience, with useful artworks and user-friendly text.

Online Dictionary of Mental Health
http://www.shef.ac.uk/~psysc/psychotherapy
The Centre for Psychotherapeutic Studies at Sheffield University, UK, runs this online dictionary. There are links to many sites offering different viewpoints on major mental health issues.

Personality Theories
http://www.ship.edu/~cgboeree/perscontents.html
An electronic textbook covering personality theories for undergraduate and graduate courses.

Psychology Central
http://emerson.thomsonlearning.com/psych
Links to many useful articles grouped by subject as well as cool, animated figures that improve your understanding of psychological principles.

Schizophrenia.com
http://www.schizophrenia.com
Information and resources on this mental disorder provided by a charitable organization.

Seeing, Hearing, and Smelling the World
http://www.hhmi.org/senses/
A downloadable illustrated book dealing with perception from the Howard Hughes Medical Institute.

Sigmund Freud Museum
http://freud.t0.or.at/freud/
The online Sigmund Freud Museum has videos and audio recordings of the famous psychoanalyst—there are even images of Freud's famous couch.

Social Psychology Network
http://www.socialpsychology.org
The largest social psychology database on the Internet. Within these pages you will find more than 5,000 links to psychology-related resources and research groups, and there is also a useful section on general psychology.

Stanford Prison Experiment
http://www.prisonexp.org/
A fascinating look at the Stanford Prison Experiment, which saw subjects placed in a prison to see what happens to "good people in a bad environment." Learn why the experiment had to be abandoned after six days due to the unforeseen severity of the effects on participants.

Stroop effect
http://www.dcity.org/braingames/stroop/index.htm
Take part in an online psychological experiment to see the Stroop effect in action.

Quote Attributions

opening quote

Abnormal Psychology

What Is Abnormality?

Investigating an indefinite concept

The scientific study of psychological disorders, or "psychopathology," is sometimes referred to as the field of abnormal psychology. One of the first major issues students of abnormal psychology encounter is that the answers to questions like "What is abnormal?" and "What is a mental disorder?" are constantly evolving. Guidelines have been established, however, that help psychologists and others diagnose and treat people suffering from mental disorders, which can cause distress, fear, and sometimes even physical pain in sufferers or those around them.

A young man in his first year at college feels sad and lonely as he tries to adjust to living away from home for the first time. A woman begins to panic when she drives over a bridge. A little boy has difficulty learning to speak. A grandmother feels disoriented and can't remember how to get home. Are these people having abnormal experiences? Do they have a mental disorder? The answers to these questions are complex and depend on who is answering them. That is because terms like "abnormal" and "mental disorder" are in part defined by social and cultural beliefs, which differ from culture to culture and change over time. This is not to say that some mental disorders might not have physical causes. Many are firmly based in biology, but it is not possible to diagnose or

identify mental disorders with simple medical procedures, such as blood tests. In many cases (for example, phobias) there may be no biological cause to detect. Even if there is a biological cause, it is often difficult for a psychologist to determine whether or not a person needs treatment, and what sort of treatment that should be. In such cases a clinician's definitions of abnormality and mental disorders and their severity are crucial.

Whether or not someone is diagnosed as having a mental, or psychological, disorder has many important implications. For example, during a trial (below), if defendants are found to be mentally disordered, they might receive a different sentence than if they were considered psychologically healthy.

"nearly half of all Americans will experience a mental or emotional problem at least once during their lifetime that, if diagnosed, would be classified as a mental disorder."
—R. C. Kessler and others, 1994

Although there is no one definitive definition of psychological abnormality, a variety of definitions have been proposed and accepted. In the United States one official definition of mental disorders that is accepted by a large number of mental health professionals, despite some critics, can be found in the *Diagnostic and Statistical Manual of Mental Disorders*—or the DSM (see box p. 9). The DSM is published by the American Psychiatric Association (APA) to help psychologists, psychiatrists, and other medical professionals identify and diagnose psychological problems.

6

quote

Each chapter in *Psychology* contains quotes that relate to the topics covered. These quotes appear both within the main text and at the start of the chapters, and their attributions are detailed here. Quotes are listed in the order that they appear in the chapter, and the page numbers at the end of each attribution refer to the pages in this volume where the quote appears.

The Human Computer

Simon, H. A. "Cognitive Science: The Newest Science of the Artificial." *Cognitive Science*, **4**, 1980, p. 7.

Turkle S. *Life on the Screen.* New York: Simon and Schuster, 1995, p. 8.

Popper, K. *Quantum Theory and the Schism in Physics.* London, U.K: Hutchinson, 1982, p. 10.

Hippocrates. *The Sacred Disease. c.* 400 B.C., p. 10.

Watson, J. B. *Psychology from the Standpoint of a Behaviorist.* Philadelphia, PA: J. B. Lippincott, 1913, p. 13.

Balzac, H. Le Père Goirot in *Revue de Paris.* 1834, p. 17.

James, W. *The Principles of Psychology.* 1890, p. 21.

Churchill, W. S. Speech given at the Lord Mayor's Luncheon, Mansion House, London, 1942, p. 23.

Attention and Information Processing

James, W. *Talks to Teachers.* 1899, p. 24.

Greene, J. and Hicks, C. *Basic Cognitive Processes.* Milton Keynes, UK: Open University Press, 1984, p. 34.

Logan, G. D. "Attention and Skill Acquisition." *At* http://www.life.uiuc.edu/neuroscience/faculty/profiles/logan.html, 2001, p. 37.

Learning by Association

Babkin, B. P. *Pavlov: A Biography.* Chicago, IL: The University of Chicago Press, 1949, p. 45.

Dewsbury, D. A. "Early Interactions between Animal Psychologists and Animal Activists and the Founding of the APA Committee on Precautions in Animal Experimentation." *American Psychologist*, **45**, 1990, p. 46.

Watson, J. B. *Behavior.* New York: H. Holt and Co., 1914, p. 50.

Thorndike, E. L. *The Elements of Psychology.* New York: A. G. Seiler, 1905, p. 51.

Skinner, B. F. *About Behaviorism.* New York: Random House, 1974, p.52, p. 54.

Skinner, B. F. *Science and Human Behavior.* New York: Macmillan, 1953, p. 53, p. 55.

Sagal, P. T. *Skinner's Philosophy.* Washington, DC: University of America Press, 1981, p. 57.

Auden, W. H. *A Certain World: A Commonplace Book.* New York: Viking and Faber, 1970, p. 60.

Rosen, D. *Psychobabble.* New York: Atheneum, 1977, p. 61.

Skinner, B. F. *Walden Two.* New York: MacMillan, 1948, p. 63.

Representing Information

Galton, F. *Statistics of Mental Imagery.* 1880, p. 65.

Kosslyn, S. M and Squire, L. R. *Findings and Current Opinion in Cognitive Neuroscience.* Cambridge, MA: MIT Press, 1999, p. 67.

Kosslyn, S. M. *Psychology: The Brain, The Person, The World.* Boston, MA: Allyn and Bacon, 2000, p. 67.

Gregory, R. *The Intelligent Eye.* New York: McGraw-Hill, 1970, p. 68

Bower, G. H., Karlin, M. B., and Dueck, A. "Comprehension and Memory for Pictures." *Memory and Cognition*, **2**, 1975, p. 69.

Wittgenstein, L. *Philosophical Investigations.* Oxford, UK: Blackwell, 1953, p. 71.

Rosch, E. *Cognition and Categorization.* Hillsdale, NJ: Laurence Erlbaum Associates, 1978, p. 73.

Estes, B. *Cognition and Categorization.* New York: Oxford University Press, 1994, p. 76.

Bruner, J., Goodnow, J., and Austin, A. *A Study of*

Thinking. New York: Wiley, 1956, p. 78.

Harley, T. A. *The Psychology of Language: From Data to Theory (2nd edition)*. Hove, UK: Psychology Press, 2001, p. 82.

Brecht, B. *Mother Courage and Her Children.* New York: Arcade Publications, 1949, p. 85.

Storing Information

Lewis, C. S. *A Grief Observed.* London: Faber and Faber, 1966, p. 89.

Twain, M. Cited in B. DeVoto (ed.), *Mark Twain in Eruption.* New York: Harper and Brothers, 1940, p. 90.

de Bono, E., *The Mechanism of the Mind.* New York: Simon and Schuster, 1969, p. 92.

Shakespeare, W. *Richard II. c.* 1598, p. 93.

Proust, M. *Á la Recherche du Temps Perdu.* 1922, p. 94.

Nietzsche, F. *Human, All Too Human.* 1878, p. 101

Traditional Chinese proverb, p. 104.

Fuller, T. *History of the Worthies of England.* 1662, p. 105.

Duhamel, G. *Civilization 1914–1917.* New York: The Century Co., 1919, p. 106.

Craik, K. *The Nature of Explanation.* Cambridge, U.K: Cambridge University Press, 1943, p. 107.

Nietzsche, F. *Thus Spoke Zarathustra.* 1883, p. 111.

Language Processing

Muller, M. Cited in N. C. Chaudhuri, *Scholar Extraordinary.* London: Chatto and Windus, 1974, p. 114.

Harley, T. A. *The Psychology of Language: From Data to Theory (2nd edition)*. Hove, UK: Psychology Press, 2001, p. 116.

Lodge, D. "Where It's At: California Language." *In* C. Ricks and L. Michaels (eds.), *The State of the Language.* Berkeley, CA: University of California Press, 1980, p. 117.

Mill, J. S. *System of Logic.* 1843, p. 123.

Mitchell, R. *Less than Words Can Say.* Boston, MA: Little Brown and Co., 1979, p. 132.

Sapir, E. Cited in L. Spier, I. Hallowell, and S. Newman (eds.), *Language, Culture, and Personality: Essays in Memory of Eward Sapir.* Menshaha, WI: Sapir Memorial Publication Fund, 1941, p.134.

Problem Solving

Thorndike, E. L. *Comparative Psychology.* New York: Prentice Hall, 1930, p. 137.

Newell, A. "Unified theories of cognition and the role of Soar." *In* J. A. Michon and A. Anureyk (eds.), *Soar: A Cognitive Architecture in Perspective.* Dordrecht, Nederlands: Kluwer Academic

Publishers, 1992, p. 141.

Schmidt, C. F. "Cognitive Architecture." *At* http://www.rci.rutgers.edu/~cfs/472_html/ CogArch/Protocol.html, 2002, p. 143.

Webb, B. Diary entry, 1893, p. 146.

Johnson-Laird, P. N. *The Computer and the Mind: An Introduction to Cognitive Science.* Cambridge, MA: Harvard University Press, 1988, p. 147.

Boole, G. *An Investigation into the Laws of Thought on Which Are Founded the Mathematical Theories of Logic and Probabilities.* 1854, p. 148.

Gigerenzer, G. Cited in G. Gigerenzer and R. Selten (eds.), *Bounded Rationality: The Adaptive Toolbox.* Cambridge MA: MIT Press, 2001, p. 155.

Arrow, K. *et al.* "Memorial Resolution for Amos Tversky (1973–1996)." *At* http://www.stanford.edu/ dept/facultysenate/archive/1997_1998/reports/ 105949/106013.html, 1996, p.157.

Pinker, S. *How the Mind Works.* New York: Norton, 1997, p. 158.

de Bono, E. *Handbook for the Positive Revolution.* New York: Viking, 1991, p. 160.

Dutton, D. "What Is Genius?" *Philosophy and Literature*, **25**, 2001, p. 163.

Glover, E. "Some Recent Trends in Psychoanalytic Theory." *Psychoanalytic Quarterly*, **30**, 1961, p. 62.

Every effort has been made to attribute the quotes throughout *Psychology* correctly. Any errors or omissions brought to the attention of the publisher are regretted and will be credited in subsequent editions.

Edward Thorndike (1874–1949).

Set Index